San Francisco's

QUEEN

OF VICE

The Strange Career of
Abortionist Inez Brown Burns

LISA RIGGIN

University of Nebraska Press | Lincoln & London

Library of Congress Cataloging-in-Publication Data
Names: Riggin, Lisa, author.
Title: San Francisco's queen of vice: the strange
career of abortionist Inez Brown Burns / Lisa Riggin.
Description: Lincoln: University of Nebraska Press,
[2017] | Includes bibliographical references and index.
Identifiers: LCCN 2017003732 (print)
LCCN 2017032325 (ebook)
ISBN 9781496202079 (hardback: alk. paper)
ISBN 9781496203052 (epub)
ISBN 9781496203069 (mobi)
ISBN 9781496203076 (pdf)
Subjects: LCSH: Burns, Inez Brown—Health. | Clinic
managers—California—San Francisco—Biography.
| Abortion services—California—San Francisco. |
BISAC: BIOGRAPHY & AUTOBIOGRAPHY / Histor-
ical. | BIOGRAPHY & AUTOBIOGRAPHY / Women. |
SOCIAL SCIENCE / Abortion & Birth Control.
Classification: LCC RG734 .R54 2017 (ebook) | LCC
RG734 (print) | DDC 362.1988/8097946—dc23
LC record available at https://lccn.loc.
gov/2017003732

Set in Fanwood by John Klopping
Designed by L. Auten.

For Vanessa and Stevie,
for making it all worthwhile.

When Frisco was the abortion capital of the United States . . . Inez Burns was the undisputed queen of the abortionists.

—Journalist Warren Hinckle, "When S.F. Was Abortion Capital," *The Independent*, November 29, 1994

Contents

Illustrations

Preface

This book does not examine the personal, social, or moral implications of abortion, nor is it a study of the women who underwent the procedure. Those accounts have been written. However, to appreciate the intense struggle between the "Queen of Abortions" Inez Brown Burns and District Attorney Edmund "Pat" Brown, it is important to have an understanding of the progression of state and federal laws governing abortion in America during this era.

Even as Prohibition became the driving force behind organized crime, state and federal statutes, together with changing social mores, drove abortionists into hiding, opened the door to increasingly dangerous and sometimes lethal practices, and resulted in abortion becoming the third-largest illegal enterprise in the nation. The attempt to pass state laws regarding abortion began as early as the 1820s and culminated in 1873 when Anthony Comstock, head of the New York Society for the Suppression of Vice, succeeded in getting Congress to pass the "Act for the Suppression of Trade in, and Circulation of, Obscene Literature and Articles of Immoral Use," which governed the procedure for most of the next one hundred years. According to historian Patricia Miller, what came to be known as "Comstockery" was significantly instrumental in driving abortion underground, leading to at least forty new anti abortion laws between the years 1860 and 1880.[1]

The affluent and racy 1920s led to a rise in the number of abortions with fees averaging from $50 to $1000. In her book *When Abortion Was a Crime* Leslie Reagan quotes an anonymous medical commentator of that decade who stated that abortion was widely practiced, discussed, and openly accepted by many who chose to overlook it and treat it as an "open secret."[2]

During the war years of the 1940s and into the more conservative 1950s a nationwide crackdown ended the relative ease with which practitioners like Inez Burns wielded their trade. The old system in which physicians, lawyers, friends, and advisors referred patients to abortion specialists practicing out of private clinics was replaced with new hospital rules and regulations. Furthermore, hospital administrators assisted the state by forming therapeutic abortion committees, which in many cases further restricted practices. In 1954 the Joint Commission on Accreditation of Hospitals (JCAH) set up standards that required consultation for practices governing reproduction, including "curettages or any procedure in which a pregnancy may be interrupted." The JCAH explained, "We are dealing here with not only prfessional [*sic*] but also moral and legal considerations."[3]

It was not until the 1960s that many states, including California, began changing abortion laws. On June 14, 1967, within six months of being elected governor of California, Ronald Reagan signed the Therapeutic Abortion Act, which provided for the well-being of the mother. Six years later, on January 22, 1973, the United States Supreme Court, in *Roe v. Wade* and *Doe v. Bolton*, in effect struck down state laws regulating abortion.

———

This is a work of nonfiction. No events have been fabricated, no names have been changed, and no characters invented. In writing this book I spent many hours conducting interviews with Inez Burns's granddaughter Caroline Carlisle, who gave me great insight into Burns's early years and private life. I also relied on evidence gathered through extensive research of archival documents, personal papers, photographs, oral histories, newspapers, and trial transcripts. Anything between quotation marks comes from letters, memoirs, or other written documents.

I am indebted to a number of people without whose help this book would not have been possible: Friends and colleagues (too numerous to list, but you know who you are) whose encouragement never wavered.

Gordon Bakken, who left us too soon, for your wonderful ideas. Stephen Bloom, who even though we chose to go in different directions, shared my enthusiasm for this story. I extend a special thank-you to Clifford Trafzer, my dedicated mentor and friend, for always believing in me. I would also like to thank my editor, Bridget Barry, for her timely edits and wise suggestions that smoothed the way for this project, and to all the staff at University of Nebraska Press who helped make it happen.

I thank my family, who kept me sane and without whose unconditional support and patience this project would not have come together. My cousin and dear friend Rita, whose steadfast strength and wisdom gave me balance. Finally, I thank my daughter Vanessa—who spent hours by my side combing through microfiche and old photographs—and my son Stevie, both of whose enthusiasm and encouragement are unmatched.

Prologue   The Beginning of the End

San Francisco, 1946:

Chief Assistant District Attorney Thomas Lynch leaned toward the witness.

"Isn't it true," he demanded, "that Inez Burns insisted on being served her morning coffee while she performed illegal surgeries on these women?"

"Yes," replied former defendant and ex-employee Madeline Rand. She glanced nervously at Inez Burns, seated directly behind the defense table, her head held high, every hair tucked perfectly under her custom-made sable hat. The same soft fur trimmed her woolen suit and draped gracefully around her shoulders, setting her apart from the rest of women in the courtroom.

"In fact," Rand continued, returning her gaze to the prosecuting attorney, "we had so many clients we were usually shorthanded and most of us had to eat on the run . . . but never Inez, she only had strong black coffee."[1]

———

The promise of a sensational story brought out journalists, lookie-loos, and the simply curious to San Francisco's historic courthouse that gray, damp February morning. The public castigation of the notorious Queen of Abortionists and her cohorts drew record crowds. Dressed in a chocolate-brown Dior suit, Inez Brown Burns was flawless and glamorous, the star in her own ill-fated drama. She sat stoically behind the defense table, her hands calmly folded in her lap. Lined up on the bench beside her were Musette Briggs, a light-skinned black woman, referred to as Burns's "understudy" by prosecutor Tom Lynch; next, the "Little Sparrow," Mable Spaulding, a shy, middle-aged introvert; then Myrtle Ramsey, not too bright by Burns's standards, but ready to do any job and designated "the cleaner." Finally, seated at the end was Joseph "the Duster" Hoff, a longtime employee and Burns's meticulous lab technician.

Ignoring the attention given to the defendants, prosecutor Lynch began by inquiring if the jury candidates knew any of the individuals from his long list of witnesses, which included eight physicians, seven attorneys, and twenty other persons of interest. He would take no prisoners, he promised, but intended to link "any and all of them" to Burns's twenty-plus-year, multimillion-dollar operation. It was a lifetime of corruption, Lynch told the court, that Burns built through backroom deals, coercion, and vice—finally brought to an end with her arrest in September of 1945.[2]

Waiting impatiently (given the list in Burns's "little black books," some no doubt with nervous anticipation), the citizenry, many whom she had previously serviced, befriended, paid off, and yes, hated and gouged, turned out to witness the most anticipated legal drama in three decades, a case that pitted the best attorneys in San Francisco against one another. The prosecution came under the capable direction of the newly elected and politically motivated District Attorney Edmund G. "Pat" Brown, who entered office pledging all his resources to "uproot the system" of graft and corruption that ate away at the moral heart of the city—starting with the queen bee of them all—Inez Brown Burns. "I, myself, along with Tom Lynch, will handle this trial," he assured his constituents.[3]

True to his word, Brown oversaw every aspect of the case with the bulk of the courtroom work falling to his chief assistant, Thomas C. Lynch. Lynch, cold and calculating by nature, was a skilled prosecutor who spent ten years in the federal courts taking down gangsters and income tax evaders. Lynch chose as his second chair Andrew J. Eyman, a capable attorney who, along with homicide inspector Frank Ahern—Honest Frank, as he came to be known—led the raid on Burns's abortion clinic.

The renowned Walter J. McGovern headed up Burns's defense team. A former state senator, pillar in the Catholic Church, and appointed president of the police commission by Mayor Angelo Rossi, McGovern was gregarious and outspoken. He relished the spotlight and was considered one of the best trial lawyers in the state. Mr. McBig, as he was known about town, had a reputation for pushing his weight around. For this trial, he chose as second chair John R. Golden, a sharp attorney who formerly worked eleven years as assistant district attorney for Brown's predecessor, the pointedly corrupt former district attorney Matthew Brady.[4]

The die was cast. Inez Burns confidently played the game as she always had—underhanded and calculating. For Pat Brown, years of careful career planning brought him to this public stage, and losing was not an option.

And so, the first of three trials began.

San Francisco's Queen of Vice

PART ONE

The Queen Bee

1   *On Trial*

This trial will be an event compared with the
beginning of an atomic chain reaction.

—*San Francisco Chronicle*

Inez Burns's first trial began on February 18, 1946, despite repeated delays
requested by the defense counsel and a last-minute flight by prosecutor
Tom Lynch to Los Angeles to force the "ailing" defendant to appear. The
district attorney's office built its case primarily on the direct testimonies of
a number of women who patronized Burns's Fillmore Street clinic, who
could identify all of the defendants. Defense attorney Walter McGovern,
not concerned with proving his client's innocence, focused his attention
on District Attorney Brown's political aspirations. McGovern strategized
to show that Brown's desire for state office motivated him to single out
Burns, the Queen Bee, to get public recognition as the law and order
district attorney who cleaned up San Francisco.[1]

With evidence tying Burns to numerous city officials and members of
the police department, the defense attorney's focus on Brown's political
ambitions was exactly the distraction his chief assistant Tom Lynch feared.
McGovern, described by one reporter as "massive and elegantly attired,"
was, according to Lynch, a very talented lawyer of the old school and a
master of "invective and the English language," which made just picking a
jury a huge challenge. Anticipating a lengthy struggle over jury selection,
the judge summoned an oversized panel of one hundred candidates from
which both sides received thirty-five preemptory challenges.[2]

McGovern began voir dire by questioning prospective jurors on the
good faith of the prosecution as well as the political ramifications of the

trial for Brown. One candidate, when questioned on Brown's campaign to be state attorney general, replied that he did not even know Brown was running. Smiling at this response, McGovern turned to the crowded courtroom and agreed, "Lots of people don't either."[3]

The courtroom took on a circus-like atmosphere as McGovern, when asking the usual questions, stopped and from out of nowhere demanded to know if the candidate knew District Attorney Brown.

"Do you know our fearless district attorney, Edmund G. 'Pat' Brown," he asked with a sly smile, "known to his friends as Buster Brown?"

This tactic completely unnerved some of the candidates, but only encouraged McGovern to elaborate even more: "Who goes about like a busy bee, flitting from flower to flower and stinging as he goes—and who may be a candidate for attorney general!" Leaning in, now commanding the court's full attention, McGovern continued in a loud voice, "And do you know his assistant, Mr. Lynch, the lean and hungry Cassius?"[4]

McGovern's theatrics did not offend or rattle Lynch, who had heard it all before. In fact, that was a kind introduction by the defense attorney, who often referred to Lynch as "the slacker" who stayed home from the war to "hold back the fog." In truth, Lynch was too old for the draft, a point unfortunately missed by most of McGovern's audience. The former senator never left any doubt who controlled the courtroom. Lynch knew what he was up against and hoped Brown would put off running for attorney general until after the Burns trial. It shocked him as much as anyone when Brown threw his hat in the ring. Much to Lynch's chagrin, one jury candidate, Jacob Barman, admitted to knowing most of the individuals on the panel, including Brown, and stated he was a member of the same political party.[5]

"When did you know him?" McGovern asked, and then without missing a beat continued, "When he was in the Republican assembly, or just since he has become a Democrat?" Then McGovern demanded to know if Barman worked on Brown's campaign.

"Not yet," Barman grinned.[6]

Unfortunate timing on Brown's part set him up to play right into McGovern's drama. Just back from the Democratic convention in Sacramento, Brown attempted to slip quietly into a seat behind the prosecutor's table in the middle of voir dire, but McGovern caught him.

"Ah, and here he comes now," the defense attorney announced as he motioned toward Brown, now settled in behind Lynch. "Do you know Mr. Brown," he asked the next candidate, pointing to the district attorney, "who sits over there?" Then, with a grand Shakespearean gesture of his hand, McGovern literally lifted Brown to his feet, still wearing a bright green, saucer-sized campaign tag around his neck that read, "Brown for Attorney General!" Delighted, McGovern asked the speechless district attorney, "Did you bring one of those for each of us?"

He was simply "magnificent," Lynch recalled.[7]

But even with McGovern's impressive orations, Lynch was up for the challenge. He knew it was a contest, in part because he had recently come from the state attorney's office and came off as cold-blooded and matter-of-fact. Staying true to his reputation, Lynch spared no one, sweeping everyone possibly connected to Burns up in his net. Physicians listed during jury examination included Burns's son, Dr. Robert Merritt, a well-respected physician and longtime resident of Santa Clara. Also, her past partners: Dr. Adolphus A. Berger, the former city autopsy surgeon; Dr. Charles B. Caldwell, currently on trial for murder; Dr. Lewis A. Stuck and Dr. Frank Paget, of Oakland; and Dr. Larry Everson, a former naval officer. City officials named included Edward Dullea, a member of the fire department and brother to Police Chief Charles Dullea; police inspector George "Paddy" Wafer; Thomas Mitchell, official from the State Franchise Tax Commission; and former San Francisco supervisor Warren Shannon and his wife Gloria Davenport Shannon. Interestingly, while the Shannons provided a substantial portion of the evidence used against Burns and were accused by her of blackmail and attempting to extort $35,000, at the last minute the district attorney's office withdrew subpoenas issued for the pair.[8]

After several days of questioning, a panel of four men and eight women, thoroughly examined and accepted by both sides, was summarily dismantled when the defense demanded to reexamine one of the women. McGovern revealed to the court that his investigator found Mrs. Bessie Peabody to be a relative of Gloria Shannon, who had promised to "blow the lid off this whole thing," and had kept this information secret. When questioned by the judge, it became clear that Peabody lied on her questionnaire in an attempt to get on the jury. With Peabody dismissed, McGovern went through five new candidates before settling on a juror that suited him.[9]

During the final days of questioning, several prospective jurors expressed their belief that laws governing illegal surgery should be modified. Leading the group, Mrs. Leah Hamilton, wife of a University of California Hospital doctor, argued that current laws were outdated and did not conform to the "social conditions of today." The judge excused Mrs. Hamilton for cause when she held firm that her beliefs might sway her verdict. Finally, a selected jury of seven men and five women heard the case in the superior court of Judge William F. Traverso.[10]

The next major hurdle involved the mysteriously unavailable Warren and Gloria Shannon. McGovern accused the district attorney's office of withholding evidence that would confirm their involvement and attempted extortion of his client. But Brown argued that the Shannons' testimony only "confirmed evidence he already had." In an attempt to ferret out the truth, McGovern kept Miss Jean Calmenson, a petite, redheaded stenographer from the district attorney's office, on the stand for an entire day. He charged that the prosecution withheld the notes of a private conversation between Brown and Burns that took place on the day of the abortion clinic raid and her arrest. After several hours of questioning Calmenson finally admitted taking notes of such a conversation and recalled Brown inquired of Burns if she knew the Shannons. However, Calmenson vehemently denied any knowledge of the district attorney mentioning money or an automobile given to Warren Shannon.[11]

"Isn't it true," McGovern pressed her, "that Mr. Brown wanted to know whether the Shannons had tried to shake Mrs. Burns down for $35,000?"

"No," she replied, shaking her head, "he didn't ask her anything like that in my presence."

"Didn't District Attorney Brown tell my client she wasn't the sort of person he expected to find?"

"Not that I recall."

"Didn't Brown tell you this was off the record and to stop writing?"

"I have no record of that," she said, again shaking her head.

Red-faced, McGovern turned to the prosecutor and accused him of withholding the transcripts of the conversation. Lynch jumped to his feet, dug through the stack of files piled in front of him, and handed one to the defense attorney.

"This is not the right conversation at all," McGovern shouted. "It's a plant!"[12]

But Lynch maintained he was under no legal obligation to give his records to the defense, and the judge agreed with him. Lynch's witness list no longer included insiders Warren and Gloria Shannon, but the prosecution did intend to call former Burns employees Madeline Rand, Kathryn Bartron, and Virginia Westrup, originally named as defendants in the case. Also listed were Peel Queen and his wife Levina, who remained fugitives after a daring late night escape, the latter named as a principal anesthetist in Burns's operation.[13]

———

The facts in the case were well established before the first trial began. Inez Burns owned and conducted abortions at the facilities located at 325–27 Fillmore Street, San Francisco and 435 Staten Avenue, Oakland. At the 6300-square-foot Fillmore Street clinic, the first floor served as a garage, the second floor a flat, connected to the third and fourth floors by a secret stairway. At times Burns allowed friends and employees to live in the second-floor flat, including Madeline Rand and Warren and Gloria Shannon. The third floor held a large reception area, kitchen, offices, and two elevated "recovery" sun porches. Bedrooms and three surgical rooms made up the fourth floor. Each white-tiled surgical room included two sinks, one large and one smaller; these fed into an oversized concrete incinerator buried in the back yard, which the staff fired up nightly to destroy the fetal remains.[14]

Burns performed the majority of the abortions, her German-made stainless steel instruments always freshly sterilized and stored in a rolled-up leather bag. Her tools of the trade included forceps, cervical dilators, a tenaculum, and uterine curettes. Over the years various nurses, doctors, and staff assisted her, including anesthetist Levina Queen, who came to Burns's clinic in October 1943 and worked from 9:00 a.m. until 5:00 p.m. six days a week, generally alongside Burns in the surgical rooms. According to Queen, the Fillmore Street clinic treated twenty to forty women on an average day.[15]

Throughout the three trials, five women testified that they visited the clinic and that Burns performed abortions on them. In addition, two women were called who refused to testify on the grounds that their testimony might publically degrade them.

Such was the case with the prosecution's third witness, Mrs. Agnes Metzil, who surprised the court when she strode down the aisle loudly announcing, "I refuse to testify. I don't want to commit a crime, but I don't want to be a public scorn!" Lynch insisted the stout, middle-aged woman take the oath and identify herself. But Metzil stared defiantly at the linen handkerchief knotted between her fingers and refused to speak until ordered by the judge to do so. The prosecutor then launched into his questions.

"Have you ever visited Burns's establishment at 327 Fillmore Street?"

"I refuse to testify!"

"On what grounds?" Lynch demanded.

"Just what I said before," the woman said, her voice now an octave higher.

"That's not sufficient, your honor!"

The judge ordered the jury out, and then explained to Mrs. Metzil that she could only refuse to testify on the constitutional grounds that her testimony might incriminate or degrade her.

"Now, do you understand that?" he asked.

"Yes, I do,"

"Okay then, state the grounds upon which you wish not to testify," the judge prompted.

"I refuse to testify, as I stated before," Metzil responded.

"I have tried to point out to you, lady, the only grounds on which you can refuse to testify is if it would tend to incriminate or degrade you." Exasperated, the judge prompted her again. "*Is* that what you mean?"

"That's right, I don't want to be degraded in public life," she nodded.

Unconvinced, Lynch glared at the defense table and said, "I'd like to know what got into her, she was all right when she arrived here this morning."[16]

McGovern smiled from across the aisle when the judge dismissed her.

In each case, the women who did testify recalled that Burns's staff admitted them into a large living room that served as a reception and waiting area. This room, comfortable and well decorated, always seemed crowded with women careful to observe the "no smoking" and "quiet" signs. From there Mabel Spaulding interviewed each woman individually in a private office to determine the length of her pregnancy, previous operations, any other medical conditions, and to fix the fee. If Spaulding found the patient prepared to pay cash, she could continue upstairs; if not, Spaulding gave her instructions to return with the money as soon as possible.[17]

Finished with the initial introduction, Spaulding or additional staff guided the woman to an upstairs bedroom where she undressed down to her slip. Then a nurse took the patient to one of the surgical rooms to be attended by Burns and blood technician Joseph Hoff, who took samples that he sent to a local lab. As instructed, the patient positioned herself on the operating table, her feet securely strapped in the metal stirrups with the lower half of her body exposed. Once the patient relaxed under anesthesia, Burns began by performing a vaginal examination. Typically, at the beginning of the abortion the patient felt a sharp pain that then subsided. The entire procedure took less than fifteen minutes, and the patient was then transferred to one of the sun porches to recover for approximately an hour. Providing all went well, the patient went home for bed rest with the following instructions detailed by Burns:

1. No tub baths, showers or head shampoos, for 10 days.

2. Take no douches for 14 days—our methods are more antiseptic than yours would be.

3. Stay in bed for 3 or 4 days. You may get up for meals and go to the bathroom, but return to bed at once.

4. Keep your bowels open—this is very important. Milk of Magnesia (3 tablespoons) or Ex-Lax. If you do not, you may have gas pains. In that case take an enema, some aspirin and use an ice bag. If this does not relieve you or you are flowing too heavy, please get in touch with us and please do not call anyone else.

5. When you leave here, you might flow and you might not. If you do, all right, if not all right. An unusual flow accompanied by cramps that continue—please get in touch with us immediately or return. If you do not flow, there is a possibility of a reddish or brownish discharge that will last for about two weeks. This is perfectly normal.

6. Your next period will be four to seven weeks from now, during which you might flow a little heavier than usual. If so, do not be alarmed. Just stay off your feet, and take care of yourself.

7. We advise no sexual intercourse for at least two weeks. Preferably not until after your next normal period.

8. If any of the above instructions are not quite clear to you, don't hesitate to ask and we will be glad to explain.

Before leaving each client received a card with a telephone number and was told to call the clinic—and no one else—immediately if anything went wrong.[18]

2   *From the Palace to a Tent . . .*
and Back Again

The town's many smoke-filled speakeasies were jammed
with hell-bent citizens out for the maximum of illegal fun.

—Dashiell Hammett

In 1910, four years after the earthquake and devastating firestorm destroyed
San Francisco, twenty-four-year-old Inez Ingenthron, like multitudes of
others, returned to the city to rebuild her life. The divorced mother of two
sons arrived via the Southern Pacific Railroad with only one in tow—the
baby Robert. Her sister Nellie, black hat and scarf blowing in the cold
ocean breeze, waited shivering on the platform.

"Where's the other one?" she asked, snuggling her face next to Bobby's
fat, red cheek. "Your letter said there were two."

"I'll send for George later," Inez said, "when I can."[1]

She never did. Two-year-old George stayed in Pennsylvania with his
father George Merritt Sr. while Inez spent the next year crammed into
her mother's two-bedroom Cumberland Avenue house along with Nellie
and their two brothers, Harry and Walter. Sharing the crowded eight-
by-ten-foot bedroom with her mother and sister, Inez never bothered
to unpack the cardboard suitcase she brought. It held everything she
owned, including the tightly bound leather bundle containing the tools
of her trade.

The stainless steel surgical instruments given to her six years before
included forceps, curettes, and dilators, and she kept each piece meticulously clean and sterile. They were all Inez needed, and within weeks

she was back in business. Back to her whispered profession—the secret, forbidden vocation that old Dr. West had taught her, and taught her well.[2]

—

Inez Lillian Ingenthron was born on September 5, 1886, in a two-room cardboard shack on the outskirts of Pittsburgh, Pennsylvania, where her parents put her to work in the local pickle factory at the age of five—or so she told her children and grandchildren. She held onto the tale so vehemently her family insisted it was true. Actually, if somewhat less exciting, official records show she was born in the city of San Francisco to Alice Bell Cross and Frederick Ingenthron, a German immigrant and cigar maker.

Inez's parents married on December 13, 1873 in Dearborn, Indiana. Seven years later the couple appear on the 1880 census as residents of Chicago along with their five-year-old daughter Nellie. It is unclear what year the family settled in San Francisco; however, they began to appear in local records living on Perry Street as early as 1888. In 1894 Inez's father died, leaving the family—which in addition to Nellie now included Harry, age seventeen, Walter, age twelve, and eight-year-old Inez—living in a small house on Howard Street.

Across town from the Ingenthrons, Dr. Eugene F. West, the distinguished (if somewhat infamous) local abortionist, who was practicing out of his office on McAllister Street when he first met Inez, openly advertised his services in local newspapers:

DR. WEST, ladies specialist, my method of curing female disorders is always reliable. Irregularities from any cause successfully overcome in one visit. Consultation is free. Come in for immediate advice, or write. Confidential office and private entrance.[3]

In 1893 Dr. West's advertisements, which often included phrases such as "all cases successfully treated," drew in twenty-one-year-old Addie Gilmour, whose death subsequently exposed West's practices in a lengthy public trial—the first of many. In this case he claimed to have cared for the girl only after an abortion, and at the request of another doctor. When Ms. Gilmour died suddenly, Dr. West colluded (police alleged) with still another physician, Dr. A. S. Tuchler, to dismember and pack the body into oilcans, which the two dumped into the San Francisco Bay. For his part, Tuchler wanted Gilmour's head, specifically the skull, to complete a skeleton he was assembling. Tuchler unceremoniously wrapped the girl's head in chicken wire and hung it underwater (apparently it was customary for local physicians and medical students to leave body parts in the bay as a way to reduce them to bone) near the town of Sausalito. Unfortunately, when discovered it caused quite a stir.[4]

A jury acquitted West and in 1902 the less-than-respectable doctor, whose incompetence and malpractice routinely kept him in the courtroom, happened upon Inez, then a sixteen-year-old, auburn-haired beauty who worked at the opulent Palace Hotel off Market Street. Struck first by her classic good looks and quick wit, West sought out her "manicure" (i.e., escort) services, which he heard would satisfy his every desire. He was not disappointed and soon became a regular customer. Inez had also heard of Dr. West, and knew why he was one of the most sought-after physicians in the city. Within a year of their first meeting she confided in her new friend that unfortunately she had found herself in a "delicate" situation and needed his assistance.

West scheduled her procedure without hesitation, but Inez refused to go through with it until he allowed her to watch an operation firsthand.

"It's not for the squeamish," he warned her.

"I'm not soft," she assured him.[5]

After observing the first surgery, she insisted on attending another, and then another. The simplicity of the procedure intrigued Inez, as well as the fact that Dr. West made in one hour what took her weeks to earn. Thus, Inez found her new profession.[6]

It did not take much convincing for the overworked physician to take Inez under his wing, first as his assistant, and then gradually as a full partner. He also recognized she was particularly talented as a surgeon—she had the "touch," he said, in her gentle hands and unwavering patience. But it was more than that; he believed she had a "sixth sense" for this unique procedure. She soon left her job at the Palace to work full time performing abortions under his watchful eye.

While murder charges piled up against the inept, aging doctor, his protégé would operate for the next thirty-five years with very few mishaps. More than likely, while Inez gained her operating skills from West, she also learned from his mistakes. With her additional income she moved from her mother's house on Howard Street into a lively, if somewhat ramshackle boarding house only blocks from the glowing lights of the city's business district. Life was good.[7]

But for Inez and the rest of San Francisco, time stopped at 5:12 a.m. on the morning of April 18, 1906, when the great earthquake and subsequent firestorm destroyed the city. Left with few options Inez, together with her mother and sister, joined three hundred thousand other refugees and made their way to temporary evacuee camps.

Nothing could have prepared Inez for the year that followed. After days of living out in the open and eating meager handouts shared with strangers, the rain-soaked women finally settled in Golden Gate Park, where they were issued an army tent and three cots. Inez stored the only belongings she managed to salvage from the fire in a wooden crate hidden under her makeshift bed. As Inez expected, thieves overran the camp, so the sisters chose their mother to stand watch while they waited in line for food, water, and firewood. This became their dreaded daily routine. Food remained scarce and fresh water even harder to come by. Soldiers who only days before were forced to shoot citizens trapped on burning rooftops now oversaw survivors, who were reluctant to pitch in, dig sanitation trenches, or clear fields. In this city within a city, the bottom feeders quickly took over, profiting off the misery of all. Inez knew she needed to find a way to earn money if she and her family were to make it beyond basic survival in the camp.[8]

Six weeks into their stay, while trudging through puddles of mud with a soup bucket clutched in one hand and the blackened hem of her skirt in the other, Inez paused in front of several young men lounging in the brief morning sun beneath a hand-painted sign that read "Bachelor's Club."

"What're you selling?" she asked a bearded young man who lay stretched out on a gray army tarp, his sleeves and trouser legs rolled up to expose pale white skin.

"Hooch . . . smokes," he smiled, pulling himself up on one arm. "You got somethin' ta sell?"

She ignored him and kept walking, but she had an idea.

By that evening a hastily made banner announcing "Tarot Card Reader" hung above her tent door. A small wooden table draped with a red silk scarf decorated the entrance, and Nellie conveniently arranged for their mother to be across camp attending evening Bible readings. Inez opened for business.

It did not surprise her that the city's displaced residents came desperately seeking answers or that her male customers usually called after dark. And it only increased business that Inez believed herself a reincarnated gypsy queen who spent a lifetime wandering the Moroccan desert telling fortunes and casting spells. She took on this new role with great vigor, wearing only black, giving séances by candlelight, and of course, secretly accommodating the pleasures of her late night customers. Within a week Nellie could take bookings only by appointment.

While Inez did not make a great deal of money, it was enough to allow the three women comforts few others could afford. Nevertheless, after a year of living in a tent, sleeping on a narrow army cot, contending with public baths and the insufferable mud, Inez wearily gathered her belongings and headed for Pennsylvania and her mother's people.[9]

———

In 1910 Inez returned to a city rising from the rubble with amazing speed. With herself and a baby to care for, she wasted no time re-establishing her network of old friendships and acquaintances. She knew she was very good at what she did and within months her client list grew faster than she could expand. One year after her return, Inez met and married William E. Brown, a sea captain seventeen years her senior. At the time, it seemed a good idea since she needed someone to be a father for young Robert. The couple added William Junior to the family the following April.

To keep her growing business in the shadows, Inez began using her middle name Lillian, and put the word out that she was a skilled "practical nurse" trained to care for women's delicate ailments. With her accumulated profits, Inez purchased her first property in 1919, a 1700-square-foot house on Excelsior Avenue that she wisely put in her own name. It was small, but it was hers.

Here in her first modest home Inez began a lifelong pattern of taking in, caring for, and supporting those in need: family members, friends, employees, and sometimes just plain strangers. In the small one-bedroom Excelsior Avenue house she made room for William's younger brother Fred.[10]

Inez managed to operate under the radar for ten years. Then in the spring of 1920 she had her first close call after being swept up in the search for nationally celebrated labor leader Edith Suter.

A Swiss immigrant, Suter came to America at the age of five, and like most nineteenth-century émigrés she experienced firsthand the degradation of severe, abject poverty. After years of working long hours in a New York City sweatshop, Suter decided she could not face quietly settling into a life of such drudgery. Following her passion, Suter took up the cause of the underprivileged and joined the United Garment Workers of America. Within a few short years she moved up through the ranks and became a greatly admired labor leader who traveled from coast to coast attending conferences and organizing workers.[11]

During the last week of April 1920, Suter made one of her regularly scheduled trips from New York to San Francisco, not for a conference, but to attend to local labor issues—at least, that was the official line she gave family members and colleagues. She even registered as usual at the Hotel Lankershim, and then she disappeared.

Two weeks later Sarah Hagen, the assistant secretary of the San Francisco Labor Council, reported her missing and a statewide hunt began. Notified by a friendly contact inside the police department, Inez promptly telephoned Hagen hoping to resolve the situation quietly.

"Miss Suter came to my home very sick," she told the assistant secretary. "I am really sorry, but there was nothing I could do."

"But how is that possible?" Hagen demanded.

"It was pneumonia," Inez said. "I'm so sorry."[12]

The following day, police investigators showed up on Inez's doorstep to investigate. According to her official statement, the labor leader appeared at her home on the evening of May 11, stating that she heard Inez was a nurse and complaining of a terrible illness. "I only agreed to take care of her," Inez told the officers, "because she was very sick and had no place to go." But when days went by with no improvement she realized the woman was in trouble and didn't have a doctor. That is when "I called my own doctor, Dr. Hans Mager," Inez explained further.[13]

According to Inez, Dr. Mager came immediately and examined Suter, determined that she suffered from pneumonia, and recommended that she not be moved. Then on the evening of May 22, the thirty-eight-year-old rallied somewhat, but died suddenly during the night. Inez directed police to the private undertaker where she had arranged for the body to be taken.[14]

The police had more questions than answers and left it to the county coroner to perform an autopsy and clear up the mystery. But the autopsy report only added to the confusion. "This patient did not die of pneumonia, and there is every indication that an operation of some kind was performed on her," the coroner concluded. "Unfortunately the body was embalmed, and therefore I cannot be sure."[15]

After obtaining the coroner's report, captain of detectives Dunan Matheson demanded Inez be brought to police headquarters, where he questioned her for an entire day. Inez, however, stood by her original statement. Frustrated, the police felt sure the labor leader died of an illegal operation, though they were unable to determine who actually performed the surgery: Inez Brown, the practical nurse, or Dr. Hans Mager, the fixer.

After hours of interrogation Inez called her attorney, Eric Rosenstern. But Captain Matheson refused to be challenged by the intrusive lawyer and threw him out of police headquarters for interfering with the investigation. Rosenstern left in a huff, only to return a short time later and accuse the detective handling the case of stealing the dead woman's valuables. "Miss Brown turned over Miss Suter's personal belongings, including a substantial amount of money, three sealskin coats, and a diamond ring to the officer," Rosenstern reported, "items that were never handed in to the police property clerk."[16]

With accusations leveled at his officers and no clear evidence to go on, Matheson begrudgingly released Inez. Reports later claimed that she gave the deceased women's furs and jewelry to the officer as a bribe.

Dr. Mager appeared at the coroner's inquest and gave his account of Suter's death. Confidently taking the stand, he refused to budge from his original story and insisted that the body (ordered immediately and conveniently embalmed by Inez) be examined further by a "proper" pathologist to determine that Suter had in fact suffered from pneumonia. The hearing took place without Inez, who insisted she had taken ill and checked herself into the Fairmont Hospital.[17]

On June 2, the coroner's jury determined Edith Suter's death was definitely due to an illegal operation, but they could not assign the responsibility to any one person. With Rosenstern's surprise accusation and no clear evidence obtainable from the body, Matheson dropped the case. He did not win this round, but he now had Inez Brown on his radar.[18]

The following year Matheson arrested Inez again when another client, Amelia Sauer, became seriously ill and ended up in Mission Emergency Hospital. But to his dismay, the judge dropped the charges when Sauer refused to testify.[19]

Over the next four years Inez operated her business with little interference and no major mishaps. She divorced William Brown and in 1924 invested the cash she had squirreled away into a 3200-square-foot, custom-built home on trendy Guerrero Street less than a mile from Mayor James Rolph's mansion. Inez personally designed the five-bedroom house, which included an oversized master suite brightly lit by large bay windows that opened out from the second floor. The headboard of her king-sized bed reached halfway up to the twelve-foot coffered ceiling and perfectly matched the pale gold velvet coverlet that set her back a thousand dollars. Off to one side of the suite two walk-in closets opened to display her growing collection of designer fashions. Builders constructed one closet to hold her extensive hat and shoe collection; the other contained a long rack of chic evening gowns, each separately bagged and labeled. More importantly, behind the silk and taffeta dresses stood a massive upright combination safe. Besides ready cash, the safe held account books and Inez's growing collection of "little black books" that listed patients, dates, referrals, repairmen, fees, and payoffs.[20]

The Guerrero Street house was her dream home, a showpiece of her talented entrepreneurship. She spared no expense and installed silky walnut floors throughout the house, all covered with rich Persian carpets that wound from room to room. A massive grand piano graced the family room, and a three-tiered Baccarat crystal chandelier lit up the entryway.

But ever the model of practicality, Inez included secret cubbyholes installed beneath the steps of the massive curved staircase, hidden hollow pockets carved into the solid walnut bannister, and slide-away running boards along the walls in the dining room. Secret places only she knew about—places to stash notebooks, envelopes containing patient cards and the weekly take, and tightly bound bundles of cash.[21]

To entertain friends and business associates she ordered the full basement finished into a smoking lounge with plush furniture, subdued lighting and a fully stocked bar, all centered around a large mahogany poker table. Her weekly games (which became legendary) began on Wednesday night and usually continued through Saturday, were by invitation only, and brought together the "who's who" of the city.

On any given week Inez entertained players who quickly became close personal friends, insiders, and network connections. These included politicians, like Mayors James "Sunny Jim" Rolph and Angelo Rossi, betting commissioner Tom Kyne, crime boss Pete McDonough, various local doctors including the county coroner (fixers and referrals), attorneys, and police officials. Fire captain Ed Dullea and a variety of beat cops occasionally joined the fun. Inez counted this in the cost of doing business: all part of keeping everyone happy, she always said.[22]

Inez made a lot of friends and acquaintances, but she trusted no one. All the daily records, including payoffs, she personally wrote in small black notebooks that she stored on the top shelf of her closet safe. She accepted only cash payments and handled all the money, putting only as much in the bank as absolutely necessary. She kept "working capital," as she called it, in the safe, and strategically distributed the rest throughout the house and in a steam trunk in the attic.

Interestingly, her proclivity toward obsessive-compulsive behavior surfaced during this time. She ordered her private bath to be equipped with three marble sinks—one to wash her face, the second for hand washing, and the third to brush her teeth. A stack of snow-white towels always rested on the stand next to the porcelain claw-foot tub. "White, only white," she told the maid. "And bleach 'em good. I don't ever want to see any spots."[23]

Tall mirrors covered the bathroom walls. She did not want to miss an added pound, wrinkle, or flaw. Each morning she religiously stripped down and faced the oversized doctor's scale that she said, "waited accusingly behind the towel rack." If her petite frame tipped the scale over 105 pounds she downed a concoction of raw eggs before her black coffee—as breakfast, and had nothing else for the rest of the day. "No man likes a fat woman," she would tell anyone listening.

According to her granddaughter Caroline Carlisle, who came to live with Burns at the age of ten, her obsession with body image only intensified as she became more involved with the Hollywood starlets who sought out her professional services. When safer procedures brought plastic surgery to society's rich and famous, Inez was waiting in line. While stars like Vivienne Segal and Mary Pickford opted for nose jobs and facelifts, Inez focused on her feet, which she described as much too wide. "They make me look like a peasant," she said.[24]

Finally, with the money to do something about it, she took a weeklong vacation to Los Angeles and had both small toes removed. Now she could easily slip into those sexy narrow heels that slenderized her calves and boosted her backside. But her "remodeling," as she liked to call it, did not stop there. Next to go were her lower ribs on each side, making the hourglass figure that she always belted in beneath custom tailored suits and flirty silk dresses even more pronounced. The facelifts came later. She religiously bathed her milky-white skin in expensive cold creams and night moisturizers and faithfully wore a wide-brim hat and a scarf to ward off sun damage. Still, the inevitable sagging and wrinkles set in, prompting her to take another vacation to Los Angeles for a touch-up.[25]

Inez had acquired expensive tastes, but the unprecedented frivolity of the 1920s brought an increasing number of clients to fill her pockets and pay the bills. Young, single women who flooded into the city looking for freedom and hoping for a good time often ended up in low-paying jobs and rooming together in rundown boarding houses. Unlike the decade before, more and more of these women spent their weekends partying and meeting local men at speakeasies, dance clubs, and burlesque shows. Others simply gave up their dreams and settled into one of the many bordellos that crowded the city's Tenderloin and North Beach neighborhoods.

Award-winning author Curt Gentry detailed this seedier side of town in *The Madams of San Francisco*, particularly the North Beach area, where he wrote, "houses of prostitution were so plentiful" that private owners had to put up signs on their front doors to distinguish their residences.[26]

Likewise, Herb Caen, longtime columnist and the accepted satirical voice of the city, who got his information from some of San Francisco's most noted insiders (including celebrated attorney Melvin Belli) described 1920s San Francisco in much the same way, calling it a "fog haunted . . . city" with the Hall of Justice being dirty and "reeking of evil." Where City Hall, the DA, and cops ran the town as though they owned it, "and they did," Caen said, with hookers by the hundreds, maybe thousands, and the "abortion mills—one on Market and the other on Fillmore [both operated by Inez Brown] . . . were so well known they might as well have had neon signs!"[27]

Inez never shied away from the spotlight and quickly joined San Francisco's privileged society. In 1928 Mayor (and future governor of California) James Rolph escorted Inez, along with madams Sally Stanford and Tessie Wall, all dressed in dazzling gowns and wrapped in exotic furs, to the Dreamland Auditorium for the annual Policeman's Ball. The results of the city's wide-open approach made Inez rich beyond her wildest dreams. To accommodate the surge in her caseload, she hired one of the city's most promising up-and-coming young physicians, Dr. Adolphus A. Berger.[28]

Dr. Berger came to San Francisco following his service in the Navy and accepted a position as house physician at St. Francis Hospital. He quickly gained a first-rate standing and retained that position until 1927, when he was appointed the city's autopsy surgeon. However, in the decades that followed, his moonlighting began to take its toll. In addition to covertly working alongside Inez, he gained a reputation as an "expert" witness who covered for other abortionists unlucky enough to end up in front of a jury. In one particular case, Berger argued the victim died of a heart ailment, "which is the most common cause for death," he pointed out, among women age 30 to 40. These autopsy reports written by Dr. Berger, the prosecutor contended, "always tend to show everyone suffering from the same ailment." Nevertheless, in and out of the spotlight Berger remained Inez's colleague for the rest of her career.[29]

3 Love Pirate

He condoned all improper acts I "may" have committed.
—Inez Brown Granelli

It did not take long for the ever-flamboyant Inez Brown to be back in the headlines. Beginning in May 1927 disclosures of her unorthodox marriage practices hit the newspapers and kept gossip columnists buzzing across five states. Within a year of moving into her Guerrero Street home she met and married her third husband, the handsome Italian playboy Charles A. Granelli.[1]

The stylish Italian immigrant co-owned a small produce company but spent most of his time at the racetrack or in local gambling joints. Still Inez, swept away by his swarthy good looks, ignored his obvious lack of income. Within weeks of meeting Granelli in the spring of 1925 she joined him on a weekend trip to the quiet vineyards of Napa Valley, where the couple said their vows. Granelli straightaway moved into her home and almost simultaneously moved his sister into Inez's Excelsior Avenue house. The following April their daughter Alice Lorine was born. Blessed with her mother's creamy white skin and her father's hazel eyes, Inez's fourth child and only girl was without a doubt her princess.[2]

Inez and Granelli spent their weekends wining and dining friends from San Francisco to Hollywood—and Italy, all on Inez's dime. Ironically, everyone assumed Granelli to be a man of means and often referred to him as "a wealthy San Francisco businessman." In truth, like William Brown before him, he had no money of his own, but he did look good for social occasions, sitting polished and smiling next to Inez in her opera box. "He's my new 'accessory,'" she whispered to friends, "bought and paid for."[3]

In fact, she even paid for his expensive 1924 Bugatti T-35 racecar. Then a year later when police arrested him for speeding, she paid the fine and bailed him out of jail. Handsome and charming, he was the perfect escort for dinner parties and late night shows. But all too soon the intrigue wore off as it always did, and her eyes were drawn in another direction.[4]

In December 1926 Granelli left for a five-month visit to Italy, where he hoped to invest—or more likely hide—$18,000 cash from his wife's business. In his absence a local politician, the handsome assemblyman Joseph F. Burns of the Mission District, caught Inez's attention. When Granelli returned the following April, he realized the suave legislator had succeeded in replacing him. "He has willfully, maliciously, and intentionally prejudiced my wife against me," the discarded Italian exclaimed.[5]

Immediately, Granelli packed up his suitcase and moved in with his sister—into the Excelsior Avenue house owned by his estranged wife. According to Granelli, the two reconciled a month later when Inez admitted her wrongdoing, confessed she "kept company" with Burns, and begged his forgiveness. But the reunion abruptly ended when Granelli discovered Inez and the charismatic Joe Burns still carrying on the affair. On November 2, 1927, Granelli filed for divorce, and two days later sued Burns for $150,000 for alienating his wife's affections. "For years he has poisoned her mind against me," Granelli charged.[6]

Granelli also demanded that Burns be forced to account for the gifts Inez lavished on him. According to the complaint, his wife not only bestowed her affection on Burns, but also gave him a $4000 diamond ring, an expensive car, and thousands of dollars in cash. Furthermore, while her husband was sporting around Europe, Inez moved the couple's considerable community assets, including 700 shares in the Bank of Italy (soon to be Bank of America) and the American Trust Company into her own name and into the names of her mother and sister. Granelli therefore requested the court restrain his wife from making any further financial moves, and finally, he asked for custody of the couple's two-year-old daughter Alice.[7]

Irate, Inez fired back with a protracted lawsuit in which she accused her husband of being in collusion with whatever "improper" associations she "may have had" with Burns or any other man. Newspaper articles from Montana to Utah announced: "Assemblyman Sued as Love 'Pirate'" and "Hubby Gets Cash to Let Wife Flirt!"[8]

"He condoned all improper acts I *may* have committed," Inez contended. She explained that in the exact wording of their marriage contract, Granelli consented to allow her to associate with Burns or any other man, and agreed he would make no complaint, providing she supplied him with sufficient money for his "support, entertainment, and dissipation."[9]

"I not only supported Charles," Inez said, "I also support all his relatives, giving them a place to live, money, and automobiles." Furthermore, the previous October, Inez revealed, Granelli attempted to extort more money from her by threating to publicly humiliate her. He warned her that he would reveal her misconduct with Burns, put her in jail, divorce her, and take Alice away. When she refused to be blackmailed, he filed his action. She promptly countersued for the $18,000 he used to finance his jaunt to Italy, for full custody of their daughter, and for all the furniture in her Guerrero Street home (valued at $12,000), as well as community property consisting of $30,000 in stocks and bonds and their interest in his Valley Produce Company.[10]

The following February Joseph Burns filed his own $75,000 damage suit against Granelli and his attorney and vehemently denied all charges. "I did not entice Mrs. Granelli to leave her husband," he stated, "or accept any gifts of automobiles, jewelry or money." After six months of fighting their case out in the newspapers, judges dismissed both Granelli's and Burns's lawsuits. According to their respective attorneys, both parties settled the matter and reached a satisfactory agreement. Granelli then refiled against Inez for desertion and misconduct.[11]

The press continued to refer to Granelli as the "wealthy" or "rich" San Francisco gentleman. However, after he started divorce proceedings against Inez his resources quickly dried up and it became obvious that she held all the power and money. Following the divorce settlement Granelli was sued by his attorney for cheating him out of his $534 fee.[12]

For Assemblyman Burns the public scandal could not have come at a worse time. Granelli's revelations hit the newspapers even as Burns campaigned to keep his state assembly seat. As public interest in the scandal swelled, Burns's popularity plummeted, causing the irate legislator to charge the accusations as "purely political" and to ask that the case be heard before Election Day. "Mr. Granelli is part of a conspiracy," Burns charged. "It's all malicious political lies!"[13]

Soon rumors began circulating that the San Francisco delegation planned to return to Sacramento without Assemblyman Burns. The prediction of Burns's isolation was followed by a brief article inviting readers to write in and "take up the defense of slot machines, punchboards, gambling . . . bootlegging and other forms of making money without formally working for a living." Politics remained as usual in the city by the bay.[14]

Burns's political death was swift and by August he lost his assembly seat. Nevertheless, Inez married him in 1932 and continued to use his lifelong political connections, which proved useful throughout the next two decades. Burns soon moved on and opened Burnell's Smokery, a cigar store (i.e. gambling joint). He later became a tavern proprietor, then bought, stabled, raced, and bet on horses— all financed by Inez's increasingly lucrative business.[15]

4   *Off the Hook*

The oldest, largest and most notorious "practitioners"
in San Francisco—were not even disturbed.
—*The Atherton Report*

In June 1936 federal investigators cracked down on a West Coast abortion
network that operated from as far north as Seattle all the way to San Diego
in the south. In a coordinated effort agents swooped into clinics, arresting
ringleaders in Los Angeles, Hollywood, San Diego, and San Francisco.
They hauled away truckloads of instruments and hospital equipment
along with rolled-up bundles of cash and boxes of expensive jewelry
(apparently used in lieu of cash payments). Authorities indicted a total
of thirty-one individuals on felony charges in a racket that brought in an
annual estimated $500,000, or $8.4 million in today's dollars.[1]

Federal agents recruited San Francisco captain of inspectors Charles
Dullea (soon to be police chief) to gather information on the ring in
his jurisdiction, which led to the arrests of two doctors and three other
persons in the Bay Area. As part of the cleanup, Dullea staged raids on
two clinics owned and operated by "Dr. Brown" (Inez Burns). At the
339 Waller Street clinic, officers found a facility as elaborately equipped
as a hospital. The other, at 327 Fillmore Street, appeared to be used as
a reception office and for convalescing. At both locations they found a
receptionist, a maid, and a janitor, but no sign of Burns.

At the Fillmore Street clinic Dullea's officers dutifully went through
the motions, replacing the receptionist with an officer and interviewing
women calling in for appointments. All day patients kept coming, police
reported, some in such desperation they willingly waited all day. "It is

evident," officers reported, "that Inez Burns must be making at least $1000 a day." Finally police convinced one patient's husband to lead them to the Waller Street clinic, where they made a show of kicking in the doors. There they found the clinic outfitted with an operating room, a waiting room, a kitchen, and bedroom/recovery rooms containing seven beds—all empty. Officers picked up Thomas Ramsey and Myrtle Wilson (soon to be Myrtle Ramsey), whom they believed to be caretakers, and charged them with vagrancy.[2]

While police spent the day holding interviews at the Fillmore Street branch, Burns, tipped off, had time to drive her recovering patients to safe locations. The officers made no arrests but confiscated $2000 in medical equipment from the empty clinic, which they stored at police headquarters. "If she tries to claim the stuff," Captain Dullea said, "we'll charge her then." Needless to say, she never attempted to retrieve the hospital equipment.[3]

It remains unclear if Burns ever participated in the vast multimillion-dollar West Coast operation that investigators brought to heel during that summer in 1936. What seems evident is that Captain Dullea protected Burns's identity from government agents. Only one year before, District Attorney Matthew Brady hired former FBI agent Edwin Atherton to investigate the excessive and blatant corruption that contaminated the city from the mayor's office down to the cops who walked the beat. In his 1937 report known as the *Atherton Report*, he pointed out that the city's abortionists paid at least $100,000 a year for police protection and remained the "surest, most discreet and regular payoffs of all." Furthermore, Atherton discovered that the newly exposed West Coast abortion ring was controlled by persons relatively new to the business, and that "the old, established . . . independent abortionists were not affiliated with this roundup . . . and were among some of the oldest, largest and most notorious 'practitioners' in San Francisco—and they were not even disturbed by this foray." Finally, Atherton noted, Captain Dullea "high-handedly intimidated" the officers who came forward and admitted to regular payoffs for protection.[4]

Ultimately, neither the attempt to shut down the West Coast abortion network nor Atherton's report curbed vice in the city. Local madam Sally Stanford, who according to columnist Herb Caen operated the "Stanford School of Advanced Social Studies," pointed out "war, depression and trouble" always brought a boom in the "sin-for-sale business."[5]

For Burns, business continued to increase, and in spite of Captain Dullea's efforts to shield her, her thriving enterprise raised eyebrows at police headquarters, where captain of detectives Dunan Matheson had kept his eye on her since the death of labor leader Edith Suter. The opportunity to pick her up came only months after Captain Dullea's bogus raid on her clinic. In August 1936 a seriously ill woman brought into the emergency room of San Francisco General Hospital complained that a visit to Burns's clinic caused her condition. Matheson arrested both Burns and her partner Dr. Adolphus Berger. But like others before her, the woman experienced a lapse of memory at the preliminary hearing (under somewhat suspicious circumstances) and police dropped the charges.

Now paying top dollar for protection, Burns no longer made any effort to hide her illicit business or her popularity. In fact she flaunted it, rubbing shoulders with the city's elite while donning imported furs, diamonds and sapphires, and wearing only designer clothes custom made for her at Ransohoff's on Union Square. She entertained frequently and could be seen dining out with friends, including madams Mabel Malotte and Sally Stanford, at local hot spots like the St. Francis. The three conspicuously chauffeured about town in her long black 1936 Pierce Arrow.[6]

With every passing year Burns's reputation grew, bringing more and more women to her door. This was a time when back-alley abortionists with little-to-no training gladly operated in the back seats of automobiles, on kitchen tables, or in garages for fifty dollars. Women desperate to end their pregnancies often ended up mutilated, in hospital emergency rooms, or even dead. Burns's years of experience and her obsession to clean and sterilize everything around her went a long way in decreasing the chance of a mishap or infection. Physicians throughout the state and beyond came to rely on her to do the "deed" they legally could not; lawyers referred clients, priests their parishioners, and mothers their daughters. Almost everyone in San Francisco knew about her and where to find her. According to reporter Jerry Flamm, "Inez was the place to go if you wanted it done right."[7]

As the 1930s wore on and the rest of the nation languished in the throes of the Great Depression, Burns stashed away wads of cash. Besides the working capital she kept in the closet safe, she sewed bills into the hem of her heavy dining room drapes and stuffed bundles of cash in the back of the grand piano. She stacked additional rolls, tightly bound with rubber bands, in shoeboxes hidden in the basement. And then there were the bricks of fifty- and hundred-dollar notes wrapped in plain brown paper and stacked neatly in a trunk in the attic. But the money just kept coming. She bought another house in the upscale neighborhood of St. Francis Wood, then another in the affluent community of Atherton. Next, a mansion on Mulholland Drive directly across from Cuban bandleader Xavier Cugat, and then a 700-acre horse ranch in La Honda near Half Moon Bay, stocked with thoroughbred racehorses, as a weekend getaway. All paid for in cash.

———

Warren A. Shannon, San Francisco city supervisor and one-time acting mayor, spent decades around city and local politics. A late bloomer, Shannon first tried his hand at selling insurance but failed as a salesman, so he joined the printing business with his brother William. Finally, at the age of forty he decided on a career in politics and boldly put his name in for lieutenant governor. Admitting he had never held office, Shannon pointed to his interest in public affairs, a wide circle of friends (which included the wildly popular Inez Burns and her husband Joe) and a good business sense as qualification enough. He lost the election, but the publicity brought him to the attention of Mayor James Rolph, who appointed him to San Francisco's Board of Supervisors.[8]

Shannon may have started his career as a civil servant late in life, but it did not take him long to become entrenched in the city's corrupt political system. He quickly became a friend and ally of Sheriff Thomas Finn, better known as "Boss Finn." It was also common knowledge that Shannon was on the take. Historian Donald Langmead stated in his *Icons of American Architecture* that Shannon, while managing the Golden Gate Bridge project, a venture that he oversaw beginning in 1925, "helped out" bridge engineer Joseph Strauss. According to Langmead, when Strauss ran into opposition to his design, he hired a fixer to bribe Shannon, who then regularly picked up "a sealed envelope with a $100 bill inside," and the resistance in San Francisco "magically" evaporated. Ten years later, the mayor honored the charismatic Shannon, now president of the Board of Supervisors, by naming him chairman of the Exposition, Affairs, and Industrial Development Committee for the grand opening of the long-awaited bridge.[9]

Unfortunately, that same year his wife, and mother of his two daughters, died following a long illness. Shannon then married three-time divorcée Elise Bennet. However, the new Mrs. Shannon filed for divorce two years later stating, "It was just a case of two nice people who couldn't get along." Not discouraged, Supervisor Shannon soon began looking for wife number three.[10]

5   "Miss X"

San Francisco Mill Operates Openly: Proprietor Boasts,
"We've Thousands of Clients!"

—San Francisco News-Call Bulletin

In the spring of 1938 Inez Burns's flagrant public parading backfired when two journalists from the *San Francisco News* conspired to write an undercover exposé about her. Reporters had certainly attempted to infiltrate Burns's operation in the past; usually she headed them off and they went away empty handed. However, this team included the relentless, award-winning journalist Mary Ellen Leary, future wife of Arthur Sherry, assistant district attorney of Alameda County. Leary set up the sting with the help of the newspaper's assistant city editor Joe Sheridan, who agreed to masquerade as her husband to bait Burns at her Fillmore Street clinic.[1]

On the appointed day, with cameramen strategically hidden, a sobbing Leary and her "husband" Joe Sheridan posed at Burns's door, ready for action. Unfortunately, two nuns blew their cover when they "walked right into their path," passing the couple on the front steps and spotting the photographer, forcing the team to come back later for a second try. Their next attempt proved successful and the pair got their story. Leary and Sheridan's article made the front page of the *San Francisco News-Call Bulletin* by announcing: "San Francisco Mill Operates Openly!"[2]

The May 4 story detailing their undercover investigation ran under the anonymous byline "Staff Writer" and described every aspect of the pair's personal visit from being admitted into the shadowy foyer, to the in-depth private interview the "pregnant" Leary underwent. "We expected to have an exciting experience," the reporters said, or at least some feeling of "self-conscious shame or nervous fear." But instead, when the undercover couple got in the door, they found the encounter amazingly simple and casual. It was all very businesslike and "about as exciting as a date with a dentist," Leary said.[3]

Their account began with the team's second covert attempt to gain entry. With cameramen in place, distraught "husband" Sheridan and "pregnant" Leary held hands in the drizzling rain as they made their way up the concrete steps to the second floor entry. When Sheridan rang the doorbell, the metal peephole cover slid back and there was a pause while hidden eyes assessed the pair before the ringing of a buzzer sprang the door open.

"Have you an appointment?" smiled a middle-aged woman in a nurse's uniform who was leaning over the second floor bannister.

"No," the "husband" spoke up for pair.

"Then just come on in here and wait," she said, descending the stairs and leading them into an airy living room with large bay windows looking down onto Fillmore Street.[4]

Business at the clinic appeared good: the journalists noted two additional waiting rooms, one to the left and the other to the right, all expensively furnished and fully occupied. In the smaller room to the left, a woman in her late thirties sat quietly folding and refolding a white handkerchief. Seated directly across from her, a plain woman of about thirty-five anxiously picked up and flipped through magazines from a side table. She then abruptly stood and walked to the window, stared down at the street below, then at the newcomers, then back to the street. After five minutes a young nurse entered, her bright red hair tightly twisted into a bun on the back of her head, the crinkling of her starched white uniform following each step.

"Your sister is all right and doing fine," she said, handing the handkerchief-clutching lady a card. "I suggest you call us in about an hour."

The nurse turned her attention to the undercover pair. "Alright, you come with me," she indicated to the "wife." "Your husband will have to stay here."[5]

To his relief, Sheridan realized the only requirement for him to hang out in the waiting room was a wedding ring. In an office down the hall, the redheaded nurse interviewed Leary from behind a polished wooden desk.

"Who sent you?" she began.

Leary quickly came up with a factious name.

"Was she a patient of ours?"

"Yes, about four years ago."[6]

Writing on a small pre-printed index card, the nurse made no effort to verify the referral and quickly moved on to establish the length of Leary's pregnancy as two months.

"It is best for you to come in within just a few days," she admonished. "Then it will be $50–$55 for the operation, and $5 for the anesthetic."

The nurse suggested she come in on Friday morning, as Saturday was so busy.

"We try to hold Saturday free for the business girls, you know."

"Friday would be fine," Leary agreed.

"You don't need to worry about anything. It's very easy, and you can be sure you will be well taken care of. We examine you that morning, and if everything isn't perfectly all right, we won't do it," the chatty nurse continued.

"We have done thousands—yes thousands and thousands—of these operations."

Leary nodded and smiled, silently taking mental notes.

"It won't be any different for you than any other girl, no reason why it shouldn't be very easy. If it isn't going to be all right, we can tell beforehand and we don't do it, so don't worry."

"Well, I am a little frightened," Leary confessed. "Can you tell me more about it—I've never done this before."

"I—I just wondered what it would all be like."[7]

With very little coaxing, the nurse settled back and gladly described the clinic's standard procedures.

"In the morning we take your blood pressure and examine your heart. Don't eat any breakfast before you come—that's because of the gas we will give you. It is more likely to make you sick if you have eaten. For the rest, even if I told you, you wouldn't understand."

"Do I stay overnight?"

"Oh, no, indeed," the nurse laughed at her naivety. "Won't take you more than two or three hours."[8]

The nurse escorted Leary back to her "husband" in the large waiting room, which now held a new occupant—a beautiful blond woman sitting quietly in a brocade wingback chair reading a fashion magazine. From the floor below, the reporters heard the doorbell ring, admitting yet another client. The pair hurried to look over the banister to catch a glimpse of the newest arrival, but only the dark flash of her headscarf could be seen as a staff member ushered her up a private back stairway.

Leary's story described Burns's clinic as reliable, and said her Mission District facility was as presentable as any other home on the block. Nevertheless, the cautious reporter signed her column mysteriously "Miss X." Fifty years later, in an interview for the Washington Press Club Foundation, Leary finally took credit for the story, remembering Burns as the "most respected" of the abortionists.[9]

Alarmed and embarrassed by the *San Francisco News* article, officers stormed Burns's clinic at noon the day after the story ran in the most "dramatic raid of its kind," according to police sources. Lieutenant Michael Mitchell, head of the operation, hid to one side of the outer door as one of his men rang the doorbell. When the buzzer released the door allowing the search team into the main floor, a wild scrabble ensued as officers swarmed from room to room and attempted to move to the upper floors. But a large, uniformed woman blocked the stairway, stalling their advance.

"What do you want?" she screeched.

"We're police officers," the inspector informed her.

"Look out up there!" the woman shouted as she ran up the stairs and disappeared down the hall. The warning shouts sent scantily clad patients scurrying through the halls and searching for exits. Off the front entry of the second floor, police found two adjoining rooms occupied by four half-dressed girls recovering in daybeds. A fifth woman was hurriedly dressing in the closet of another room. They found four more in two additional side rooms. Police reports described the women as attractive and all under the age of thirty. Several began to cry as officers hustled them into the large waiting room for questioning.[10]

Leaving his officers to interrogate the patients, Lieutenant Mitchell trapped Burns at the top of the stairs, where she was guarding a locked door that led to the third floor.

"Who are you?" She demanded. "What do you want?"

"Open that door," Mitchell ordered.

"Why don't you just go away?" Burns shouted back. "I'm just trying to rent some rooms here."[11]

When the officer attempted to physically move her aside, Burns violently kicked out, connecting the point of her leather work shoe with his left shin. Finally, after a two-hour standoff, she consented to unlock the door and two more patients and a nurse filed out. On the third floor, police found what Lieutenant Mitchell later described as a large, airy room, "scrupulously clean and completely outfitted as a hospital." White-tiled from floor to ceiling, the operating room contained two large surgical beds surrounded by bottles, bowls, basins, and stainless steel surgical equipment. Two additional recovery rooms adjoined the hospital room, making a total of eleven more beds on the third floor.[12]

Even as police conducted their search, new clients continued to ring the front doorbell, a husband returned to collect his wife, and a dutiful sister sat waiting on the front steps. Officers collected each patient's name and address and then released them. The report showed that the women came from various parts of the state including two patients from Oakland, two from Monterey, one from Bakersfield, and one from Napa. Tip-off reporters Sheridan and Leary recognized one of the twelve questioned as the beautiful blonde they observed in the waiting room the day before.

Police arrested Burns, who insisted her establishment was only a massage parlor, along with her nurse, Margie Silver, who claimed she only lived there. "Why are you doing this to me?" Burns demanded. "This is a clean house, I've never killed anybody up here."[13]

Charles Dullea, now promoted to captain of inspectors, announced to reporters that the police department had closely watched Burns since they raided her place two years before. He further explained that following this most recent arrest he notified the State Board of Medical Examiners, who put its own investigator, Thomas Hunter, on the case. The district attorney charged Burns and her nurse, Margie Silver, after police obtained collaborating statements from her patients caught in the raid. Within hours Burns posted $500 bail for each of them.

Initially, this latest arrest did not look good for Burns. However, when the preliminary hearing commenced on the morning of June 1, Inspector George Engler, who participated in the raid, had an unexplained lapse of memory and testified he had no actual knowledge of abortions performed at Burns's clinic. Furthermore, of the women found at the clinic and questioned, nine claimed to be just "visiting," two who admitted they came for operations gave fictitious addresses, and one slipped away. The judge dismissed the case.[14]

Burns escaped prosecution again, but Mary Ellen Leary's news story and the subsequent raid brought her to the attention of federal tax authorities. Almost immediately investigators began auditing her business records and tax returns going back ten years. Within months the Bureau of Internal Revenue filed charges of tax evasion against her for the years 1934–36 and set bail at $10,000.

After federal investigators spent months combing through her bank statements, receipts, and invoices, they realized they could only verify a small portion of her suspected income. In the end they determined her gross income for 1934 to be at least $45,000—or $41,000 with deductions—leaving her owing $6,000 in taxes for that year and an additional $3,600 for 1935.

The following year, when the average yearly family income was just over $1500 and despite Burns's claims that she was "only a poor woman trying to rent some rooms," government agents assessed her 1936 assets at $202,900, or $3.4 million in today's dollars. Burns paid her back taxes without hesitation.[15]

6   *The Fixer*

Inez is an artist. . . . If you knew the prominent families
that have been saved from disgrace by her you would think
differently.

—Joseph F. Burns

Following the 1938 raid on Inez Burns's clinic, Thomas Hunter, the
detective hired by the State Board of Medical Examiners, began a full-
scale investigation. While staking out Burns's Guerrero Street home
he spotted an expensive car driven by a young woman parked in the
driveway. Hunter ran a trace on the suspicious car and discovered it
was registered to ex-assemblyman Joseph F. Burns. When the detective
questioned Burns, he reluctantly admitted he was Inez's husband. "Yes,
I'm her husband," he conceded. "Inez is an artist," he continued, "and
she is doing a service for the public." But Burns adamantly refused to
give the identity of the young woman driving his car. "She's not mixed
up in this thing at all," he insisted, "she just borrowed my car to move
some of her things."[1]

The ex-politician, who quietly worked behind the scenes operating his
cigar store on Mission Street, feared this latest incident with his wife's
operation would pull him back into the spotlight. "I tend to my business
and she tends to hers," he told the investigator, as he attempted to drive
the young woman away, "and I don't pay any attention to what she does."[2]

Hunter sensed Burns was hiding something, and dug around until he
uncovered the dirt. He soon discovered several accusations of bribery
had been leveled against Burns while he served as an assemblyman,
most notably on fish and game legislation. Burns vehemently denied

the charges, and they were ultimately dropped. Hunter also found that Burns had a longtime association with the South of Market Street Boys, which one newspaper dubbed "San Francisco's own Tammany Hall." The Irish club's membership included former mayor and then California governor James Rolph, heavyweight champion James Corbett, and major league pitcher Frances "Lefty" O'Doul, to name a few. In January 1938, Joe Burns joined his fellow "Boys" as they crowded into St. Agnes Church and then marched two-by-two through the rain down Golden Gate Avenue to honor their fellow brother, the infamous city boss, sheriff Tom Finn.[3]

While Joe Burns denied taking bribes, he could not refute evidence of his involvement in a longstanding and well-organized clique for fixing local juries. In fact, Burns, known in not-so-polite circles as the Fixer, was still reeling from a jury tampering conviction and fine of $500 handed down only months before. As it turned out, investigators caught Burns when he fixed the jury (twice) in the paternity case of his friend, San Francisco County betting commissioner Tom Kyne. Graft investigator Edwin Atherton found it usually went down in this way: the accused gave Burns a list of the jurors, who he then selectively matched with those "related to" or "connected to" someone in his extensive network. To avoid leaving a paper trail, he called in a favor to a friend, who then called another friend or relative, and so on. Lack of evidence made it almost impossible to trace it back to Burns. When all else failed, he could "fix it" using his connections with local mobsters.[4]

The ex-assemblyman refused to comment on the judgment except to say, "What's this town coming to anyway? I wish they'd just leave me alone!"[5]

PART TWO
Edmund G. "Pat" Brown

7 *"Five-to-One" Odds*

California politics are peculiar and dangerous.

—Lord Bryce

By 1935, thirty-year-old lawyer Edmund G. "Pat" Brown already had a taste for politics. Determined to get his foot in the door of city government, he worked incessantly meeting people, networking, getting-to-know and being known in his hometown of San Francisco. To that end, he joined numerous organizations including the Elks, the Marina Boosters, the Haight-Ashbury Neighbors, the Knights of Pythias, the Junior Chamber of Commerce, and the Community Chest. In July of that year, he organized the New Order of Cincinnatus, a San Francisco–based reform group of young, politically minded professionals. Although the group showed mixed results in early elections, their efforts put Brown in the spotlight. He issued statements to the press, posed for photographs, and spoke at public events. Just as importantly, various members of Cincinnatus became lifelong friends and supporters of Brown.[1]

As the hardships of the Depression dragged on throughout the 1930s, Brown, like many other politically active professionals, began to have serious doubts about his party's policies. Motivated for change, he, along with other free market Republicans, moved to join Roosevelt's Democratic "New Dealers." As Roosevelt's second campaign began gearing up, Brown readily changed his party affiliation from Republican to Democrat without much "alteration to his centrist point of view." According to California State archivist and historian Kevin Starr, this détente between parties served to structure and nurture Brown's political career for decades to come.[2]

In 1938, after working tirelessly on the campaign of Governor Culbert Olson, Brown spent months unsuccessfully pitching himself for a job at the state house in Sacramento. Rejected, he complained to a friend, "I have been using all the pressure that I can think of to bring my abilities to the attention of the governor." Getting nowhere, he concluded, "I found I have wasted a lot of effort." Undeterred, Brown turned his strategy toward establishing a political career at home.[3]

In the late spring of 1939, Brown approached San Francisco district attorney Matthew Brady for a position as deputy district attorney. When Brady turned him down, Brown decided to run against Brady in the next election. It was well known when Edwin Atherton investigated and reported on the district attorney's office in 1937 that he exposed widespread corruption and accused Brady of an array of inappropriate activities ranging from misappropriation of funds and ineffective management to just plain laziness. In truth, the detailed and extensive Atherton Graft Report, according to Kevin Starr, did not accomplish much and only managed to slow the city down "somewhat," proving that San Franciscans "preferred their . . . system of organized vice."[4]

When he first entered politics, Pat Brown had to contend with his own father, Ed Brown, who owned and operated the Padre poker club on Eddy Street. *Chronicle* reporter Jerry Flamm, whose father was a San Francisco beat cop from 1921 until 1955, insisted Ed Brown owned several shady operations prior to the poker club; he had been a bookmaker, ran cigar stores (fronts for illegal Klondike and Bull dice games), and local theaters. When Pat Brown entered the race for district attorney, he asked his father to close down the Padre club. The elder Brown agreed, saying he did not want to do anything to interfere with his son's political career. But after spending a night thinking over his father's meager situation, Pat Brown reconsidered. "Gee, I thought . . . I'm taking away the only joy he has out of life," Brown said, and returned to his father's downtown hotel room to tell him to keep the club open even if it cost him the election. But when he arrived his father was nowhere to be found. Brown eventually located him back at the club, which he found open and operating as usual. "He never had any intention of closing it," Brown later recalled.[5]

In running for district attorney, Brown knew he faced an uphill battle against decades of accepted organized corruption. Nevertheless, during his campaign Brown publicly commented on the *Atherton Report* and his rival, District Attorney Brady. According to Judge George Harris, who served as a state and federal justice during Brady's tenure, Matthew Brady was very politically astute and a city institution. Nevertheless, Brown charged the longtime district attorney with "incompetence and stupidity," and declared him "criminally negligent in permitting things to go on and letting police take money." In the end, Brown did not win this first election, having virtually no experience in criminal law. Still, he remained determined to run again and promised San Franciscans that politics and crime would change under his watch.[6]

For some time Brown looked with great admiration across the bay to Alameda County's no-nonsense district attorney Earl Warren. Warren was a "broad-shouldered district attorney" who "was building a marketable reputation by relentlessly prosecuting con men and women, bunco artists, prostitutes, bookies and racketeers," and he had been "hailed for running the best D.A.'s office in America," according to historian Roger Rapoport. And Brown found in Warren the role model he needed to clean house in San Francisco.[7]

Four years later a more seasoned Brown challenged Brady again. This time armed with new party support, he enjoyed the backing of popular Democrats and the exposure and networking from Cincinnatus. Following Warren's lead he ran under the slogan, "Crack Down on Crime. Pick Brown This Time!" While campaigning, Brown told packed wartime rallies, "There is no organized crime in San Francisco; the crime is all organized by the police department!" He charged that politicians and cops winked at favored abortionists, bookmakers, gambling parlors, and two-dollar whorehouses.[8]

As the days counted down, Brown tracked the election results in local newspapers. Disappointed when he saw that early polls favored Brady, he borrowed a tactic used by city boss Pete McDonough and took $500 from campaign funds to betting commissioner Tom Kyne's place and placed a bet on himself at "five-to-one" hoping to drive down the odds. Using the fifty ten-dollar tickets from the bet, Brown devised a scheme for campaign workers: handing out the tickets, he promised, "If I win you get $60!"[9]

Four days before the election, the pro-Brady *San Francisco Examiner* ran Brady's charge of Brown as being the "tool of local criminals" even while "he boasts his civil mindedness." Days later the *Examiner* reported Brown filed incorporation papers for two "social clubs" that were merely shady covers for poker joints trying to hide behind the allowed private-club-limited gambling laws.[10]

Irate, Brown went on the defensive and responded in a radio broadcast only hours before the polls opened. "The incumbent," he charged, "dug through old records and was only able to come up with these routine activities, which were entirely legal." More importantly, Brown pointed out, the city's gamblers "know exactly where they stand with Mr. Brady."[11]

On the morning of the election, the results remained uncertain. Brown voted early, and with little else to do the rest of the day decided to play a round of golf. Trailed by photographers, he and wife Bernice teed off at the city's Lincoln Golf Course. An excruciatingly close race continued until well after midnight when the final count came in. Brown's efforts paid off; he won the election by a slim margin of only 7102 votes. For the rest of his political career, Brown played golf on Election Day.[12]

———

Standing in the rotunda of San Francisco's Hall of Justice that cold, foggy morning in January 1944, Pat Brown gave his first inauguration speech. Proud in his perfectly tailored, double-breasted suit, he straightened his tie, then promised the citizens by the bay that as district attorney he would turn their city around, and that he personally would seek the "full penalty of the law" against those who deliberately, maliciously, and repeatedly committed crimes.[13]

In the years to come, many felt Brown did not act as vigorously as he might have. In reality, he already aspired to the state attorney general's office. Of course, it was plain to his family and colleagues that what he really wanted—and had always wanted—was to be governor. Even from the cramped quarters of the San Francisco district attorney's office, his assistant Tom Lynch remembered him gazing out the window to the Bay Bridge and beyond.

"You know Tom," Brown said, "I can almost see Sacramento from here."[14]

———

In 1941, sixty-four-year-old city supervisor Warren Shannon was past his prime, but the popular politician still seemed a good catch as a husband when he met and married Gloria Davenport, daughter of famed political cartoonist Homer Davenport. Three years later, after serving six terms on the board of supervisors, he retired to operate a downtown Oakland cigar store. It was not the life Gloria Davenport had envisioned.

Unfortunately, Shannon's cigar store, like his return to private life, soon proved a failure. After only a year the career politician found himself broke and deep in debt with nowhere to go. Desperate, he turned to lifelong friend Inez Burns, who without hesitation offered the destitute couple a free apartment, purchased them an automobile, and gave Gloria Shannon a job. The couple gratefully accepted her hospitality and moved into the first-floor flat of her Fillmore Street abortion clinic. But the Shannons, it seemed, could not catch a break, and within a year police raided the clinic and arrested Burns. Amidst the confusion the resourceful couple managed to slip away and hide out at Oakland's Lake Merritt Hotel for the next three months. According to the hotel manager, the pair spoke to no one, rarely left their room, and checked out around 8:00 a.m. on November 30, 1945, leaving no forwarding address.[15]

8   A "New Broom"

Pat Brown . . . was considered by more than one politico a
virtual traitor because he attempted to do something about
corruption.

—Charles Raudebaugh

Progressive Era politics brought many significant changes in the areas
of vice reform, suffrage rights, labor legislation, and alcohol control—at
least on a national level. Even in the state of California, this movement
successfully propelled reformer Hiram Warren Johnson into the governor's seat in 1911. By 1913 California state legislators passed the Red Light
Abatement Act, outlawing prostitution, and six years later ratified the
Eighteenth Amendment, prohibiting alcohol.

Nevertheless, San Francisco, where gambling houses, speakeasies, and
brothels abounded and where abortionists and prostitutes openly plied
their trades, successfully retained its reputation as a wide-open town. In
fact, it was well known that city officials often got elected on a promise
to protect vice and fight any threat of moral reform.[1]

Even Pat Brown, when he reflected back on his work as district attorney,
saw it more as one of "tolerance . . . of prostitution and gambling." But
with regard to abortion and police corruption, he had no patience.[2]

Brown knew he faced decades of organized corruption. Former district
attorney Matthew Brady, elected as the county's chief prosecutor for two
decades, presided over a city as corrupt as any large metropolis at the
time. "There were 150 whorehouses in the city and bookie joints were
everywhere," said reporter Charles Raudebaugh, who started working for
the *Examiner* in 1926, and payoffs were considered just "the cost of doing

business." But Brown knew, as did everyone else, that convicting Inez Burns, who for at least fifteen years operated her Fillmore Street clinic with near complete immunity, was "the necessary first step in cleaning up" the city. "Burns was a very good abortionist," Brown admitted, "with a good reputation." Nevertheless, by the time he became district attorney "her business had become flagrant and out of control." Resolute, Brown stated, "I took her out of business . . . [because] she was corrupting the police department." Even her husband, ex-assemblyman Joe Burns, played poker with the deputy fire chief and the brother of the chief of police. "They were very, very close," he said. "This couldn't happen anywhere else in the country!" She needed to go.[3]

Newspapers across the city quickly dubbed crime-fighting Pat Brown and his longtime friend, Assistant District Attorney Tom Lynch, the "new broom" in town. Following his election Brown immediately began a media campaign charging San Francisco abortionists with taking the lives of eighteen thousand unborn children a year—four thousand more than the fourteen thousand actually born—and naming Inez Burns as the Queen Bee of them all.[4]

The battle only began with eliminating abortionists. In San Francisco the scandal "was not in the idea of having an abortion," another of Brown's assistant district attorneys, Norman Elkington, said, "but the corruption that went along with it." Politicians received campaign contributions from those involved in the abortion business, and the police took payoffs "from the top to the bottom." The district attorney's office estimated Burns paid out thousands of dollars every week to police and city officials.[5]

Finally, in September 1945 Brown's office hatched a plan to raid Burns's main clinic at 327 Fillmore Street. The police had raided Burns three times in the previous ten years, and with the exception of a $10,000 fine for evading taxes in 1939, she managed to escape unscathed. Brown intended to change that. He selected a small group of men from the district attorney's office and the police department to secretly plan and carry out the raid and to follow through with arrests. "Good Roman

Catholics," Brown said of his handpicked force of men he knew Burns could not pay off.[6]

But Brown's best-laid plans backfired and Burns, tipped off, escaped within minutes of the police search. Still, all was not lost when the team's steadfast leader, inspector Frank Ahern, suggested, "Let's go over to Guerrero Street [Burns's home], and see what's doing." Leaving part of his crew at the Fillmore Street clinic, Ahern took a select group of plainclothes policemen to Burns's custom-built mansion. While his officers hid behind manicured bushes, Ahern rang the doorbell. When the unsuspecting Burns answered the door, Ahern shoved his way inside to find all her nurses and orderlies still dressed in their white uniforms and waiting for the call that they could safely return to work.[7]

Ahern placed everyone under arrest as his men searched the house. What they found shocked the city and set District Attorney Brown up for a yearlong battle in court. In Burns's "extremely large," double-locked, walk-in closet, as Ahern described it, he found a locked safe. Lynch, who had prosecuted Burns years before for federal tax evasion, still had the combination, and upon opening it found it packed with over $300,000 in cold, hard cash. Elkington turned the money over to Ahern. "We knew what was there and we didn't want to be responsible for that money," he said. The search uncovered evidence that even more cash—once hidden in the attic, the grand piano, the basement, and sewn into the drapes—was now missing. The prosecution later produced evidence that Burns, when tipped off, managed to relocate an additional $450,000 that was now missing. Together with the money found in her safe, the district attorney's office estimated she had a grand total of just over $750,000 in cash, or over $9.8 million in today's money. Ahern later testified that Burns offered him one of the wrapped bundles of cash—at least $50,000, he estimated—to "forget the whole thing."[8]

"There's a big chunk of money upstairs," she said.

"I don't want a chunk of your money," Ahern replied.

"You don't want a—say, what's your name?"

"My name's Frank Ahern."

"Oh," she nodded. "We've all heard of the honest cop."[9]

More important than Burns's stash, Ahern discovered a stack of thin, black, bound notebooks on the top shelf of her safe. In one sweep he solved the mystery everyone in San Francisco had speculated on for years: the existence of Burns's "little black books." They were all there. Each filled with carefully recorded dates, names, amounts, referrals, local physicians, payoffs, and personal notes in her own graceful handwriting. Expanding his search throughout the house Ahern found more notebooks—some going back decades—hidden in the cubbyholes between the floorboards of the stairway, in secret cutouts carved into the banister, and in the dining room buffet cabinet.

When Brown publicly revealed that he had Burns's notebooks, nervous tremors went through the state. A week later he disclosed that "various prominent persons" had attempted to pressure him into quashing the investigation. Others, he revealed, went so far as to threaten him with "coercive measures," telling him it would be politically dangerous for him to prosecute Burns.

Brown described Burns's notebooks as a powder keg, replete with the names of prominent women from San Francisco, Los Angeles, Pomona, and Hollywood. He calculated from the number of entries in the daily logs that Burns oversaw between thirty and forty abortions a day at the Fillmore Street clinic alone, with ordinary clients paying $75 to $250 each, while the more socially prominent paid as much as $1000 ($12,000 in today's dollars). According to Burns's granddaughter Caroline Carlisle, the list included such Hollywood greats as Rita Hayworth and Olympic figure skater Sonja Henie.[10]

But in the weeks that followed, and as the case drew more and more public attention, Brown began noticeably distancing himself from the topic of the "little black books." He hedged around inquiries from reporters and declined to name persons in public life with whom Burns associated. Instead he vaguely confirmed, "She definitely has connections," and sidestepped questions involving movie stars, stating, "I can't go any further at this time."[11]

Without a doubt Burns was well known; people came from all over the country to see her. Primarily, said Lynch, because she was good. "She had two full floors filled with every type of medical instrument imaginable," he said—everything she needed. But as the preliminary hearing drew nearer, Brown became even less forthright about the contents of Burns's private books. After teasing the media for weeks, he never made public the names of the prominent citizens listed in her journals. Instead, he announced, "We intend to strike at every element directly connected with this abortion racket," and added, "I would like to emphasize that the names of persons on the periphery of the case will be kept out of the proceedings. . . . We don't intend to involve anybody who doesn't deserve to be."[12]

In the end, Brown decided his office held more than enough evidence to pursue the case without using the incriminating notebooks at all, and he promised to turn them over to the Bureau of Internal Revenue as evidence to go after Burns for income tax evasion. "Mrs. Burns paid some $50,000 'additional' income tax last year," Brown charged, "and made a profit of over a million dollars."[13]

Within days, the arrest of Burns made national news and *Time* magazine deemed San Francisco cops "connoisseurs of human frailty," stating it should be no surprise that they found Burns operating an abortion clinic equipped with three fully functional operating rooms and sitting on a cache of money. The article blamed the city's complete lack of principles on the decline of morals during wartime.[14]

Brown's office initially arrested and held a total of eight individuals, including Burns's employees Madeline Rand, who attempted to sell her testimony, and Rose Queen, alias Levina Garcia, alias I. P. Blanchett, alias Levina Queen, whose husband stalled the police at their front door long enough for her to escape over the back fence. Eventually Brown released three, including Rand and Queen, who became key witnesses for the prosecution. At the arraignment on December 17 Burns, along with Musette Briggs, Myrtle Ramsey, Joseph Hoff, and Mabel Spaulding, was charged with conspiracy to commit abortion and practicing medicine without a license. The next day Inez Burns, aka Inez L. Brown, aka Inez Brown Burns, aka Lillian Brown, aka "Dr. Brown," aka Amy Dutch was released on $5000 bail.[15]

Brown felt secure that he had a solid case. His evidence included records taken in the raid and photographs of the complete layout of Burns's four-story clinic: three hospital-grade operating rooms, nine recovery rooms downstairs in addition to the six more his officers found upstairs, and two elevated rooms constructed into "recovery" sun porches. In the kitchen they seized expensive sterilizing equipment and uncovered a hidden door that led to a secret stairway and an "escape" apartment on the lower level. And hidden in the back yard behind the ivy-covered fence, past the perfectly sculpted rose bushes, was a large concrete vat buried deep beneath the manicured lawn—a fire kiln used to burn the fetal remains.[16]

"We have receipts, case history cards of patients," and logbooks tying everything together, making "a complete case," Brown said. Furthermore, he announced, every indication of this case implied it would reach the highest "brackets of officialdom." This included the same individuals who put pressure on his office to quash the Burns investigation. "We will spare no effort or expense to get to the higher-ups in this vice ring," Brown promised.[17]

9   *Cops and Robbers*

What Started the Abortion Inquiry? "An Honest Cop!"
—*San Francisco News*

The chain of events leading up to the raid began on the evening of
September 23, 1945, in San Francisco Central Hospital Emergency
room when police officers came to question a young Oakland housewife, Gerrylee Marsigli, admitted after suffering the adverse effects of an
abortion. Upon hearing Marsigli's statement, the officers quickly called
in homicide inspector Frank Ahern.

Based on information taken in the young woman's statement, Inspector
Ahern promptly posted an officer down the block from Burns's clinic
with instructions to keep a running log of all activities and any known
identities of those frequenting the clinic. Three days later, on the morning
of September 26, Assistant District Attorney Tom Lynch received a
phone call from homicide inspector Al Corassa informing him that chief
of police Charles Dullea would like him to come to police headquarters
directly. In the meeting that followed, Dullea announced the time had
come to "knock the place [Burns's clinic] over," and said he planned to
go immediately to make the arrests. On his way to the basement garage
of the Hall of Justice, Lynch handed the keys to Burns's clinic, which
he still had from his days as a federal prosecutor, over to Ahern, then
slipped into the coroner's office to telephone District Attorney Brown
and let him know "the deal" was on.[1]

When the team arrived at Burns's clinic and found it deserted, Ahern,
along with his squad of plainclothes police, found and arrested Burns
and her crew at her Guerrero Street home. He also recovered crucial

documents, some of which he believed Burns took from the clinic during her getaway.[2]

Eyewitness to Burns's escape Oscar L. Tennant was one of the first called to testify at her hearing. Tennant operated a garage across the street from Burns's clinic, and he often repaired and stored her car there. Tennant recalled that he received a strange phone call at his shop around 9:45 a.m. on the day of the raid.

"As I recollected it," he testified, "somebody asked if Joe Burns was there."

According to Tennant, Joseph Burns was already at the garage waiting for the call. "He [Burns] probably anticipated the call, ya see, I'm pretty sure of it," Tennant told the judge, because when Burns hung up the phone he blurted out, "There may be somebody coming out from the district attorney's office, there's going to be a raid!"[3]

Anticipating action across the street, Tennant watched from his garage window. Within minutes he observed three individuals jump into Burns's 1940 Buick Series 90 limousine, already conveniently parked facing the street, and speed away. As the car flew past him the garage owner recognized Inez Burns and Joe Hoff, the "technician" from the clinic, in the front seat.

Confirming Oscar Tennant's timeline, officers recorded the time of Burns's departure at approximately 9:55 a.m. Furthermore, on the day before the raid, the officer on watch logged fifteen women entering the clinic between nine and ten in the morning, but on the day of the raid, only four patients showed up. According to Assistant District Attorney Norman Elkington this confirmed his theory that someone initially alerted Burns hours, maybe even days, before the final warning.

In addition, police recovered a message jotted down in Burns's handwriting that she attempted to swallow when officers searched her. When Ahern snatched the incriminating note from Burns's mouth, he saw it revealed confidential police investigation details including the officers involved, the name of the Oakland housewife (Gerrylee Marsigli) who filed the complaint, and the names "Delano" and "Bruno," two local thugs working at the Stardust Bar who referred Marsigli to her. When questioned, Burns refused to discuss the note and claimed she received an anonymous tip from a "drunk" she could not identify.[4]

The timing of the call to Oscar Tennant's garage and Burns's subsequent getaway became even more significant as the investigation revealed it was not until 9:30 a.m. on September 26 that Brown's handpicked team reached a final decision to raid her clinic. According to Elkington, those select few present included Chief Dullea, Lynch, homicide inspectors Frank Ahern and Al Corassa, and police captains Barney McDonald and John Engler. Seventeen minutes later, Ahern and his men descended on Burns's establishment to find she and her cohorts had slipped away.

With the clinic abandoned, Lynch directed the officers to scour the 6200-square-foot facility and collect evidence. To Lynch's delight, even as the police hauled operating tables and oxygen tanks out the back, pregnant women continued to come in the front door. To catch Burns's patrons in the act, he set up a stenographer from the district attorney's office to play receptionist at the big desk in the clinic's plush waiting room. For the rest of the day unsuspecting women lined up and volunteered to answer such questions as: "How long do you think you've been pregnant?" "Have you been here before?" and "How much did you pay last time?" Potential clients never realized they were now on the prosecution's witness list.[5]

In the weeks that followed, acting police chief Michael Riordan tried to wash his hands of further investigation into the tip-off allegations. He instructed his officers to ask Burns only one question: "Did you receive any information from anybody, or from anybody in the police department, about the raid proposed against your place?"

Burns flatly replied, "No."

Chief Riordan stated his satisfaction that the investigation of a leak in the department was resolved.[6]

Brown, determined to get answers, subpoenaed Burns to testify before the grand jury investigating the corruption angle of her case. But she remained tight-lipped, citing her Fifth Amendment right not to incriminate herself. Relentless, Brown pressed forward, requesting that Superior Court judge Edward P. Murphy force her to answer his questions, but Burns stuck by her "anonymous drunk" story. Enjoying the fanfare, Burns emerged from the courthouse with her head held high. Speaking to reporters crowded under rain-soaked umbrellas, she called it "unfair" for the district attorney to demand she appear as a witness when she was a defendant in the upcoming trial. She also filed an insurance claim for jewelry that mysteriously disappeared during the raid. "I don't believe it!" Chief Dullea said, when hearing of her claim, and retorted, "It's odd that she made no report to the proper authorities."[7]

Elkington continued piecing together his list of all persons who participated in the raid or who knew about it. When asked by reporters if he believed the list included the person responsible for the tip-off, Elkington solemnly replied: "You can draw your own conclusion."[8]

Later, Elkington's list expanded to include the Stardust bartender known simply as "Bruno" and identified only through Burns's handwritten note. By Burns's second trial, police had arrested Vincent Bruno as part of a statewide drug ring. It became clear Bruno not only worked as the middleman for Burns, but also for the mob.[9]

With public interest in the case growing steadily, and to further ensure the integrity of the investigation, Judge Murphy placed a gag order on Elkington's witness list and the grand jury proceedings.[10]

———

Now under the scrutiny of the grand jury, the city's policemen attempted to clarify their personal involvement with Inez Burns. Among the officers privy to the raid, police inspector on robbery detail George "Paddy" Wafer admitted to playing poker, pinochle, and cribbage at Burns's house over the past six years. According to Wafer, players usually arrived around 7:30 p.m. on Wednesday nights and entered through a rear door to the game room located in the basement of her Guerrero Street home. But Wafer denied any knowledge of illegal activity and pointed out his lifelong friendship with Inez and her husband, Joe. Other officers also admitted participating in these card games, as did fire captain Edward Dullea. After questioning his men Chief Dullea admitted his officers "used very poor judgment," but decided no disciplinary action was necessary. With regard to his brother, Dullea said he "had no control over his actions."[11]

Although not included in the invitation-only card games, Officer Stephen Flahaven lived next door to Burns's clinic for over three years. He also denied any knowledge of illegal activity. "If I had a suspicion of anything unlawful at the Burns' place, I would have notified my superior officer immediately," he said. And then there was police sergeant Glen Hughes, Burns's brother-in-law. He claimed he never stepped foot in Burns's house, and said he had "no knowledge" of her operation.[12]

Members of the fire and police departments were not the only ones on the exclusive list of attendees to Burns's weekly games; some of the city's most prominent professionals joined in as well. These included a dentist and various local physicians who said they played pinochle, hearts, and poker for small stakes along with city supervisor Warren Shannon. The fuss over the card games infuriated Burns.

"So what? Some cops came over—and Ed Dullea?" She declared, "Why, they've all been friends of ours for many years. . . . It's too bad we can't have a little game of cards once in awhile."[13]

The weekly poker games proved just the tip of the iceberg. On one occasion, several officers from the local precinct pulled a practical joke on Burns after she refused to buy a block of ten thousand tickets for their annual policeman's ball at a dollar each. To get even, they alerted the newspaper to a dead body in Burns's basement. When reporters came sniffing around, their commotion practically shut down her business for an entire week.[14]

While Chief Dullea obviously turned a blind eye to the activity at Burns's clinic, he was still respected as a rough-and-tough Irish cop. Norman Elkington considered Dullea one of the best police chiefs the city ever had and credited him with keeping San Francisco relatively free of mafia influence. Nevertheless, like most of the community Dullea saw Burns's work as a necessary evil, something to be ignored and tolerated—that is, until Pat Brown stepped in as district attorney.[15]

Unable to ignore the grand jury investigation and after weeks of pressure, Chief Dullea summoned all his department captains to headquarters and instructed them to "clean house." Further public accusations by Brown forced Dullea to order his men to cooperate and "ferret out any sources of crime." Reluctantly, he affirmed the San Francisco Police Department's willingness to give evidence before "lawfully established tribunals" when called upon to do so.[16]

Despite Chief Dullea's halfhearted attempts at reform, Brown sensed a lack of enthusiasm for his cleanup efforts and once again turned to the press. "Anytime you have something illegal running in a city for a long period of time, someone is being paid off," he told reporters. "It's either the district attorney, the police, or some public official." According to one insider, Burns stated it cost her $20,000 a month for protection to run her business, including $5,000 to every politician running for office. Furthermore, Lynch uncovered that Burns paid off the county coroner to "fix" death certificates and to swap organs from her deceased patients with those from other cadavers before examination. Feeling the growing public scrutiny, San Francisco mayor Roger Lapham and Jerd Sullivan, president of the police commission, got in on the act and declared they too welcomed an investigation.[17]

Brown made his goals clear. He would dismantle the entire corrupt city network, including the police officials on Burns's payroll, and he pledged all his resources to uproot the system. Still, he saw no benefit in kicking a few beat cops off the street when the problem started at the top. Even Walter McGovern, former police commissioner and Burns's trial attorney, referred to San Francisco's police department as a "honeycomb of honesty."[18]

Angered by Brown's accusations, Mayor Lapham, who won his seat by exposing the rampant vice ignored by his predecessor Mayor Angelo

Rossi, went public and pointed out that if the district attorney held any evidence he should stop wasting everyone's time and act on it. "If there is anything wrong going on I'm just as interested in knowing as anybody else," he declared. "Why just talk about it? Take some action, that's his job!" But regardless of Lapham's arrogant posturing, everyone knew the only thing that changed in the mayor's office was, as one reporter put it, "the window dressing of Lapham's colorful personality."[19]

Police Commission president Sullivan, who according to police reporter Charlie Raudebaugh was "apparently one of the few" unaware of the corruption in the city's police department, sided with Lapham, adding, "It's all news to me; I told Buster Brown if he's got a beef, he should take it before the grand jury." Chief Dullea joined with the mayor and police commissioner. "Let him name the individuals," Dullea challenged. "If I knew, I would immediately prosecute them."[20]

Undaunted, Brown responded by reminding them, "Anytime you have something illegal running in a city for—say twenty or thirty years— someone is being paid off." He then included in the probe bail bondsman Edward "Red" Maloney, who rather industriously arranged Burns's bail prior to her booking at the city jail.[21]

Brown continued to put pressure on witnesses, convinced someone knew about the telephone call that led to Burns's ten-minute warning and the frantic attempt to destroy evidence before the police arrived. On February 7 fourteen policemen, led by Chief Dullea, filed before the grand jury to disclose what they knew, then brusquely pushed past waiting reporters. "Nothing new has developed," was all the grim-faced chief would say.[22]

Finally, public pressure to assist with Brown's investigation led Police Commissioner Sullivan to write a letter to the district attorney promising his cooperation:

> I feel it has been the desire of the present police commission and your office to cooperate 100 percent. . . . You, a district attorney, have your

own investigation; we have neither the funds nor the manpower to conduct an investigation of our own department. I hope that if you have—say evidence that would indicate some particular officer or officers who have been taking money for protection of the abortionist, you will make it available to us and I assure you that we will take steps to bring the accused to trial.[23]

Brown responded with a declaration of faith that 99 percent of the police were honest. He also reaffirmed his intention to go for the "larger fry" and not the cop who takes $20 on the street.[24]

After repeated leaks to the press, Brown's assistant Norman Elkington, designated to head up the investigation and prosecution of the police tip-off angle of Burns's case, told reporters no further public comments would come from the district attorney's office. "We'll get nowhere fast if we announce our plans in advance," he said.[25]

Brown further ordered all aspects of the investigation hereafter handled exclusively by Homicide Inspector Ahern—one of the few officers on the force he trusted.[26]

10 *Disappeared*

The grand jury has been pretty wishy-washy. . . . They found the Burns case a case of dynamite and ducked it as best it could!

—*San Francisco Call*

Following Inez Burns's September 1945 arrest, the district attorney's office spent hundreds of man-hours meticulously preparing a strong case against her. When the grand jury convened, Brown, confident the proceedings would be sealed, included Burns's "little black books" with the evidence presented. But when the jurors refused to indict her, citing lack of evidence, Brown discovered his key piece of evidence—the books themselves—had disappeared at the last minute, only to turn up days later.[1]

When the grand jury handed down its decision, Brown expressed his shock and anger. Even without Burns's journals his office held more than enough evidence to go to trial. He suspected someone paid off the jurors. He had no clear evidence, but everyone in the district attorney's office could see things did not add up. "I do not intend to dismiss this case," Brown told reporters, "and I have no comment to make—at this time—on the grand jury's refusal to act."[2]

Upon further inquiry Brown discovered that some of the jurors even questioned the validity of the investigation, and at least three of the nineteen members never showed up to vote. The district attorney's office also learned that Burns hired one juror, Harry J. Daniels, as her personal realtor, and following the grand jury's ruling he made substantial commissions from sales of her properties. Rumors of corruption aside, Brown was more determined than ever to stamp out Burns and her influence. Using his authority as district attorney, he bypassed the grand jury and filed the case with the municipal court.[3]

Burns's preliminary hearing before Judge Harry A. Neubarth began on November 26, 1945. The first witness, Gerrylee Marsigli, testified of her ordeal leading up to her late-night visit to Central Hospital, which triggered the raid and Burns's subsequent arrest. According to Marsigli, when she arrived at Burns's clinic defendant Mabel Spaulding greeted and escorted her to a large living room used as a reception area. At least fifteen women waited there silently in compliance with strategically placed wall signs. It was then, Marsigli stated, that she panicked, pushed past Spaulding, and demanded to be "let out." Spaulding permitted her to leave without incident.[4]

Marsigli returned two days later. On her second visit Burns's staff questioned her at length and entered her personal information on a filing card before admitting her. Additional staff helped her change into a hospital gown, Marsigli said, and then led her into one of the upstairs operating rooms where Musette Briggs positioned her on the operating table and covered her face with a wire ether mask. Once again Marsigli panicked. This time she told "Dr. Brown" she could not go through with the abortion. Burns did not perform the procedure on her, but Marsigli testified that this time Burns's staff did not allow her to leave for several hours, saying she "might make trouble" in her condition. Days later Marsigli suffered a miscarriage at Central Hospital, where she received care from Dr. Joseph Visalli. At the hospital she admitted visiting the Fillmore Street clinic and identified "Dr. Brown" as Inez Burns from photographs shown to her by police officers.[5]

Marsigli's testimony brought several clashes between the defense and the prosecution. Burns's defense attorney, James Brennan, insisted Tom Lynch did not prove an abortion took place. Lynch reminded the court that clear evidence showed the miscarriage resulted from her visit to Burns's abortion mill, a statement the judge allowed to stand. The defense in turn tried to shake Marsigli's testimony.[6]

"Were you wined and dined by the district attorney's office?" Defense Attorney Brennan asked the witness. Without waiting for an answer, he continued, "Were you fearful of the authorities because you knew you had committed a crime going to this place?"

"Well . . . yes," Marsigli admitted, stating that she also took lunch with Brown's staff three times and she signed a statement for authorities while still in the hospital.

"Jeepers," Marsigli protested, "I can't remember the exact conversation."[7]

Brennan alluded to a conspiracy at the district attorney's office and demanded copies of her statement, which Lynch objected to based on confidentiality. Again, the judge sided with the prosecution.

The next day Marsigli reported that a man accosted her on the street when she left the Hall of Justice following her court appearance. She told police that as she left the courthouse and walked down Kearny Street, a middle-aged man grabbed her arm and roughly pulled her close to him.

"I want to talk to you," he whispered.

She tried to jerk away, but he continued to hold her.

"You better be careful, you're going to be sorry—you're in for a lot of trouble."[8]

The next morning Lynch revealed to the court that his wife had received threatening phone calls at their home as well. "You tell your husband he'd better mind his own business," a male voice warned. Judge Neubarth ordered police protection assigned to the Lynch family, Marsigli, and any other witness who wished it.[9]

Assistant District Attorney Norman Elkington then came forward and revealed that he too received threatening calls. "Okay, wise guy!" a hoarse voice said, "Would you like to know what the odds are on you around town?"

"Yes, I would," Elkington challenged.

"It's ten to one," the caller laughed.[10]

The hearing continued and a second witness for the prosecution told an almost identical story as Marsigli. This time the defense demanded to know the names of the doctors who referred her. While laws protected patients of abortion, the physicians or "repairmen" called upon to treat patients with complications had a legal obligation to report the illegal operation immediately—but almost none did. The young divorcée testified that two doctors referred her: one in Oakland, and one in Redding. She did not recall the name of either physician. The defense then pushed the witness to divulge the name of the father of her child. She repeatedly claimed that she could not recall his name either. A third witness told much the same tale, but this time the witness was unable to identify any of the five defendants.[11]

After hearing the prosecution's argument, Judge Neubarth determined they had enough evidence to hold Burns and her four employees over for trial.

———

In January 1946 a new grand jury was selected. In addition to their other duties this jury would investigate the official protection and reported police tip-off angle of the Inez Burns case. Pat Brown made it clear that this time he would "get to the bottom of this" with all "its ramifications." The new jury impaneled by Judge Edward Murphy worked closely with the district attorney's office and agreed that the first item on their agenda would be the Burns case. "I don't believe any of us want another *Atherton Report*," Brown threatened. It made for good reading, he added, "but it did not improve the conditions in the city very much."[12]

Brown took no chances this time, and he demanded to be part of the jury selection process. He questioned and dismissed several candidates, including former mayor Angelo Rossi, who admitted he was a friend of Burns and that he personally appointed former state senator Walter

McGovern as police commissioner. (With a trial now imminent, Burns hired McGovern to replace James Brennan.)

"He [McGovern] has also been your friend for many years, hasn't he?" Brown inquired of Rossi.

"He has," replied the former mayor, "just like yourself."[13]

1. Inez Burns's abortion clinic, located at 325–27 Fillmore Street in San Francisco's Mission District, was the largest and most well-known of her facilities. BANC PIC 2006.029:127616-C.02.02-NEG Box 922, Courtesy of the Bancroft Library, University of California, Berkeley.

2. The elegantly furnished reception room of Inez Burns's 327 Fillmore Street clinic included "No Smoking" and "No Talking" signs. BANC PIC 2006.029: 127616.04.04-NEG Box 922, Courtesy of the Bancroft Library, University of California, Berkeley.

3. Detectives inspect one of Inez Burns's Fillmore Street clinic operating rooms during the raid in September 1945. BANC PIC 1959.010: 140948.8:3-NEG Box 180, Part 2, Courtesy of the Bancroft Library, University of California, Berkeley.

4. The day after journalist Mary Ellen Leary's story made the front page in the *San Francisco News-Call Bulletin* in May 1938, Inez Burns's clinic is raided and she (center) is arrested along with her nurse Margie Silver (foreground). BANC PIC 2006.029: 96227.06.06-NEG Box 684, Courtesy of the Bancroft Library, University of California, Berkeley.

5. Inez Burns, far left, and her codefendants Mabel Spaulding, to Burns's imme-
diate right; Myrtle Ramsey, center; Musette Briggs; Joseph Hoff, far right, in the
courtroom following their indictment in December 1945. District Attorney Pat
Brown and his assistant Tom Lynch (seated) are watching from the far right.
BANC PIC 2006.029: 127616-A.02 NEG Box 922, Courtesy of the Bancroft
Library, University of California, Berkeley.

6. Following Burns's September 1945 arrest, detectives escort her and a suitcase of cash from her Guerrero Street home. BANC PIC 2006.029: 127616.04.02-NEG Box 922, Courtesy of the Bancroft Library, University of California, Berkeley.

7. In 1924 Inez Burns custom built a 3200-square-foot home on trendy Guerrero Street. BANC PIC 2006.029: 127616-B.04.01-NEG Box 922, Courtesy of the Bancroft Library, University of California, Berkeley.

8. (*opposite top*) District Attorney Pat Brown interviews ex-supervisor Warren Shannon and his wife, Gloria, to assess the evidence they collected from Inez Burns's clinic to support Gloria Shannon's 10,000-word manuscript, *My Memoirs in the Midstream of Life After an Intimate View of San Francisco's Slaughter-House for Babies.* BANC PIC 2006.029: 127616-A.03-NEG Box 922, Courtesy of the Bancroft Library, University of California, Berkeley.

9. (*opposite bottom*) District Attorney Brown kept the contents of Inez Burns's "little black books" out of evidence during her trials with the exception of a few choice pages. This selection lists clients, including Dixie Wilson with the notation "Sally's" referring to madam Sally Stanford, and was used as evidence during the testimony of former employee Levina Queen. Burns also noted the total of the day's take with $125 specified as "payoff." BANC PIC 2006.029: 127616-G.05.03-NEG Box 922, Courtesy of the Bancroft Library, University of California, Berkeley.

10. (*above*) Inez Burns and her codefendants wait outside the courtroom in San Francisco's Hall of Justice. Right to left are laboratory technician Joseph Hoff, receptionist Mabel Spaulding, caretaker Myrtle Ramsey, Inez Burns, and her assistant Musette Briggs. BANC PIC 2006.029: 127616-A.05.02-NEG Box 922, Courtesy of the Bancroft Library, University of California, Berkeley.

11. San Francisco sheriff Dan Gallagher and sheriff's matron Bernadette Monaghan escort Inez Burns from the California Institution for Women at Corona to testify before the 1954 grand jury investigating police corruption. BANC PIC 2006.029: 131354.08.01-NEG Box 1040, Courtesy of the Bancroft Library, University of California, Berkeley.

PART THREE

The Supervisor and the Socialite

11 *Houseguests*

San Francisco's Slaughter-House for Babies.

—Gloria Davenport Shannon

On November 30, 1945, key witnesses in the Inez Burns investigation—former San Francisco supervisor and onetime acting mayor Warren Shannon and his self-aggrandizing, would-be socialite wife, Gloria Davenport Shannon—skipped town, leaving District Attorney Brown no alternative but to issue a nationwide search.

Ever the resourceful couple, the Shannons stayed out of sight, waiting patiently for the right moment to inject themselves into one of the biggest publicity-driven vice scandals that ever rocked the city of San Francisco. They did not have to wait long; at Burns's preliminary hearing defense attorney James Brennan accused the couple of secretly turning over Burns's personal records to the Bureau of Internal Revenue in an attempt to procure the 10 percent reward promised to whistleblowers. Furthermore, Brennan claimed, the double-crossing pair attempted to blackmail Burns for $35,000, threatening to give additional information to the district attorney's office, including a manuscript and explicit photographs of her activities at the clinic.

Burns knew of the couple's betrayal and her attorney advised her first to pay them nothing, and second to sell the property. She took the first piece of advice, but not the second. She refused to pay the couple, although she conceded she made "little gifts" of $100 per week to Mrs. Shannon for working as the doorkeeper and $1300 to Warren Shannon to purchase an automobile. Then six months after the extortion attempt police raided the Fillmore clinic.

Brennan confirmed rumors that the Shannons lived in the lower flat and had accessed the clinic through a secret stairway that led into a pantry closet in the kitchen. "The lower end of those stairs," Brennan said, "led right into the Shannon's bedroom. All they had to do was make use of them at night when there was no one around." He also acknowledged the existence of a book manuscript that Gloria Shannon had "shown to lots of people, not only here, but down in Los Angeles and in Hollywood."[1]

During the hearing, Brennan succeeded in connecting the shady couple to Burns and her operation through prosecution witness Edmund A. Scott, the owner of Grant Drug Store, located on the corner of Haight and Scott Streets. The druggist said he recognized the former supervisor and his wife and identified them as frequent customers who had left a book and photographs of the Fillmore Street clinic lying on his counter. "Isn't it true," Brennan demanded, "of your own knowledge that the Shannons were trying to shake down Mrs. Burns for $35,000?" But before Scott could reply, prosecutor Tom Lynch vehemently objected to the question.[2]

The couple's attempted shakedown of Burns, the defense asserted, discredited any statements they made against their former friend and landlord. When asked to comment on the charges, District Attorney Brown would not confirm or deny the allegations. However, he did go on record to report that Burns paid an additional $26,000 in federal taxes since her arrest in September, stating he believed the payments may have stemmed from a "tip made by Warren Shannon or his wife."[3]

Next, a spokesperson for the Treasury Department came forward but he would not finger the Shannons specifically either, and only confirmed reports that the large sums of money found during the raid, along with the large amount of cash Burns put up for bail, brought her to their attention. He also said they had an open investigation on her going back to 1940.

Considering the defense's allegations, Brown promised to submit any evidence to the grand jury that "appears sufficient to warrant" an investigation of Warren Shannon or his wife in the attempted blackmail of Burns. Ironically, on the morning following Brennan's allegations the Shannons disappeared from their Oakland hotel, leaving Brown no choice but to concede his office did not have sufficient time to connect them to the Burns case before the current grand jury.[4]

Not everyone let the Shannons, Pat Brown, or the grand jury off so easily. In the first week of December 1945, the *San Francisco Call* ran an editorial demanding answers to the obvious questions on everyone's mind:

I THE SHANNON INCIDENT—*Why were not the Shannons questioned BEFORE the trial?* Was Mrs. Shannon actually a receptionist for Mrs. Burns and did she receive remuneration for her work? Did the Shannons pay rent to Mrs. Burns for their living quarters? In all fairness to the public and the Shannons, these questions should be answered. One would think the Shannons would DEMAND a public statement issued on these matters.

II THE TIPOFF—Mr. Brown issued a statement charging there had been a tipoff and that more and better evidence could have been secured from the clinic had there been no tipoff. *Who tipped off Mrs. Burns?* Association of high police officials with known criminals is not one way of allaying public fear of rackets and gangsters. It IS necessary that high ranking officials should not even be suspect and their associates should not be persons who might believe that police friendship could be protection for their not too lily white purposes.

III THE GRAND JURY—In its handling of these related subjects (and to those who know, they ARE related) the County Grand Jury has been *pretty wishy-washy*. The jury found the Burns's case a case of dynamite and ducked it as best it could. They have not seen fit to bring into daylight some of the matters discussed here. Judge McWilliams has certainly heard some of the rumblings of these atomic matters and has failed to chastise the grand jury or supplant the membership. We do not know that San Francisco can have a pure government, but we think—and the public (or that part of the public that is informed) also thinks—that it could be better than it is.[5]

12 *On the Lam*

We are unappreciated confidential agents working for the
people of San Francisco.

—Gloria Davenport Shannon

As it turned out on November 28, two days before Warren and Gloria
Shannon skipped town, Pat Brown requested an all-points bulletin on
the pair, but Police Chief Dullea refused, demanding a formal, written
request. Hours later, with the proper request in hand, the police chief
again stalled, claiming his office could not locate the license plate number
for the Shannons' car. Finally, on the morning of November 30 a dispatch
with attached photographs of the couple went out. Brown missed the
fugitives by mere hours.

In the dispatch Brown asked to be notified directly if the Shannons
were spotted. Almost immediately, his office began receiving tips of the
pair hiding out in any number of places from Florida to Mexico. In an
attempt to draw them out Brown went public, stating that no charges
had been filed and that he anxiously "wanted to talk with them." In fact,
he promised that at a moment's notice he would fly immediately to their
location. "I want the Shannons primarily as witnesses," he reaffirmed.[1]

On the morning of December 1 the pair was spotted one hundred miles
south in the oil town of Bakersfield, holed up in the run-down San Padre
Hotel. Officer E. A. Coutts, dispatched to stake out room 801, found the
couple registered under the name Mr. and Mrs. Cooper. The Shannons
knew Brown desperately wanted to speak with them, as evidenced in a
letter Gloria Shannon wrote to her sister days later in which she excitedly
recreated the morning's events: "We got up at 6:00 a.m. and saw the

headlines . . . bigger than when the war was declared: 'Statewide Search for Shannon,'" she wrote. Then the duplicitous pair (with their fourteen pieces of luggage) attempted to sneak out of the hotel, but the plainclothes Coutts caught them. "Warren told him we were going to see a lawyer who is a state senator and was a district attorney," Gloria added, "and after that, we promised to return to San Francisco." Warren Shannon told Coutts they intended to seek the senator's advice, as they had a few "sensations of their own" to introduce into the Inez Burns case and they did not want the prosecution to drag them in "through the back door."[2]

Senator Jesse R. Dorsey, who said he had been friends with Warren Shannon for "some forty years," met with the couple and then proceeded to throw the police off their trail by telling officers that "as far as he knew" the Shannons left town around eight thirty that morning. But a staff reporter for the *Bakersfield Californian* who staked out Dorsey's residence identified the Shannons' 1938 black Buick leaving the senator's house over an hour later heading for the Mexican border. The fugitives' promise to return to San Francisco left Brown waiting impatiently in his office until late that afternoon.

According to Warren Shannon, the senator advised them to get out of the state, as the district attorney had not yet issued a subpoena or warrant for them. When Brown heard the Shannons solicited the help of Senator Dorsey, he angrily retorted, "Pull or no pull, the court and grand jury will get all the facts in this case." The following day he issued a subpoena for the fleeing duo.[3]

From their hideaway across the border, Gloria Shannon continued to write her sister Mildred, confiding, "We are out of touch with the world here. . . . We don't know what they say." She then set Mildred up as a confidante to relay messages to Senator Dorsey by way of special delivery. "He will send a letter with the news in it to you, then you send it here to us [by] air mail special delivery," she instructed.[4]

Over the next two weeks, Warren and Gloria Shannon kept on the move, always one step ahead of Brown. Finally, low on cash and tired of life on the lam, the ex-supervisor and his wife, whom Tom Lynch referred to as "that big, noisy broad," telegraphed from their hideout in Chihuahua, Mexico, promising to telephone when they crossed the border into Texas. In the meantime, Gloria Shannon kept information flowing through long, detailed letters to Mildred: "The D.A.'s office has been trying to find me. This I do not want for him [to do] as what he started he cannot finish due to her [Burns] pull. . . . However, I will appear for dear old Uncle Sam . . . and be his star witness." With regard to her manuscript, she confided, "I got a wonderful writer to do it. . . . I wish you could have seen Sig (identified as a Hollywood screenwriter) when he read it. I thought he would die! I could get much for it but it's not safe."[5]

When the weary pair pulled into El Paso's Hotel del Norte they kept their word and contacted Brown, agreeing to meet him in Phoenix and "assist in every way possible" his efforts to put Burns away.[6]

Anxious to get the Shannons' statement, Brown immediately requested emergency permission from the chairman of the board of supervisors to leave the state with his assistant Lynch. They flew to Phoenix the next day to interview the couple, who now maintained they feared for their lives if they returned to the Bay Area. Gloria Shannon, who worked for a brief time as a receptionist for Burns's clinic, also claimed to have observed an abortion and promised to give Brown receipts totaling more than $3000 per day that she had secreted out of the clinic. She also claimed she witnessed payoffs to dirty cops and had knowledge of the alleged police tip-off of the September 26 raid.[7]

Fully aware of the Shannons' proclivity for the spotlight, Brown raced south to meet up with the pair hoping to rein them in before they could make any more public statements. He arrived too late. On December 20 the *Arizona Republic* announced that two of California's most important witnesses in the "San Francisco Abortion Mill Case" came to town for a private meeting with District Attorney Pat Brown, and declared themselves ready and willing to testify before the grand jury. Then, in a scheduled press conference with local journalists, the couple went on record pledging their intention to cooperate fully and denying any wrongdoing that might taint their testimony. Warren Shannon spoke specifically to the charges leveled against them by Burns's defense attorney James Brennan, "Who, by the way," he added, "was my best friend too."[8]

According to Shannon, all the allegations were completely false. Besides, he confided, the couple had insider information that the case might fall apart, leaving Burns's defense team no alternative but to set up a "smoke screen."

"We are unappreciated confidential agents working for the people of San Francisco," Gloria Shannon added. Finally, the novice photographer/writer announced she planned to publish her scandalous tell-all book and launch a nationwide lecture tour based on her "covert employment" at Burns's clinic. [9]

Inviting reporters to their hotel suite, Gloria Shannon basked in the limelight of her newfound celebrity. "You would have thought I was Greta Garbo or someone, the way she [Burns] complimented me," she confided. Referring to herself as "one of the state's principal witnesses," Gloria Shannon described how she duped Burns, who took "a liking" to her and nicknamed her "law and order." But now, she insisted, her only goal was to "finish off abortion" throughout the nation. Furthermore, she would not permit anyone, including District Attorney Brown or the grand jury, to examine her ten-thousand-word manuscript, *My Memoirs in the Midstream of Life after an Intimate View of San Francisco's Slaughter-House for Babies*. "It's documented with records from Burns's establishment, and by pictures I took with my own little Brownie," she said, "and the records include some very interesting facts on Mrs. Burns." Shannon then described letters "from *Literary Digest*, *True Stories*, and two others," which she insisted had asked her to send the manuscript to them.[10]

Exasperated at the Shannons for undermining his case, Brown made it clear when he arrived in Phoenix that he wanted to get their "full statement before anyone else talked to them" and to look at Gloria Shannon's purposed manuscript.[11]

After two lengthy conferences with the couple, Brown stated that he felt confident their meetings were productive and added material to his case against Burns. He did not confirm whether Gloria Shannon allowed him to peruse her manuscript, only that he was confident the pair intended to cooperate fully and would return to San Francisco of their own volition. "Mrs. Shannon's story is both shocking and disgusting," he reported.[12]

Brown also promised the couple full physical protection "including a guard," should it be necessary. According to Mrs. Shannon the couple received a threatening phone call while at the Santa Rita Hotel in Tucson on their way to Phoenix. "The operator reported that a caller had a message for me," Mrs. Shannon said, "to the effect that it would be much better for me to take the call unless I wanted things to get worse than they already were." But the threat did not deter Gloria Shannon from her mission to "blow the lid off" the whole abortion racket in San Francisco. "I'd get chummy with Jack the Ripper," she loudly proclaimed to reporters, while standing next to her silent but smiling husband. "Nothing but an act of God would prevent my return," she insisted.[13]

When District Attorney Brown returned to San Francisco he announced that his meeting with the couple went well, and they were on schedule to tell everything they knew about the Burns case before both the new grand jury and in the trial set to begin in February. Brown reiterated, "They are willing and anxious to give us all the information they have."[14]

Unbeknownst to Brown, however, while he and Lynch traveled back to San Francisco the Shannons made their way back to the city by way of Los Angeles. During their stopover the pair dutifully called ahead to the district attorney's office to confirm that they were to testify before the grand jury scheduled to convene on January 7, and to request that a hotel be ready for their arrival. Then, before the couple made their way north on Highway 99, Warren Shannon, ever the politician, dropped a note in the mail addressed to the *San Francisco Chronicle*.

The letter detailed the couple's confidential interview with Brown and once again addressed the "shakedown" charges made by Burns. Shannon also used this opportunity to establish his wife's pedigree for future book interests: "My wife, Gloria Davenport Shannon, is the daughter of the late Homer Davenport, famous political cartoonist, who made his start in San Francisco. She is also the cousin of the late Charles Warren Fairbanks, vice president of the United States under the late president Theodore Roosevelt, also a man of reputed integrity."[15]

Finally, Shannon asked readers not to misconstrue their continued absence. They had requested that the district attorney come to Phoenix to meet with them, he insisted, and the couple had volunteered to return to answer any and all questions put to them by the grand jury.

—

Back in the city the pressure from the district attorney's office, the media buildup, and her imminent trial prompted Inez Burns to bring in the big guns—she replaced her attorney, James Brennan, with former state senator Walter McGovern. Burns's decision to hire McGovern was not happenstance; she had a long acquaintance with the ostentatious attorney, who had also represented her longtime friend, ex-bail bondsman Pete McDonough.

Against McGovern's advice, Burns, angry at being branded "vicious" in articles published in local newspapers purporting to detail Gloria Shannon's experiences, decided to counteract the publicity through her own handwritten, three-page letter to the *San Francisco Chronicle*:

Dear Sirs, the statements about me made by Gloria Shannon are all untrue and nothing but vicious lies, the ravings of a woman gone insane over money! If they were not lies, would I have refused to give the Shannons the money they demanded?[16]

After addressing the extortion attempt by the Shannons, Burns detailed her friendship with the couple and stated that she knew Supervisor Shannon going back many, many years. Furthermore, the couple not only "sat at my dinner table," she declared, but she purchased them an automobile because Warren was an "old man with one eye and his wife was a cripple." She closed the letter by explaining, "When they lost their cigar store in Oakland, and had no place to go—they begged me for shelter and I took them in off the streets . . . and as a reward they tried to blackmail me!"[17]

Fully enthralled by the attention, Gloria Shannon bustled to the press, "You want a good story?" she told them, "You just wait 'til we tell what we know—we're going to show this town what atomic power really is!"[18]

13 "The Prophet"

If they'd put you and that "used up" old battle axe of yours in S.Q. [San Quentin] they'd get the real crooks.

—Signed, the Prophet

Warren and Gloria Shannon pulled into town on December 30, at which time Warren Shannon held a press conference to confirm that they had indeed received subpoenas to appear before the grand jury. He also took this opportunity to accuse the entire San Francisco Police Department of being privy to Inez Burns's operation. When asked if *he* knew about the abortion mill during his tenure as a supervisor, Shannon told reporters that it was common knowledge to himself, the other eighteen supervisors, and the chief of police. Furthermore, he named police chiefs going back to Dan O'Brien (appointed 1920), indicating they all knew about Burns. "In my opinion it was generally known by everyone in the city of San Francisco," Shannon said. When twenty to thirty women go into a place every day, it is bound to attract attention, he continued, "and a policeman lived in the house next door to Burns's place. . . . Every cop on the beat must have known—it would be a poor police force if they didn't know!" Pat Brown, ever more frustrated with the Shannons' public posturing, demanded the pair make no more public statements and confined them to sworn, written declarations in his office.[1]

On January 9, 1946, the new grand jury was impaneled and Brown declared them ready to address the Burns corruption and payoff case. He lost Burns's abortion case with the previous grand jury, but had confidence this handpicked jury would thoroughly investigate "no matter who was involved."[2]

In the days leading up to their scheduled grand jury testimony, the Shannons once again claimed they received anonymous threats. They told the district attorney's office of a recent phone call offering them money to keep quiet. The anonymous caller warned, "It's better to be the horse's neck than to be a dead horse." The couple went on the record that they hired attorney H. R. Hubbard to protect their interests and shield them from indictment.[3]

Regardless of the Shannons' unsubstantiated claims about the phone call, their return coincided with a threatening letter mailed to the *San Francisco Chronicle* that was addressed to "Crooked Warren and Wife."

"Listen you dirty mick," the handwritten letter began. "If they'd put you and that 'used up' old battle axe of yours in S.Q. [San Quentin] they'd get the real crooks. You and her will be punished by the everlasting God alone—sickness and financial ruin will hit you." The anonymous author, angry at Burns's arrest, pronounced the Shannons cursed "by the poor girls who, do [sic] to Mrs. Burns not running, have to go have their bastards born in this overcrowded bastard world—rite [sic] alongside real bastards like you!"[4]

The *Chronicle* never printed the sinister note, mailed on January 1 and signed "the Prophet" over a poorly drawn all-seeing Eye of Providence, but promptly turned it over to the district attorney's office. Coincidently, according to the Shannons, as the couple quietly enjoyed New Year's Eve dinner the evening before at a North Beach café a man identified only as Frenchy but known personally to Warren Shannon placed a shiny new bullet on the table in front of them. "Happy New Year to me, but not to you," he said, and smiled.[5]

A week later the Shannons gave a private deposition in their attorney's office that revealed new disclosures involving threats against their lives and attempts to buy off their testimony. Their statement disclosed prominent names and secretly recorded conversations. During his deposition Warren Shannon also disclosed a private loan for $100,000—repaid at $150,000—from former bail bondsman and crime boss Pete McDonough to Burns. McDonough flatly denied the charge.[6]

It was an undisputed fact that Burns enjoyed friendships with many individuals in high places, and Pete McDonough was one of them. By the time Mayor James Rolph was elected in 1911 McDonough had established a network throughout the police department that allowed him to monitor and oversee the city's vice operations with mutual profitability for both the brass and the rank and file in the police department. One of San Francisco's most acclaimed attorneys, Jake "the Master" Ehrlich, described the power of Pete McDonough and his brother Tom in his autobiography, *A Life in My Hands*:

> These squid-handed brothers supervised the many-splendored nightlife in San Francisco. They kept an eye on the take of every hustling girl . . . knew to the dollar how much Russian Mike or Bones Remmer folded into their pockets . . . had the drawings of any burglary, con-game, or safe blowing that happened, before it happened. They had their own lawyers, created judges and uncreated them . . . got city ordinances passed or defeated. . . . They laundered soiled money, cooled overnight beefs . . . and, oh yes, they wrote bail bonds.[7]

Conservatively dressed and looking like one of the stockbrokers on Montgomery Street, Pete McDonough had only one conviction in his long career, the result of a 1923 bootlegging charge by federal agents. But a petition for clemency proved McDonough's impressive reach; it contained the signatures of a former governor, the mayor, the police commissioner, three congressmen, twelve judges, the vice president of the Bank of Italy, and the district attorney. McDonough, touted in the 1937 *Atherton Report* as the city's "fountainhead of corruption," lost his bail-bond broker's license in the meager cleanup that followed, but one of his relatives, Edward "Red" Maloney, quickly applied for and got a license in his name. This was the same Maloney who mysteriously managed to arrange Burns's bail before police booked her in the city jail. According to one *San Francisco Examiner* reporter, throughout Burns's three trials in 1946, "the house of McDonough was still in business."[8]

Pete McDonough addressed Warren Shannon's accusation as having about as much "foundation as a possible charge that I am responsible for the 'sneak' attack of the Japs on Pearl Harbor." He did, however, confirm a longtime friendship with Burns and admitted he helped arrange a bank loan for her to pay her income tax.[9]

Immediately following their deposition, the Shannons were supposedly hit with yet another threat. Two days before their scheduled grand jury appearance while the pair made their way with their lawyer to the district attorney's office, a postal worker stopped them in the corridor. He handed Warren Shannon an envelope addressed to the couple, which postal inspectors had intercepted. Shocked by the slanderous nature of the letter, the Shannons met with District Attorney Brown immediately. Along with the letter, the shaken couple presented a written statement to Brown in which they accused a "key figure on the defense team" of collaborating with a city official in an attempt to influence their testimony. Furthermore, the Shannons declared, if that did not work, the defense team planned to find a way to physically intimidate them.

According to the pair, the accused individual promised he could "fix" the press, the grand jury, and the district attorney. In an attempt to obtain evidence against the witness fixer, Brown agreed to wire the couple's hotel room before their scheduled meeting with the unidentified crooks. Unfortunately, the recordings produced nothing to support the Shannons' charges.[10]

Upon hearing the allegations, public defender Gerald Kenny and defense investigator Eugene Aureguy came forward to refute the Shannons' accusations of tampering. Kenny, who local attorney Melvin Belli referred to as the "most placid of public defenders," stated he ran into the couple in the courthouse elevator, where they inquired about restaurants in the area and asked if Kenny could help them find a ride. Kenny told Brown the Shannons also asked him to recommend an attorney. Kenny stated that he then called investigator Eugene Aureguy, who had been tailing the couple on behalf of the defense team. Aureguy came immediately and picked up the Shannons outside the courthouse. Aureguy claimed the couple also asked him to recommend an attorney.[11]

But according to Warren Shannon, Kenny approached them in the lobby of the courthouse and offered to introduce them to an associate who wanted to help them. Kenny then took them to a nearby bar and made two phone calls, after which Aureguy duly arrived. Warren claimed the investigator drove the couple around the city, using the time to threaten and attempt to bribe them.

The Shannons alleged that Aureguy told them they should retract all earlier statements concerning Mrs. Burns and her establishment—including any statements made to the district attorney. They must also refuse to testify by invoking their constitutional right not to incriminate themselves upon appearing before the grand jury. He said money would be provided to compensate them, and he threatened them with bodily injury if they refused.

The investigator flatly denied the allegations. As he recalled it, the pair asked him whether or not they should testify and he gave them no advice of any kind. "If this is the way they want to play now, we'll expose some matters which will involve not only Mr. and Mrs. Shannon, but the entire Shannon family as well," Aureguy asserted.[12]

Defense Attorney McGovern had hired Aureguy, a leading West Coast private investigator, to "protect Burns's interest" and to dig up dirt on the Shannons. McGovern then held the information in reserve in case Brown attempted to use the couple as witnesses at the trial.[13]

Regardless of the accusations, on January 16 Brown publically expressed his hope that he would finally be able to present his full case to the grand jury following the Shannons' testimony. "I want the Shannons to tell the grand jury all they have told me of their personal observations when they lived in the flat below Inez Burns's abortion clinic," Brown said, "and anything they have to say regarding the shakedown charges."[14]

But within days and seemingly from out of nowhere, everything the Shannons had done—all the scheming and planning building up to their grand finale—began to crumble when newspaper reports surfaced that put Burns's $1300 gift to Warren Shannon together with a settlement negotiated by her attorney, and shone a light on the weekly payments to Gloria Shannon that the couple claimed they only used for entertainment. Added to the Shannons' already questionable reputation, the reports provided doubts for both the district attorney and the grand jury as to the couple's value on the witness stand. Upon hearing the latest accusations against the Shannons, the grand jury wasted no time in announcing they would postpone hearing the couple's testimony until further notice. Likewise, Brown began distancing himself from the pair and refused to take their telephone calls.

In a desperate attempt to get before the grand jury, the Shannons went on the defense and made more public statements, but to no avail. Seeing their dream withering away, Gloria Shannon took action and initiated support from the city's clergy, begging for their help in an open letter to the *San Francisco Examiner*:

Dear Sirs . . . Please help denounce these criminals and their conspirators . . . and support us and the prosecution from your pulpit. . . . I have taken upon myself the initiative in exposing the monstrous abortion racket . . . as I have a deep and sincere feeling that I want to do something to justify my place in this world. . . . I have undertaken to gather and hope to publicize information concerning the notorious abortion mill of Inez L. Burns . . . and I am aware of the danger that confronts anyone in this city who dares to expose organized, protected crime.[15]

Her lengthy diatribe included an attempt to publicly pressure the district attorney's office and the grand jury. "They have already started their malicious conspiracy to disqualify me as a witness . . . and possibly my good husband," she accused. Shannon alleged the existence of a sinister plot to let the "abortionist go free" and instead prosecute both her and her husband. She never identified who "they" might be, but ended the letter by pointing out, "a criminal setup such as Burns's abortion mill could have not survived long without protection."[16]

14 Death House

I am the greatest abortionist in the United States!

—Inez Brown Burns

The Shannons returned to San Francisco low on cash and with no source of income or future prospects. As if as an answer to prayer, William Randolph Hearst approached Gloria Shannon and purchased the copyright to her manuscript for the *San Francisco Examiner*. To the Shannons' great delight—and to Pat Brown's equally great chagrin—the first chapter ran on January 20, 1946, with front-page headlines announcing: INEZ BURNS' HOUSE OF HORRORS!

Shannon's blatantly exaggerated and dramatic tale was prefaced with an editorial notation describing her exclusive story of Burns's abortion mill as one told with all its "sordidness, its tragedies, its callousness, and its undermining of public officials and underlings through 'payoffs.'" The editor praised Mrs. Shannon as a member of a distinguished American family and the daughter of a famed American cartoonist, and credited her with the moral fortitude to raise public consciousness by making available to the *Examiner* her manuscript of personal knowledge and observation.[1]

Her story began with the revelation:

Every fifteen minutes a baby went to it's [sic] death! A river of blood ran out of that house . . .

It is such a quiet looking place. The curtains, newly laundered, are crisp and homelike and the tan stucco has a modest appeal. You'd think honest people lived there, kind and happy people. But, things very appalling go on behind those doors . . . like murder. For this "House of Death" is Inez Burns's abortion mill at 327 Fillmore Street. Inez Burns, whose business cards read, "Inez L. Brown, Designer," but, who proudly and openly boasts, "I am the greatest abortionist in the United States!" And whose intimates include men who hold, and who have held, key positions in San Francisco society.[2]

Shannon recognized immediately what a great story she had in the secret life of Inez Burns. She began her tale by describing the first time she met Burns in the fall of 1944 while dining out one evening with her husband at the Fairmont Hotel. According to Shannon, Burns, a longtime friend of her husband, stopped briefly at the couple's table to chat. Her first impression of the beautiful, strikingly dynamic woman wrapped in an expensive ermine fur was one of awe and admiration. That particular evening Burns wore a magnificent diamond and ruby ring with matching diamond dress clips that flashed and danced in the evening light. Still, it was Burns's "hard and wise, glittering eyes" that fascinated Shannon the most.

> Well preserved for her fifty-eight years, Inez was a marvel of tensely controlled nerves and shockingly callous temperament. After our brief introduction, she abruptly stopped and frantically looked around, her face white. "Good God!" She said in a hoarse whisper, "Where's my purse!? My day's receipts are in it—$5,000!"

> Rushing back to her table, Burns created instant commotion throughout the restaurant until her black suede Hermès bag was found under a nearby heap of furs.

> "Thank God," she sighed in relief. "Now, listen, Warren, I'm in a great deal of difficulty and I want you to come out to the house tomorrow night to see me. And, gee—your wife looks just like Lillian Russell. Bring her along with you!"

I was quite taken with this amazing woman, but, if I had dreamed of the horror that night would lead to, I would never have looked on that woman's face.[3]

Gloria Shannon's story included the couple's first call to Burns's house and later her clinic. Prior to their visit Warren Shannon explained to his wife that Burns's obvious wealth came from her being "San Francisco's leading abortionist." He assured her he had no knowledge of Burns's current problems and did not want to, saying, "She knows I have neither political power or interest to help her."[4]

Fascinated by Burns and eager to get closer, Gloria Shannon persuaded her husband to keep the appointment the following evening at Burns's Guerrero Street home. When the couple arrived a maid led them upstairs where they found Burns dressed in a pink silk nightgown and matching bed jacket comfortably lounging on her rose satin bed. Looking disheveled, her auburn red hair tossed loosely around her pale face, Burns sipped from a scotch tumbler and then took a long drag on her cigarette before launching into her current difficulties.[5]

"Warren," she said, sitting up and leaning forward intently, "I'm in a dreadful mess. Out of the goodness of my heart, I took in a young navy doc [Dr. Loraine Everson]—he was highly recommended by a friend ... someone, I've known for years, you know, or I never would have used him," she assured Shannon. "I promised him half the day's 'take,' and I signed a two-year contract with him." Burns paused to light another cigarette. "But, like a fool, 'the Little Sparrow,' Mabel, showed him the envelopes," she said, glaring through a cloud of gray smoke.[6]

Inez then reached her hand under the side of the bed and pulled out her purse, retrieving a white packet that she handed to Shannon. She explained that the daily envelopes had a written record of what came in and what went out. At the end of each day Mabel put the patient cards and the money into the envelope, which Burns took home so that the cards could be filed and the "glantham" put in the safe.[7]

Gloria Shannon's interest grew. "Glantham?" she asked. "What is that?"

"That, my dear," Burns revealed with a smile, "is our secret word for money." Unfortunately, Mabel had unwittingly shown the daily envelopes to Everson, forcing Burns to pay him $58,000 for three months of work.[8]

"As if that wasn't enough," Burns continued, moving to the edge of the bed, her pink bed jacket falling from her shoulders, "he kept a diary and is demanding $25,000 more or he's threatening to go to the IRS." Exasperated, she looked to Shannon. "What am I goin' to do?"[9]

Warren Shannon hesitated to get involved in Burns's legal troubles. "You need to ask a lawyer," he offered. Burns concluded that yes, she could get "Walter McGovern to take care of it." The clandestine meeting was interrupted when Burns's husband, former assemblyman Joe Burns, rushed into the bedroom and scolded his wife for "airing her dirty laundry" to the whole world. But Burns quickly backed him out the door, cursing in his face and reminding him that if she had married "someone with brains, she wouldn't have to work so hard to keep him, the bar, and the horse ranch going!"[10]

Burns quickly regained her composure and sent Warren Shannon downstairs with Joe to join the weekly poker game. "I have some work to do," she said, turning to his wife. "Why don't you come along with me?" Dumbfounded, Gloria Shannon inquired how she could possibly be of help. "You can be 'law and order,'" Burns laughed.[11]

Gloria Shannon secretly wondered if Burns was a fool to take a total stranger into her confidence and her illegal operation. But no one, not even the Shannons, mistook Burns for a fool, and she certainly was not one. Merely confident in her powerful influence, Burns knew she paid well for protection, and protection she got. In thirty years, she had been arrested three times and the charges had always been dropped. Burns knew she was above the law and took every opportunity to flaunt it.

Gloria Shannon found Burns's clinic had a clean, pleasant exterior, and was located in a respectable neighborhood. But according to her manuscript, civility ended there. "There was no decency, no cleanliness, no human consideration for pain," she wrote.[12]

She described the clinic's surgery rooms as filthy, with the bedsheets left unchanged for up to ten days, where "one girl gets out, and before the bed can be smoothed, another topples in." Burns did not allow disinfectants as they rotted the linens, Shannon noted, leaving the main surgery room (located on the top floor and set back to escape being seen from the streets) cluttered with towels from the operating tables, which Burns allowed to be changed only when red with blood. Shannon portrayed Burns as a strange, clever surgeon with a wicked temper "but deft hands, and torrential energy" as she sat on a stool before the narrow operating table for up to six hours every day.[13]

According to Shannon, Burns enjoyed her work, even allowing friends to casually drop by while she was in surgery. On one occasion a bank teller stood at the table while she finished an operation and nonchalantly discussed a will he had drawn up for her children. Another time a policeman in full uniform stopped by and was told to go "right on up."[14]

Shannon said she was disturbed by many of the patients she found at the clinic, particularly the underage girls she described as "frightened and bewildered kids" who believed themselves smart, but never dreamed life had such ruthless consequences.[15]

One day a white slip of a thing, not a day over fifteen years old came rushing up the steps. She had big blue eyes and stringy blond hair. She was late—six weeks, she said. There was only one boy . . . and it happened only once—she wasn't even quite sure it had happened. She wasn't sure of anything except the $70 she had tied in a grimy handkerchief—crumbled fives, dollars, and quarters.

Mabel Spaulding, who sat at a desk at the entrance, opened the handkerchief, counted out the money and shook her head. "Not enough!" She said.[16]

Mabel Spaulding, a pasty-white-faced, fifty-six-year-old widow who pounded through the halls in her official white sharkskin uniform, served as both receptionist and bookkeeper. She had worked for Burns for eighteen years and stayed on call twenty-four hours a day. Sarcastically nicknamed the Sparrow by Burns, Shannon recalled Spaulding as ruthless and unmoved by the girl's tears. "Get out!" she shouted to the distraught girl. "You got yourself in this mess; now you can do your crying out on the street."[17]

Wives came too, Shannon noted, many with an older child or two in tow who ended up playing on the kitchen floor amidst the scurry of attendants and the clatter of instruments. Sometimes couples came in together, but Spaulding sent the men to the drugstore across the street with instructions to wait at the soda counter.[18]

The *Examiner* published the first two chapters of Gloria Shannon's memoir late in January 1946 while memories of World War II still lay like heavy clouds over the city. Returning soldiers, weary in ragtag uniforms, wandered the streets, reminders of the 300,000 who never returned home. Front-page headlines gave daily reports of death, war-crime trials, and refugees. Port cities like San Francisco became rendezvous points and centers for international conferences. Politicians, preachers, and salesmen capitalized on this vulnerable atmosphere, winning converts using patriotic and onerous themes. Likewise Shannon, desperate to generate interest in her tell-all book, incorporated any means necessary to catch the public's attention. Along with her graphic and untrue details, she used recent revelations of German war atrocities and cleverly incorporated details of Nazi death camps into her manuscript, even comparing Burns to the hated, infamous Irma Grese, "the Beast of Belsen," who only six months earlier stood trial for the torture and death of innumerable Jewish women.[19]

The allegations detailed in Shannon's exposé tipped the district attorney's hand; the memoir also opened up a number of new avenues for investigation. Along with detailed information of underage girls, organized gambling, and police payoffs, Shannon secreted photographs of documents out of Burns's clinic.[20]

The *San Francisco Examiner* ran the first two chapters of Gloria Shannon's manuscript on the front page on January 20 and 21, 1946, and promised subsequent chapters in the days to come. But when eager readers picked up the paper on January 22, chapter three was missing without explanation. Gloria Shannon had finally been silenced.

Upon seeing the proverbial silver coins slip through her fingers, Shannon anxiously sent word to Brown via her attorney with more detailed observations collected during her tenure as Burns's receptionist, and again she refuted any charges of wrongdoing. But Brown remained evasive and only confirmed that the couple remained on the schedule to testify before the grand jury, the date now postponed—in case the jury preferred to wait until after the Burns's police tip-off investigation.[21]

During the last week of January 1946, Brown and his assistant, Tom Lynch, appeared before the grand jury and delivered a complete statement including "all collateral matters" with regard to the Burns corruption case. Following the meeting, the panel squashed previous plans to call Warren and Gloria Shannon. Jury foreman Henry Maginn reasoned, "We are not going to waste time listening to gossip not substantiated by evidence." The district attorney concurred, asserting Gloria Shannon did not have any new information, and therefore the grand jury chose not to hear her testimony. Furthermore, he did not plan to call either of them as a witness in the upcoming Burns trial. "We know everything that Mrs. Shannon has written," Brown declared, "and we won't be calling them as witnesses."[22]

Brown cancelled the subpoena for the Shannons altogether. A month later, in late February, only days before the trial began, he attempted to contact the couple. He said he hoped to "fill in some gaps" in the evidence and to clarify such things as the code words the Shannons alleged Burns employed at the clinic, such as "glantham" for money and so on. "I've asked them to call me—collect—from wherever they are," Brown said.

But the Shannons were long gone, last heard from passing through Chicago, presumably on their way to New York. Two weeks later the couple's attorney filed a lawsuit against the pair for non-payment of fees.[23]

PART FOUR

A Grand Fight

15 *The Lone Holdout*

A gross miscarriage of justice. . . . A case undone by
influences that go hand-in-hand with the tremendous
financial power wielded by that Burns woman!

—Pat Brown

Inez Burns's first trial, which began before Judge William F. Traverso on
February 18, 1946, ended two and a half weeks later on March 7. As the
drama played out in the courtroom, it continued to make headlines in
local newspapers, where the legal theatrics, titillating tidbits, and insider
gossip kept readers begging for more.

Daily features captivated local residents with descriptive and embellished accusations, particularly Gloria Shannon's exposé. It and various
other articles so prejudiced the proceedings that the judge admonished
jurors to determine the case based on the evidence and not on newspaper
stories. Pat Brown even approached local editors to say his office was
investigating mysterious and intimidating telephone calls to witnesses
spurred on by the tabloid news. Even so, the stories kept coming.

Shannon's "tell-all" manuscript was by far the most shocking with its
alarming and embellished details of a heartless and mean-spirited Burns,
who performed hundreds of operations under the most unsanitary and
humiliating conditions. Other reports, while also scandalous, held that
Burns's clinic appeared "more efficient and sanitary than many . . . of
the regular hospitals in the city."[1]

Testimony and evidence produced at the trial also demonstrated
that Burns ran a well-organized, clean operation frequented by women
primarily from the middle and upper classes. Local laboratory technician

Franklin Dare testified that Burns, posing as a gynecologist named Dr. Brown, came to his office and engaged his services to test the slides of 356 patients for infection and "social diseases"—all in one month. Next, testimonies given by Stuart Oxygen Company driver Louis Maniscalco and Grant Drug Store owner Edward Scott detailed large shipments of medical and cleaning supplies routinely delivered to both her Fillmore Street and Oakland clinics.[2]

Scott, whose drugstore stood just three blocks from Burns's main clinic on Fillmore Street, had supplied Burns for the past fifteen years, and further testified that he knew Warren and Gloria Shannon and that the couple lived at Burns's Fillmore Street flat. He even described photographs of the facility and a book the couple left on the counter at his drug store. Louis Maniscalco stated he delivered medical gasses to the Fillmore Street address at least twice a week, and he produced receipts signed by various people over a two-year period. A third deliveryman, Joseph Zich, also identified each of the defendants as accepting and paying for supplies. He specifically pointed out defendant Joseph Hoff as the "older gentleman" from the clinic who wore a hearing aid and a rubber apron.[3]

The prosecution also presented evidence from these witnesses that linked Burns to the ownership of a second "personal service" business in Oakland. According to public records, Inez and her husband Joseph Burns owned both facilities—the Fillmore Street clinic and the Oakland clinic (listed as the office of Dr. Frank E. Paget, a partner of Burns)—as community property.[4]

Incredibly, none of these witnesses admitted to any knowledge of the type of business Burns operated. Maniscalco, who made regular deliveries of oxygen tanks to the clinic, claimed no knowledge of the defendants, their names, or the purpose for his oxygen.

"What did you think the place was?" defense counsel asked.

"I hadn't the least idea. . . . My only interest was my job," he replied.

"Well, you didn't think it was a saloon, did you, or a cocktail bar?"

"I had no idea," Maniscalco held firm, "just made my deliveries to the kitchen."[5]

Joseph Zich admitted he knew about Burns's operation, but only through "hearsay" and he "got the hell out of there" after his deliveries. Pharmacist Edward Scott sold Burns enough drugs to supply a hospital, yet he also claimed to have "no idea" that abortions were being performed there.

Next to take the stand, John Englis, repairman and manager of the San Francisco Surgical Company, testified that he knew Burns going back to 1933, but as "Amy Dutch." Like Englis, Herman Weniger, a manufacturer of surgical instruments, told the court he repaired and duplicated surgical devices, such as extraction forceps used in abortions. However, Weniger testified Burns's employee Joseph Hoff picked up and delivered the instruments to him, and paid with a check signed "Mrs. Brown."[6]

Burns's onetime partner, naval officer Dr. Larry Everson, who promptly vanished after an unpleasant run-in with Burns in the fall of 1944, proved the most challenging witness on the prosecution's list. According to Tom Lynch, who managed to keep Everson's name out of the newspapers, the young doctor from Treasure Island helped out from time to time and then came in as an equal partner with Burns, collecting $58,000 for three months of work. However, when Everson realized that Burns shorted him he demanded an additional $35,000 for his daily journal, causing Burns to fire him. The two eventually reached an agreement in which the doctor received $12,500 (or $25,000, depending on who you believe) and Burns got the diary.[7]

In the raid on Burns's home the district attorney's office confiscated Everson's incriminating orange notebook and found it filled with lists of names, hospitals, dates, times, and cryptic phrases like "almost the big sleep," as ex-supervisor Shannon and his wife, Gloria had described.

Brown had the diary, but to use it as evidence his office needed to authenticate it by placing the author at Burns's clinic, and investigators could not find the doctor or get anyone to give up his name. Brown's team interviewed Burns's associates for weeks before the name Everson came up and matched local medical records with a Dr. Loraine Everson—a woman, or so they thought. Everyone was convinced except investigator Frank Ahern, who believed things did not add up, so he kept digging. Over the next several weeks he scoured through medical school yearbooks from coast to coast and found the doctor—a man after all—in Madison, Wisconsin. But when Lynch finally managed to get Everson on the phone, he found the doctor completely uncooperative.[8]

The district attorney's office had no real evidence against Everson. Still, they needed to verify his handwriting to use the diary in Burns's trial, so Lynch and his assistant Jack Eyman caught the next plane to Madison, where they tracked down the doctor through a wedding photograph posted in the *Wisconsin State Journal*. According to Lynch, the newspaper's editor also divulged local suspicions about Everson, and Lynch promised him the lead when the story broke. Then Lynch and Eyman, posing as pharmaceutical salesmen, went to Everson's office and attempted to get his signature. Unfortunately for them, the doctor caught onto their ruse, smiled, and showed them the door—but not before Eyman slipped the doctor's ink blotter off the desk and into his pocket. It was enough for the court to authenticate the diary, which the prosecution then used as evidence in the testimonies of former employees Madeline Rand, Levina Queen, and Kathryn Bartron.[9]

The first of Burns's former employees to take the stand for the prosecution, Madeline Rand, gave a surprising and appalling account of her time at the Fillmore Street clinic. Of all the witnesses, the former defendant and ex-friend of Burns gave one of the most damning testimonies of the trial. Rand identified all the defendants and Burns's partner Dr. Paget (not on trial), who she described as having the disgusting habit of eating lunch in surgery while patients were on the table. Under cross-examination, defense attorney Walter McGovern inquired if *she* ever ate lunch in the surgical room.

"Yes, in the kitchen," Rand replied.

The defense attorney pressed her, "Anywhere else?"

"Well, yes," she reluctantly admitted. "In the surgery."

McGovern then asked if this happened with patients on the table and how often. "At least once a week," Rand confessed. "The place was very busy and everyone was rushed and short-handed."

Not satisfied, McGovern wanted to know if this was true of all of the staff.

"Yes," Rand said. Later she admitted Burns never ate in the surgery room, but only drank her morning coffee there.[10]

Rand testified her job, for which she was paid $200 per month, included advising exiting patients on postoperative care using directions given to her by Burns. She told the court she tended to the women after they had stabilized, at which time she instructed them to rest for at least forty-eight hours and not to wash their hair for at least one week. More importantly, she reminded them they must call the clinic and not their family physician if any complications arose. At least half of the women, she explained, vomited before they left the clinic.

Rand's testimony included detailed descriptions of cleaning the surgery rooms, and contrary to Gloria Shannon's tales of filth and contamination she described sterilizing the instruments following each of the twenty to forty operations a day. "She [Burns] told me she wanted me to keep the place clean and showed me how to organize the instruments in the sterilizers," Rand explained to the jury.[11]

On redirect Rand claimed Burns instructed her to change the linens only when they were "badly soiled." But in the end, it was her vivid account of surgical waste disposal that brought gasps from the crowded courtroom. Rand explained Burns's painstaking directions on cleaning the tables with antiseptic and rinsing the rubber surgical pads, first into buckets positioned at the foot of the surgical table, and then into specially designed refuse sinks.

"What material did you see in the buckets?" Lynch asked.

"Mucus, blood, and the eyes of the fetus," Rand replied, looking away from the stunned jury.

Lynch raised his hand to signal the witness to pause, allowing the impact of her words to sink in.

"And then?" he prompted.

"Mrs. Burns' instructions were to use the small sink for shorter cases," she continued, "and on the cases that took a long time, she told me to pour it into the large sink—the one with the large mouth channel, because everything could pass through that one." Rand claimed she had no knowledge where the pipes from the sinks emptied. But she did admit to assisting in the operating room alongside defendant Musette Briggs, who occasionally relieved Burns, administering ether and working with patients to keep them quiet during surgery.

"Were you present when [patient] Phyllis Miller was in the large surgery room and did you hear her conversation with Mrs. Burns?" Lynch asked.

"Yes, Mrs. Burns told Mrs. Miller to be quiet if she didn't want the police to come," Rand said, "and I tried to quiet her down."

Rand further described a road trip in Burns's car with prosecution witness Virginia Westrup. The two women drove from San Francisco to Albany, New York to escort a patient, Mrs. McCauley, to the clinic. Following McCauley's surgery, Rand testified, Burns soothed the frightened woman, telling her, "Everything will be alright now, everything is out, and everything will be alright."[12]

In his cross-examination, defense attorney McGovern went after Rand to expose her motivation for turning states' evidence against his client, especially after she begged the defendant for a job. Rand reluctantly admitted she approached Burns for work because she found herself broke with three children and a drunk husband.

"Didn't you tell Mrs. Burns after the arrest that if you did not get $2000 you would go to the district attorney's office?" McGovern demanded.

"No," she said.

"When you went down there who did you meet?"

"I met District Attorney Brown."

"Did he hand you any election cards at the time?" McGovern smiled.

Rand finally admitted the defendant had accused her of stealing money from patients' purses while she worked at the clinic, and together with her husband she had contacted Burns's former attorney to demand money in exchange for her testimony.[13]

The next former employee to take the stand, Kathryn Bartron, a registered nurse at St. Francis Hospital, worked as first assistant anesthetist to Burns. Bartron, originally hired by Burns in 1934, left after two years and then returned in 1943 on a part-time basis. On the first day of Bartron's testimony, McGovern objected fifty-six times, including several demands for a mistrial by the first break at 2:30 p.m. The judge overruled fifty-four of them, but the defense attorney's disruptive tactics worked. Barton became overwhelmed and fainted twice before McGovern had a chance to cross-examine her. After a twenty-minute delay, she returned to the stand and admitted she also accepted several gifts from Burns including an expensive pin, a dress, and a fur coat. "Did you thank her at the time, or are you thanking her now?" McGovern wanted to know.[14]

One of Burns's clients, twenty-two-year-old hairdresser Anita Kelly, testified only in the first trial. Despite extensive efforts by the court to locate her for the second and third trials, she vanished and left no forwarding address. Kelly's statement detailed her September 1944 visit to Burns's clinic and the serious inflammation that followed and put her in the hospital for twenty days. Kelly pointed out Mabel Spaulding as the person who paid her $300 medical expenses and slipped an envelope containing an additional $100 under her pillow while visiting her in the hospital. But during cross-examination, McGovern managed to shift the focus from his clients and onto the young woman's marital status and recent sexual activities.

"On September 1, 1944, you were pregnant," McGovern asked, "before you were married?"

"Yes," Kelly admitted, nodding her head.

"How many men did you have intercourse with prior to the time you became pregnant?" He wanted to know, "so that I can get a list of those men."

After considerable prodding by the defense attorney, Kelly named a young service man and told how many times she had met with him prior to becoming pregnant, but she would not disclose the name of the physician who recommended her to Burns's facility.

"I suppose everybody has known about that place for a long time," was her only response.

"Did you pay Dr. Diller out of that $300?" McGovern asked.

"That's right."

"And he knew nothing about you going there before you went?"

"No."

"I just wanted to clear that up," McGovern added, "I happen to be a friend of Dr. Diller."[15]

Dr. Theodore Diller took the stand to corroborate Kelly's story that he treated her following her visit to Burns's clinic, and that he determined the cause of her illness was "instrumentation." After Dr. Diller admitted Kelly to Mt. Zion Hospital, he told the jury, he called Burns to discuss the girl's case and requested she come to his office.

"I told her she [Kelly] was quite ill and low on funds, and needed considerable hospital care, which would be quite expensive."

According to Diller, Burns appeared cooperative and concerned about Kelly's welfare. In fact, the following day she came to his office, offered to pay the hospital bill, and laid a stack of bills on his desk.

"What did you do?" asked Lynch.

"I told her I wanted nothing to do with it, but to go to the hospital and make arrangements there," Dr. Diller assured the court.

"Did anyone from the district attorney's office threaten you with arrest for failing to report this case?" McGovern interrupted.

"I reported the case to the police," Dr. Diller replied, "as a matter of routine."[16]

Newspaper headlines called Burns's operation "big business." Indeed, evidence at the trial proved she was very successful and in spite of the large overhead in protection payoffs, she accumulated a tremendous amount of wealth. Prosecution witness William St. Claire, a clerk for Bank of America, identified eleven deposit books and testified to accepting large deposits from both Burns and Mabel Spaulding at least three or four days a week. "It was always in cash, never in checks," St. Claire told the court.[17]

At the end of the eighteen-day trial, and after an hour and a half of instruction, Judge Traverso turned the case over to the jury of seven men and five women. If convicted, Burns and her four codefendants faced two to five years in prison.[18]

By the middle of the first day of deliberation members of the jury reported they remained at an impasse. But Judge Traverso ordered them back to the drawing board, and finally locked them up at the Whitcomb Hotel for the night. In the early hours of the morning their vote stood 10–2 to convict, then 11–1. The following day the jury returned to the courtroom three times, once asking to see the pages from the "little black books" containing the names of patients, and another time requesting a complete review of the judge's instructions.

According to the foreman he used every pressure and device to bring a consensus. At one point two female jurors took it upon themselves to convince the lone holdout, Mrs. Anna Linder, by taking her into the corner and going over every aspect of the case with her item by item. Linder even voted one of the defendants guilty on one ballot, but then withdrew her vote as a mistake. When the group demanded to know why she refused to concede to a guilty vote, she stubbornly replied that she "considered it her constitutional right to refuse to vote!" The jurors eventually ostracized her by making her eat lunch at a table by herself.[19]

At 5:00 p.m. foreman Jacob Abrams again sent word to the judge that the jury remained deadlocked and "further deliberation would be hopeless because [one] juror refused to discuss the evidence." Seeing no hope of moving forward, Judge Traverso dismissed the jury. After weeks of testimony and thirty hours of deliberation, the jury hung at 11–1 to convict.[20]

The holdout, Mrs. Anna Linder, a widow and mother of five, said she refused to vote guilty because as she understood (or misunderstood) it the jury was required to acquit all five defendants or find all five guilty. In fact, it was more than likely that Mrs. Linder understood the judge's instructions and the law perfectly—her late husband had been a criminal attorney. "She admitted they were guilty to some of us, but said she would not vote for it," revealed one juror. Another member described the jury room battle as a "dogfight" in which one disgruntled juror became so enraged, "I thought he was going to choke her [Mrs. Linder]." Another member, who initially wanted to keep deliberating, eventually gave up along with the rest of the jury: "We could have jumped from the window one by one or collectively and it would not have moved that woman," he said.[21]

Lynch, angered by the verdict, pointed out that the judge's instructions remained perfectly clear and had been read and reread to the jury, and allowed a guilty verdict against any two or more of the defendants. Outside the courtroom, very relieved defendants Musette Briggs and Myrtle Ramsey excitedly slapped Mrs. Linder on the back when she declared, "I was the one!"[22]

The following week, Lynch questioned a friend of Burns who drove Anna Linder away from the courthouse. "She appeared to be under a terrible emotional strain," the unnamed friend explained. "Mrs. Burns's son suggested that I drive her home. So I did."[23]

District Attorney Brown called foul, pointing his finger at "sinister influences" going as far back as the 1945 grand jury that were still at work to defeat the administration of justice. "This was the best and most carefully prepared case presented since I assumed office," he told reporters and branded the verdict a "gross miscarriage of justice." A case undone by "influences that go hand-in-hand with the tremendous financial power wielded by that Burns woman!"[24]

After the judge dismissed them the jurors informally discussed among themselves the possibility of whether or not there had been a "fix." Several discounted this theory, saying they took a total of eighty-five ballots with the first being 8–4 to convict and then settling on 11–1. But Brown suspected something was awry and privately interviewed each of the jurors to determine any evidence of misconduct in the jury room and to find out if anyone had illegally approached them. Anna Linder eventually confessed she was not the only acquittal vote, and said that another member gave her "secret encouragement" to stick with her decision. The unnamed juror promised her if she changed her vote to guilty he would change his vote to non-guilty, thus hanging the jury under any circumstance.[25]

Brown's heavy-handed approach with the jury brought outrage from other members of the legal community, who criticized his actions as seriously threatening to the jury system. Undeterred, Brown demanded a transcript of the defense's closing arguments to see if any action might be taken against McGovern. The defense attorney did not call any witnesses or present any evidence at the trial; instead, he based his entire strategy and closing argument around establishing Burn's operation as a "necessary evil," with the whole town in on the conspiracy. According to Brown, McGovern, an officer of the court, asked the jury to disregard their oath when he pleaded with them to find Burns innocent even if they thought her guilty.[26]

"I don't mind if he attacks me and my motives," Brown said, but when "as an officer of the court, he asks the jury to pervert its oath, that's going too far."

"He can't get away with that kind of stuff," he added.[27]

Lynch took the opportunity to announce that there would be a new trial with "further indictments." While he refused to expound on his statement, including the alleged payoffs and the ongoing investigation into the police tip-off, he did issue a warning: "We are going into all implications of this case now."

Brown's comments on rumors of tampering angered McGovern, who took his outrage to Judge Traverso.

"Your Honor, I have no hope—no hope! That anything can shut Mr. Brown up!"[28]

———

Two weeks after the jury came back without a verdict, Gerrylee Marsigli, whose complaint launched the investigation and raid on Burns's clinic, attempted suicide. The continued publicity of the trial strained her already-rocky marriage and led to a divorce from her longshoreman husband. On March 17 the despondent twenty-one-year-old housewife checked into a seedy hotel on Eddy Street, swallowed concentrated ammonia, and ended up back in Central Emergency Hospital. She refused to discuss her situation with police and repeatedly asked to speak with Assistant District Attorney Tom Lynch.

"I'm just tired of it all," she said.[29]

16   *"Accomplices and Co-Conspirators"*

They're all guilty under the law.

—Judge Herbert C. Kaufman

District Attorney Brown quickly refiled Inez Burns's case, and the second trial began on May 13 in Judge Herbert C. Kaufman's courtroom. The press reported that Burns, in addition to wearing the presumption of innocence, wore a "sprightly new green and white hat"; the other female defendants wore the same hats as in the first trial.

This time Walter McGovern's defense strategy focused on implicating Burns's clients, along with the physicians (repairmen, as Burns liked to call them) and those who referred women to the clinic, all as collaborators who also violated the Medical Practices Act. "It is our contention that there are a great many people who ought to be charged here," McGovern told the court.[1]

The judge agreed and upheld the defense's argument that many of the prosecution's witnesses were themselves accomplices and co-conspirators according to their own uncontradicted testimony. In an out-of-court press conference Judge Kaufman stood by his decision, stating that the testimonies of the women who obtained illegal operations at Burns's clinic and those who claimed to have worked there "must be viewed with distrust."[2]

McGovern's strategy "to be fair" with everyone connected with Burns's operation worked. Nevertheless, the judge dismissed several prospective jurors after they sided with a particularly vocal candidate, Mrs. Mayerson, who agreed with the defense and wanted to see "the same treatment" for all. Alarmed, prosecutor Tom Lynch asked Mayerson if she ever discussed the case with anyone. She replied that she had, and quickly volunteered her viewpoint: "I personally feel that these defendants are no more guilty than the women who go to them," the mother of two declared, "and I'm not sure I could be fair as a juror." At this Lynch jumped to his feet and demanded to know if this was a fixed opinion among the group.

"She has stated the law," Judge Kaufman interrupted, and said they were all technically "guilty under the law."

"It's not the same offense," Lynch snapped.

Mayerson's comment set off a firestorm of controversy lasting several minutes until Judge Kaufman's gavel calmed the group and he addressed Mayerson's outburst. The judge stated that he agreed that perhaps as a "matter of fair play" all concerned should be brought to trial, but he admitted, "As a practical matter, sometimes that can't be done." McGovern was thrilled with the willingness of the jurors to try the case, as he put it, "in the good old American way."[3]

This gave Defense Attorney McGovern the confidence to announce he planned to again rely solely on his final arguments, seeing that the prosecution's case remained legally unsound and depended largely on the testimonies of accomplices. As in the first trial, McGovern presented no evidence or testimony, but instead used the prosecution's own evidence against them. "By the prosecution's own figures 187,500 women aborted at the Burns establishment in the last 25 years," McGovern declared, yet of the seven who were brought to testify, "none were from Nob Hill or even the city of San Francisco."[4]

He pointed to this discrimination as an example of the district attorney's office seeking to send "a few goats to jail" while allowing the women who sought out Burns's services, and the firms who supplied her clinic, to go free. Furthermore, McGovern demanded all witnesses excluded from the courtroom during the trial, including the two exceptions requested by Lynch—homicide inspectors Edward Pensat and Frank Ahern. When Lynch insisted, McGovern agreed to compromise. "We have no objection, of course, to Officer Pensat," the defense attorney asserted. "He has a very high reputation." Lynch declined McGovern's obvious invitation to debate Ahern's character and conceded for him to leave the courtroom.[5]

The prosecution presented the same evidence and witnesses they had in the first trial, bringing this second trial to an end on May 26. McGovern closed by adding Abraham Lincoln's words to his long list of quotes and concluded by advising the jurors, "When your time comes to die, you'll do so more easily if you have tempered justice with mercy." Lynch quickly rebutted with a terse analysis of the defense's tactics, which he called a combination of "sarcasm, sympathy, solicitude, sophistry, and even Shakespeare" in an attempt to prove his client did not do it. "Or, if she did," he added, "she did it beautifully."

"McGovern's philosophy," he continued, "is that it [Burns's clinic] was a fine place rendering a public service." If that were true, he added, "San Francisco would be the only community in the United States openly sanctioning the violation of the law."[6]

Like the first jury, this jury could not reach a verdict. Under guard at the Whitcomb Hotel while they deliberated, foreman John O. Wagner reported them hopelessly deadlocked by the second day and requested a dictionary. Judge Kaufman refused, stating nothing in the code provided for a deliberating jury to have a dictionary. Wagner then returned with a request for the judge to repeat his instructions on the admissibility of evidence. The eight men and four women never wavered from their orig-inal vote of 7–5 to convict, forcing Judge Kaufman to dismiss them at 9:00 p.m. on May 28 without a verdict. This time the five holdouts said they did not give great consideration to McGovern's elaborate closing argument, but attributed their decision more to Judge Kaufman's instructions, in which he told them to distrust the testimony of prosecution witnesses as accomplices—specifically, former patients.

Once again the district attorney's office, along with inspectors from homicide, quizzed the sympathetic jurors. "I refused to believe any of the evidence," stated Oscar Nelson, the unofficial leader of the group, "including the testimony of police inspector Frank Ahern." And the medical equipment found at the clinic "could have belonged to her son," he added.[7]

District Attorney Brown announced that he set the case for retrial. "If the views of the two juries, which have already tried this case, are an indication of how this community as a whole feels about accommodating the open violation of the law," Brown told reporters, "then we have no choice but to try it again."[8]

As the case dragged on for the better part of a year, the continuous publicity left Burns and her family vulnerable, and her Guerrero Street mansion and Fillmore Street clinic became targets for curious neighbors, the media, and criminals. During the summer of 1946, out on bail and awaiting her third trial, Burns retreated to Los Angeles to stay with her daughter, Alice. On the night of June 3, thieves broke in through a basement window of her Guerrero Street home and made off with suitcases loaded down with eight fur coats, $3000 in cash, and a diamond wristwatch, among other valuables. This was the second break-in since Burns's arrest.[9]

—

Fifty-five miles north of San Francisco in the sleepy town of Santa Rosa, retired businessman Vincent Rossi waited patiently for his morning paper to thud against the front door. He was particularly interested in the daily updates of the ongoing Inez Burns abortion trial.

Only months before Rossi had moved his family from Chicago to the warm, Spanish-style community where he paid cash for a modest house on Bryden Lane. Rossi stayed to himself, quietly enjoying his gardening or reading peacefully on his porch swing. His wife, Lena, the more social of the two, could be seen at community picnics or shopping in town, and her fancy Chrysler Town & Country Sports Coupe was often seen parked in front of St. Rose Catholic Church. In the evenings, neighbors observed the Rossi family frequenting the drowsy downtown cafés.

Vincent Rossi sometimes drove into San Francisco on weekends to meet friends for dinner at the Poodle Dog, or for drinks and late night card games at LaRocca's Corner Bar. But mostly these trips gave Rossi an opportunity to case the city's more lucrative businesses—specifically the abortion clinics.[10]

17 *A Grand Fight*

> It was generally agreed in town that Inez had never lost a
> single patient—she was considered the best.
>
> —Reporter Jerry Flamm

When the third trial began on September 10 before Judge Robert McWilliams, both sides appeared ready to make a deal and end this yearlong battle. The following day Defense Attorney McGovern approached District Attorney Brown with an offer that would allow Inez Burns to plead guilty to misdemeanor charges with a penalty of nothing more than fines—no jail time. According to the defense, both Brown and his assistant, Tom Lynch, agreed to the deal pending a final decision by the judge.

Judge McWilliams hoped to preside over a high-profile case, however, and refused to discuss a settlement. When McGovern heard the judge's decision, he promptly demanded McWilliams disqualify himself for "prejudice and bias." McWilliams had formerly worked with Lynch, who, as a federal prosecutor, had successfully convicted Burns of tax evasion. To avoid any conflict, the judge reluctantly removed himself. "I think it exceedingly unfortunate that you waited until this time to object to my trying this case," Judge McWilliams told McGovern. "You should have objected several weeks ago." The district attorney's office then categorically denied they had reached settlement. Lynch confirmed the defense made an offer, but said, "It never got beyond the vapor stage, and no one in the district attorney's office would ever agree to anything less than a felony charge in the Burns case."[1]

The defense quickly realized their strategy in removing Judge McWilliams backfired when Superior Court judge Edward P. Murphy decided to take the case. Murphy, concerned that Burns's third trial might go in the same direction as the first two trials, stepped in and took control. He resigned his position as presiding superior court justice and had his replacement, Judge Alfred J. Fritz, assign him to the case. Judge Murphy, with his by-the-book reputation, was the very justice the prosecution wanted to hear the case.[2]

Judge Murphy began by giving an hour-long address to the jury, in which he admonished them to report any attempt to influence their decisions during this trial. "If anyone approaches you directly or indirectly during this case, it is your duty to report it to me at once, anytime of the day or night," he cautioned. "The law is very strict about this." Next, the judge, and not the court clerk, who normally read the charges, read and explained each charge against the defendants in which they "knowingly, willfully, unlawfully, and feloniously" committed said crimes.[3]

Then Judge Murphy, aware of McGovern's reputation for dancing around the law, preempted the flamboyant defense attorney from swaying this jury with an emotion-packed closing argument by questioning the panel repeatedly on their attitude toward the law prohibiting abortion and making it clear: "You cannot simply say, 'I don't like this law and won't abide by it.'"[4]

After the judge swore in the selected jurors, the court discovered that one, Thomas J. Furner, faced felony hit-and-run charges. Following several conferences with opposing counsel, Judge Murphy asked Furner if he did not think it would be wise to excuse himself under the circumstances. "My attorney advised me that jury service would be legally okay," Furner responded, "but I'll do whatever you wish." Judge Murphy dismissed Furner and replaced him with an alternate. The defense adamantly objected to replacing a sworn juror, a move they later used as the basis for appeal.[5]

In a bold attempt to eliminate any jury tampering, Judge Murphy ordered the entire jury locked under guard at the Whitcomb Hotel throughout the entire trial, an action that had not been used with a San

Francisco jury in thirty years. However, throughout the trial the judge did allow the sequestered jury to engage in recreational activities. Escorted by the superior court bailiff, they attended the ballet, went to movies, and to baseball games. Still, McGovern attacked the judge's decision, stating, "In totalitarian countries this was called protective custody."[6]

Both Lynch and McGovern understood the high stakes involved in the Burns trial. Both were determined to win, and filled all three trials with their incessant bickering. In the third and final trial, both attorneys spoke out of turn, shouted insults, and stalled the proceedings. Beginning with Lynch's first witness, McGovern repeatedly interrupted, claimed hearing difficulties, and continually objected from the defense table. The unnerved and goaded prosecutor soon began addressing the defense counsel and not the court.

"I object to this line of questioning as leading and suggestive," McGovern interrupted the prosecution's first witness for the thirteenth time in less than ten minutes.

"I don't think it's leading and suggestive," Lynch responded, turning to McGovern.

"Well, that's immaterial," Judge Murphy stepped in. "Let's start off peacefully. I don't want any objections unless they are valid, and I presume the senator [McGovern] will not make them unless they are."

"That's right, I never did in my life," the defense attorney responded.

Judge Murphy continued, turning his attention to the prosecution table.

"And I don't want any leading questions, Mr. Lynch. Try this case as both of you know how to try a case and we won't have any trouble."[7]

The judge's reprimand did nothing to curb the daily sparring that entertained the overcrowded gallery and fed the media frenzy. And the testimony of former friend, employee, and defendant Levina Queen pleased the crowd even more.

Following the September 26 raid, members of the San Francisco Police Department arrived at Queen's exclusive Forest Hills home with a warrant for Queen's arrest. But her husband, Peel Queen, stalled the unsuspecting officers at the front door while his wife escaped out a rear basement window and over the back fence in a fur coat (and little else). Queen confessed to hiding out in the city and fleeing first to New York, then to Florida. She finally turned herself in after Lynch assured her he would dismiss all charges if she testified for the state. True to his word, Lynch dropped the warrant only minutes before she took the stand.[8]

Like Kathryn Bartron, Levina Queen was a highly skilled anesthetist. In September 1943 she was working at the Brooklyn Eye and Ear Hospital when Burns tracked her down and convinced her to return to San Francisco and work for her. Burns then paid all her moving expenses. Under direct examination, Lynch pointed to Burns and her codefendants seated behind the defense table and asked Queen to identify each of them.[9]

"We will stipulate they were all warm friends," McGovern interrupted drily.

"I'd like to do this on my own, if you don't mind," Lynch shot back, but then moved on to his next point. He established that Queen worked for Burns as far back as 1935, before Burns contacted her again in the fall of 1943.[10]

"She asked if I would please come, that her anesthetist had passed away, and she was very busy," Queen recalled of their telephone conversation. The shapely brunette crossed her legs as she sat in the witness chair. Cocking her head to one side, she stared down Burns's dark glare. In an exaggerated Brooklyn accent, Queen described her work at the clinic and identified the instruments used there. Still, as when Madeline Rand testified, it was her vivid description of fetal tissue extracted from patients that brought whispers from the spectators.

"What parts of the fetus have you seen removed?" Lynch wanted to know, "and what was done with the material?"

"Well, the head and face, the arms and legs and genital organs," Queen explained, shifting in the witness chair, smoothing out her navy wool skirt. "They were drained into a bucket at the bottom of the table and then poured into a sink."

"By whom were these removed?"

"Mrs. Burns, and well, the men I saw there."

"By anyone else?" Lynch continued.

"Is there a purpose in protecting the names of the men?" McGovern interrupted from the defense table.

Lynch ignored the defense attorney and approached the witness with his final question. "Do you know of any women who were worked on by Inez Burns who were not pregnant?"

McGovern jumped to his feet in protest. "How would she know if they were pregnant or not?" he demanded, only to be quickly overruled.

"Well, yes," Queen admitted, "there were cases Mrs. Burns referred to as "Emmas" or "Emilys." They were not pregnant."

"Were surgical instruments used on these women?"

"Yes."[11]

This answer brought a stunned silence to the courtroom.

The prosecution then passed a page torn from one of Burns's "little black books" to the jury. Written in Burns's hand along with details of the daily take was noted "Emily verified" next to the name Norma Hilton.[12]

The witness was then turned over to McGovern, who attacked her relentlessly in his cross-examination. Queen, whom he amusingly referred to as "Madam," acknowledged living rent-free in Burns's first-floor flat at the Fillmore Street clinic, in addition to her $600 monthly salary—four times the salary she received from Brooklyn Hospital.

Furthermore, she admitted that her duties along with administering anesthesia included assisting in abortions by inserting cervical dilators and vaginal speculums. Finally, Queen identified three male physicians who worked at the clinic during her time there: Dr. Samuel Stern, Dr. Frank Paget, and naval officer Dr. Larry Everson.

According to Queen, Dr. Paget—an older, heavyset man with hearing aids—frequently worked at both clinics, while the handsome, young Dr. Everson, whom she described as tall, blond, and wearing a military uniform, came only to the Fillmore Street clinic, where he worked for approximately five months. McGovern asked Queen to identify Dr. Everson's handwritten diary, the orange notebook taken in the raid of Burns's Guerrero Street home.

"Madam, would you know Dr. Everson's handwriting if you saw it?" The defense attorney asked as he rifled through the exhibits displayed by the prosecution.

"I don't believe I would."

"Where did you see this book?" McGovern asked Queen, holding up the orange notebook.

"Mr. Lynch showed it to me when he visited me."

"When we had lunch," she added.

"Really?" McGovern wanted to know. "Anything else?"

"Did you have dinner as well?"

"No," Queen blushed at the implication.[13]

In the end, in spite of McGovern's overt courtroom tactics and heavy-handed cross-examinations, Queen—together with Madeline Rand and Kathryn Bartron—tied each of the defendants to Burns's operation and described the nature of her business there.

All three of these witnesses gave one defendant, Mabel Spaulding, particular attention. According to houseguest Gloria Shannon the fifty-six-year-old widow endured relentless taunting from Burns. Although bullied by her boss, the gray-haired widow worked as the receptionist/bookkeeper and apparently wielded significant power at the clinic. It was Spaulding, they testified, who usually greeted the girls in the waiting area, took their histories, estimated the length of their pregnancies, and then set the abortion prices. This information, carefully recorded on preprinted index cards, was sent up to Burns in one of the operating rooms. Often Spaulding guessed wrong, though, and after physically examining patients Burns sometimes demanded $50 to $100 more when she discovered pregnancies further advanced than estimated.

When former patient Dorothy Kuykendall—identified only as Mrs. D. K. in the newspapers—testified for the prosecution, she confirmed this arm-twisting payment approach. The pretty, dark-eyed waitress took the stand and told a simple, yet typical story. Separated from her husband for six months, she met a local miner who, when he discovered her condition, refused to give her any money. Two doctors, she testified, recommended Burns's establishment, but Burns turned her away on her first visit and told her to "come back with the other $50." Later she returned with the required amount of $150 and got the abortion.[14]

McGovern's cross-examination of Kuykendall was especially grueling. He demanded to see a receipt for the clinic charges and for her to prove she was actually even pregnant at the time.

"You say you became pregnant, but your husband was not responsible for your pregnancy, isn't that correct?" He asked.

"No, it wasn't him," Kuykendall admitted.

"Then will you tell the ladies and gentlemen of the jury who this man is you claim was responsible—was the man related to you?" McGovern demanded.

"Of course not!"

Knowing that Kuykendall was reluctant to testify, McGovern continued to press her.

"Did Mr. Eyman [from the district attorney's office] and Mr. Ahern [from the police department] tell you they were going to subpoena you to testify in this case?"

"I don't remember."

"Well, don't you remember them telling you that if you didn't come and testify they would cause you trouble?"

Again, Kuykendall could not remember such a conversation.

"Do you recall telling them you didn't want to be a 'stool pigeon' or an 'informer'?" McGovern wanted to know, moving closer to the witness stand.

"Do you remember that?"

"No, no," she answered again, shaking her head emphatically.

"Did you at any time receive money from anyone connected to the district attorney's office in this city?"

"No."[15]

When the young waitress admitted she did not earn much money, McGovern wanted to know where she got the $150 she claimed to have used to pay for the abortion, for which she had no receipt.

Not getting a satisfactory answer, McGovern proceeded to describe for the jury the special contingency fund given to District Attorney Brown to prosecute certain high-profile cases such as this one. He then asked the witness again if anyone from the district attorney's office ever referred to money in a conversation with her or talked of giving her a reward for her testimony.

Before Kuykendall could answer, Lynch jumped to his feet objecting. The judge agreed that McGovern's questioning was out of line and immaterial. Nevertheless, the defense attorney pursued the issue with his usual flamboyance.

"Of course, but only if the court wants to listen to me," McGovern continued. "She claims she paid $150 and has no receipt. But that's only her word."

Irritated, the judge raised his hand to stop McGovern again.

"It certainly can't be charged that she got it from the district attorney's office," he pointed out, "because they didn't know anything about it."

"Well, I don't know about that," McGovern said, pausing to look knowingly at the jury. "I have information that I don't want to discuss at this time."

Red-faced and exasperated, Judge Murphy cut him off. "I don't know what information you think you have," he bellowed, "but as far as the $150 she got to pay for the abortion, and where she got it, we are not concerned with!"[16]

The next witness, Virginia Hufft, like Kuykendall, was further along in her pregnancy than she originally thought.

"She [Burns] told me I was over two months," Hufft testified. "She accepted the $150 that day and told me I was to come back with the additional $50 the next morning."

"Describe what was done to you," the prosecutor prompted.

"She took gauze dipped in an oily solution and packed it inside."

"Did you have any conversation with Mrs. Burns?"

"She told me that I needn't worry, that she had been doing this for twenty-five years and had never had a slip-up."

Hufft described being given a white robe after surgery and sent to rest on a sun porch that was occupied by five other recovering women resting in single beds.[17]

The next witness, Dorothy Taylor, described much the same attitude during her visit to the clinic. Young and unmarried, and referred by her company physician to Burns, she was first admitted by Musette Briggs, who set the fee at $125. But after examining Taylor, Burns demanded more money. According to the clinic's policy, Taylor returned the following day with more cash and obtained an abortion. When she was ready to leave Mabel Spaulding instructed Taylor to telephone "if anything happened" and gave her the "Inez L. Brown, Designer" card.

One week later, Taylor returned to the clinic extremely ill and "a young blond doctor" (Dr. Larry Everson) diagnosed her as having appendicitis. Defendants Joe Hoff and Musette Briggs drove her to St. Francis Hospital where a nurse waited with a wheelchair to take her up the back elevator to a room. Briggs registered Taylor as "a friend," gave her own personal address, and paid $50. Taylor stayed in the hospital under the care of Dr. Thomas O'Connor for ten days but was never officially admitted. During her stay, Taylor received several telephone calls from Burns's clinic. She testified that she never received a bill for her hospital stay or from the doctor. Under McGovern's exhaustive cross-examination, this witness admitted the prosecution showed her photographs of the defendants and told her their names.[18]

Prior to coming to court, Taylor testified, she received a warning not to be a witness in the case. She described a man and two women who approached her at work whom she believed connected to the Burns trial. Although she had never seen them before, the trio told her she had committed a felony when she had the abortion. McGovern fought vehemently to have the girl's statement stricken from the record, but the judge refused, allowing only the portion "connected with the Burns trial" taken out.[19]

Of the patients who testified, Dorothy Kuykendall and Dorothy Taylor received promises of anonymity in exchange for their testimony. However, unable to avoid the persistent media attention, Taylor's attending physician, Dr. Thomas H. O'Connor, a prominent doctor in the city and member of the board of trustees at St. Francis Hospital, remained hesitant to take the stand. Lynch quickly discovered the difficulty of dragging a man of his reputation into the glaring spotlight of a public abortion trial. Initially, O'Connor refused to appear, and Lynch received an anonymous warning that he would never "practice law in this town again" if he pursued him. With Brown's support Lynch persisted, and the reluctant doctor testified that he examined Taylor at St. Francis Hospital on February 10, 1945, after, he assumed, the physician's exchange admitted her. O'Connor stated that he treated the girl not for an appendicitis but for "an acute inflammation of the uterus," which he believed an instrument caused.

Under McGovern's cross-examination, O'Connor admitted he did not know precisely what caused the girl's condition, allowing McGovern to press forward.

"Now, could this infection have been caused by, this is a rather delicate subject, at the toilet . . . ?"

"No," O'Connor replied emphatically, "not that I've ever heard of."[20]

O'Connor released Taylor after ten days of observation. While Taylor told the court she never received a bill from Dr. O'Connor or the hospital,

O'Connor testified he sent a detailed invoice to 1060 Pine Street, the home of defendant Musette Briggs.[21]

Like the other patients brought to the stand, Winnie Bell Frazee testified her examination by Burns showed her pregnancy more advanced than she thought. However, Frazee did not return to the clinic with more money. Instead, her family physician, Dr. Wald, admitted her to St. Mary's Hospital, where he performed a legal abortion. According to hospital records Frazee, past her first trimester, came to the hospital more than once with a complicated twin pregnancy and hemorrhaging. Anxious to prove Burns showed good judgment when she turned Frazee away, McGovern led the witness step-by-step through her ordeal at St. Mary's Hospital.

"Didn't he [Dr. Wald] tell you that you were past three months pregnant, and he would not give you an abortion?" McGovern asked Frazee. "Then you went back to St. Mary's Hospital three or four days after visiting the Fillmore Street clinic?" The witness admitted she saw Dr. Wald before going to Burns's clinic, but said when she returned home from the clinic she began to miscarry. Then approximately five days later she went to the hospital.

"Isn't it true that when you went to St. Mary's Hospital part of a fetus was removed from your body—a leg of the fetus?" McGovern continued.

At this, the witness caught her breath, unable to answer the question.

"Didn't the doctor tell you when the hemorrhage occurred just part of the body came out, leaving the head?"

"I don't know," Frazee whispered, flustered and dazed.

Judge Murphy had heard enough and raised his hand to stop McGovern. "That's going too far," he cautioned.[22]

The State rested its case with San Francisco pathologist Dr. Jesse L. Carr, who identified the numerous medical instruments placed into evidence by the prosecution. Of the state's thirty witnesses, five were women who admitted to using Burns's services at the Fillmore clinic, three were former employees, and the rest consisted largely of salesmen who admitted furnishing drugs and other medical supplies to Burns.

Homicide inspector Frank Ahern, the arresting officer, became the final witness called prior to Carr and described for the court the events on the day of the raid. The prosecution carefully kept Ahern's testimony from wandering into the areas of police payoffs still under investigation by the grand jury, but local journalist Charles Raudebaugh also speculated that the prosecution held back from saying too much about police involvement in order to avoid a public break with Police Chief Charles Dullea.[23]

According to Ahern on the day of the raid he, Assistant District Attorney Tom Lynch, and officer Martin Lee hid out of sight about two blocks from the Fillmore Street clinic beginning at 10:00 a.m. until they got the go-ahead at 3:00 p.m. At that time Elkington, Eyman, stenographer from the district attorney's office Jean Calmenson, and three more police officers joined them. The team found the clinic deserted and Ahern spent several minutes trying to open the front door using keys provided by Lynch. But he found that Burns had changed the locks and they were unable to gain access. Ahern explained to the court that he then stationed two officers at the clinic and took the rest of the crew to Burns's Guerrero Street home, where District Attorney Brown and additional officers met them.

At Burns's house Ahern first questioned her blood technician Joseph Hoff, who nervously produced pay stubs from his wallet totaling $400 per month for "dusting," he told the officer. Next, Ahern quizzed Burns in her second-floor bedroom suite and examined the contents of her walk-in closet. Pushing aside carefully bagged designer gowns, Ahern said, he located a large black safe, which he opened using a combination also supplied by Lynch. The four-inch steel door opened to reveal neatly stacked bundles of cash, the handwritten diary of Dr. Loraine Everson, and several black notebooks containing notations in Burns's handwriting. The officer testified that he confiscated everything, including any medical related material he found throughout the house.

Lynch painstakingly walked Ahern through each piece of evidence, which included detailed photographs of secret passages as well as surgical instruments, additional notebooks that were found under the slates in the stairway, sterilizers found in the buffet cabinet, and medical supplies located in the bookcase. Burns claimed all the items either "belonged to someone who had long been dead" or were stored there for her son, Dr. Robert Merritt.

"Your honor," McGovern pleaded, "in the interest of time, we stipulate that Mr. Ahern was there with police officers, Mr. Brown our district attorney, Mr. Lynch and Mr. Eyman, and a number of other assistant district attorneys, and that they removed from these premises practically everything except the ventilation and it is now here in the courtroom."[24]

But Lynch was just getting started. Ahern did a step-by-step description of the furnishings, drugs, supplies, and equipment he found at both locations. The entrance door to the Fillmore Street clinic, he noted, was equipped with a peephole covered with a brass slide, and the door to the top surgical floor was securely locked with the key pinned to the inside of a drape. And leading up the stairs Burns had posted signs stating, "Absolutely no visitors upstairs, positively no exception," and "Positive silence in the surgery room—and that means you!" In a second-floor closet behind a false wall with a hidden door, Ahern testified, he uncovered a dark narrow "secret escape stairway" leading to the flat below. McGovern strongly objected to the word "secret," which the judge allowed stricken from the record.

Despite the loud objections from the defense table, Lynch had officers lug in armload after armload of boxes, bags, cartons, jugs, notebooks, ledgers, stethoscopes, microscopes, and instruments wrapped neatly in a brown leather pouch with the name "Inez L. Burns" inscribed inside, all to the front of the courtroom. Another bundle of stainless steel instruments found hidden in the secret staircase also accompanied the display, along with yet another set found under the bathroom sink of the flat occupied by Warren and Gloria Shannon. Adding to the rubber surgical mats, brown glass jugs of antiseptic solution, and an oversized sterilizer (McGovern objected to the word sterilizer—it was eventually defined as a large metal object), officers rolled a large anesthetic apparatus into the courtroom on wheels clinking and rattling like an old hospital gurney, all which grew into a mountain around Ahern's legs.

Documents in the haul of sixty-five exhibits included paycheck stubs, a payroll checkbook, account books, daily ledgers, and a box of printed filing cards for listing information from prospective clients—the pre-printed questions included "referred by" and "commission to." During McGovern's cross-examination, Ahern admitted he found and removed the notorious "little black books" belonging to Burns, which were not in evidence.

"Do you see any of those notebooks in the courtroom today?" McGovern wanted to know.

"No, sir," Ahern admitted.

"Well, where are the books hiding?" McGovern demanded.

"There're not hiding, I have them in my possession," Lynch interrupted.[25]

The black notebooks, along with Dr. Everson's orange journal, became the subject of great interest and speculation by the public following District Attorney Brown's press conferences, where he threatened to expose their contents. The prosecution admitted only a few pages from the notebooks into evidence and only at the first trial—just enough information to confirm the identity of the five women who testified, along with the corresponding dates, payments, and treatment. The prosecution excluded all other patients from the record. Lynch never made any attempt to establish authorship of those obviously belonging to Burns— written in her hand, and containing her personal notations—nor did he reveal the identity of Dr. Everson, but referred to his journal as "the diary of the young doctor."[26]

He offered one notebook entitled "Inez's Advice" into evidence; it contained her "specific directions." Another book listed Burns's "rules of procedure" instructing her employees to "never take a patient you think you can't face again; follow your hunches; and don't forget the black list."

Written on the back of the notebook entitled "Inez's Advice" were the names of local physicians (fixers), the cities where they operated, and the amount to pay each. The orange notebook, previously established as the journal of Dr. Everson, included a page of "troublesome cases." Among them was a Livermore woman with the notation, "finally got $2000 (all bills) was in San Jose hospital almost two months—almost the long sleep! Infection in bloodstream before the work." Some pages included personal notations, Burns reminding herself to keep a close eye on the financial records: "They are going to try and bluff me out!" She wrote, "Handwriting is on the wall! Even changing marking cards." Another notation put Burns's share of the take for one day at $1155 and for $1010 on another day. Also noted was $3750 that went out for the month as "overhead." Following the first trial Brown opted to remove even these two notebooks from evidence in an effort to keep the identities of prominent patients and corrupt officials secret.

McGovern cross-examined Ahern at length, dryly referring to him as "honest Frank" and "the William Jennings Bryan of the police department," all over the vehement objections of the prosecution. But McGovern could not rattle the big, Irish cop, who only reddened slightly at the defense attorney's repeated mockery. In the end, McGovern's sly reference to Ahern's claim of refusing Burns's $50,000 in cash stuck; Honest Frank was a nickname reporters latched onto and one that stayed with the officer for the rest of his career in law enforcement.[27]

18 *The End of the Road*

A long, gruesome, bloody, macabre road.

—Judge Edward P. Murphy

Defense Attorney McGovern always insisted that "the little lady" (as he called Inez Burns) and her four codefendants were anxious to take the stand and tell their side of the story. But in the final days of the trial after the prosecution finished with their witnesses and presented their evidence McGovern announced, as he did in the first two trials, "In view of the total insufficiency of evidence, we, too, rest." Later, he assured frustrated journalists that it was the proper thing to do when the prosecution did not prove their case, either legally or in substance.

Nevertheless, McGovern's closing statements always delighted reporters, courtroom enthusiasts, and zealous followers of the case. He thundered around the courtroom pointing out co-conspirators and corrupt officials while accusing Pat Brown and the district attorney's office of turning the case into a personal crusade.

"This persecution," McGovern told the jury, "has all the background of a private, personal fight—an unfair, unequal, unjust, and un-American conflict! And you should refuse to take part in this political conspiracy." Then with hands thrust deep into his pockets, eyes reverently downcast, and pacing back and forth, McGovern painted graphic pictures of a wartime city, conjuring up vivid memories all too fresh in the minds of the jurors.[1]

"These women were caught up in this war just like our soldiers," he told them, and they too wanted to do something patriotic, and yes, some of them went overboard, he admitted, sadly shaking his head. Others even went to bars, lonely during the war, and were seduced, and some were even raped—but all were "particular victims of the war."

Stopping directly in front of the jury box, McGovern brought his narrative full circle by creating a hypothetical girl "close to each of you," he said while pointing at the panel. What if she became "the victim of an assault by a man whose race or physical background she did not know?" he asked. Now, with the men and women of the jury theoretically in need of Burns's services, he held their attention. McGovern then brought it home. "Ask yourself," he challenged them, "if you would allow this girl, who *you* are responsible for, to bring a child into the world, or would you take steps to stop it?"[2]

Unable to discount the damning testimonies of salespeople, repairmen, bank clerks, and clients, McGovern admitted Burns's establishment ran "wider open than City Hospital or San Francisco General Hospital." But he appealed to them as citizens of San Francisco, a city known for tolerance and cosmopolitanism, to recognize that it allowed Burns to operate as "a necessary evil." Furthermore, he reminded them, if the city's officers seemed in agreement with this trial it was only because they went along with the "peanut politician," Pat Brown, who sought to further his political ambition over the broken bodies of unfortunate women. "Don't be taken in by stool pigeons," he begged the jury, pointing to the former employees who turned "traitors and crossovers"—Madeline Rand, Levina Queen, and Kathryn Bartron. McGovern reminded them, "Even Judas had the decency to hang himself!"[3]

At the conclusion of his lengthy closing, McGovern shamelessly praised the previous administration of Matthew Brady, but condemned District Attorney "Buster Brown" for his neglectful inaction against Burns for the past twenty months. Quoting from Dante, he told the jury, "Ambition feeds on strange foods."

Dropping his final bombshell, McGovern implied that Burns was on "such unusually intimate terms" with Assistant District Attorney Tom Lynch, whom he referred to as "detective gumshoe," that he had keys to her apartment only to find that she had changed the locks on him. "You should draw whatever conclusion that your 'life experience' will justify from that particular situation," he said, turning to pointedly stare at the red-faced prosecutor.[4]

Gesturing toward the sixty-year-old defendant, her head newly decorated with a somber, black-plumed hat, McGovern pleaded, "Hasn't she been punished enough? Hasn't she suffered enough? Look at her poor wrecked body. She is past the noontime of life, past the summer. The shadows of her life are falling toward the east! Obviously, she hasn't a great deal of time to stay here." His voice rising, and with dramatic hand gestures, he demanded to know how the people of San Francisco could find Burns guilty and excuse themselves. "How can the people of this city look at her and say that for the past twenty years she has gone and done these things and not say, 'We permitted you to do it'?" McGovern's final statement provoked Judge Murphy to instruct the jurors that they would receive their legal pronouncements from him, and "not from counsel."[5]

Lynch did not bother to address the defense's latest insinuations but quickly rebutted McGovern's justification of Burns's illegal activities. "It was a cold-blooded business," he told the jury. "This is a case about money," and "not if a woman was sick . . . simply, how much money did she have." The pattern of criminal conspiracy is complete, Lynch declared, and while he could not produce a motion picture of what went on at the clinic, he could produce the players: Mrs. Spaulding, "the custodian of cash," took the money then turned the patient over to Joe "the Duster" Hoff, "who did his dusting with a microscope." Next, the patient went upstairs, Lynch continued, to the surgical rooms where sometimes Inez Burns, "the star," did the work and sometimes Mrs. Briggs, "her understudy," performed the operation. Finally, Myrtle Ramsey, "the caretaker," helped them bathe and sent them home.[6]

Lynch challenged McGovern's contempt for the legal system. He told the jurors McGovern had no defense and therefore appealed to their passion, prejudice, and civic pride. He accused the defense of using tactics to draw attention to District Attorney Brown, Judge Murphy, former district attorney Matthew Brady, and even to castigate the police, all in an effort to hide those truly guilty. "Mrs. Burns was not engaged in a public utility for the public welfare," he reminded them.[7]

Finally, Lynch took full advantage of the rare silence from the defense table. Speaking in a direct, firm voice, he told the jury, "Not one single person has come upon this stand to deny one single word of the testimony." Lynch ended his closing argument with one parting shot directed at the defense table. "And Inez Burns didn't go there just to drink coffee in the operating room in the morning."[8]

On September 26 the jury retired to deliberate at 4:20 p.m. Within half an hour they confirmed they had reached a consensus, but sent a note to the judge asking to review a number of exhibits including photographs of Burns's establishment, Everson's diary, and other material seized in the raid. The prosecution offered no objection to the request for evidence, but McGovern voiced his concern that it was all "highly irregular."[9]

At 10:50 p.m., after only six and a half hours of deliberation, the jury of seven men and five women returned a verdict of guilty of conspiracy to commit abortion and to practicing medicine without a license. Burns sat in silence; the conviction came one year to the day after the raid on her Fillmore Street clinic.

Upon defense counsel's request, Judge Murphy polled the jury. Each spoke up quickly and remained firm in their vote with the exception of Mrs. Elizabeth Moses, the wife of a physician, who hesitated, refused to look up, and spoke so low he asked her to repeat her statement. Eventually, she too confirmed her vote. Judge Murphy denied McGovern's request that his clients remain at liberty on bail and ordered Burns and her four codefendants into the custody of the sheriff. As the members of the jury filed out of the courtroom, they agreed to say nothing of their deliberation and refused to speak to the press. Only the foreman, Sverre Kloster, came forward. "I hope I never have to go through that again," he told reporters.[10]

Four days later the final scene of this long drama began with the court clerk calling out the names of each defendant as they stood to hear their fate. District Attorney Brown watched from the back of the courtroom as his assistant, Lynch, spoke for the prosecution, saying, "The people are ready."

With his usual flair and dramatic bearing, the former state senator stood and addressed the court. "I would like to state that after conferring with other counsel interested in this case, and with the defendants themselves, we are more than convinced we stand on solid ground for reversal of this verdict," he said, then reviewed in detail the defense's view that the court erred when it dismissed juror Furner after the swearing in of the jury. Confident in the appellate court, McGovern stated, he advised Burns and her codefendants not to jeopardize their position by seeking a new trial or probation. "These five defendants were not tried according to the principles of common law that subsequently were written into the Constitution of the United States and the Constitution of the State of California," McGovern concluded, then sat down.[11]

"I am ready to pronounce judgment," Judge Murphy said.

"Step up, ladies and gentlemen," McGovern commanded the defendants with a grand gesture of his hand. Dazed, Burns and her four codefendants walked up to the bar.

The judge then read off the convictions and sentences for all five defendants—each sentence to be "not less than the minimum (two years) nor more than the maximum (five years)," as provided by law. McGovern asked for and received a stay of execution pending his appeal, but Judge Murphy adamantly denied bail.

"Does that mean bail in any amount?" the defense attorney asked.

"In any amount," the judge replied.[12]

When Judge Murphy left the bench, the courtroom erupted as family, friends, and reporters pushed toward the stunned defendants. All five broke down, cried, and held relatives for a final few moments of solace.

This last day proved a sensational finale for the avid crowd who had followed the case from its beginning. When bailiffs attempted to clear the courtroom, they found sightseers had blocked the exits used to return the defendants to their cells. Finally, they cleared a path, and officers guided Burns and her codefendants out of the court and back to jail.

The next day, the *San Francisco Chronicle* proclaimed, "One of San Francisco's oldest and best-known institutions came to the end of the road yesterday." In an interview following the conviction, Brown refused to comment on any pending deal with Burns in exchange for her testimony in the current police graft investigation. However, he told reporters, "It wouldn't surprise me if something developed." According to the district attorney, Burns "threatened to do some talking" if she was sent to prison. Many people "will probably come to a parting of ways before this is all over," he predicted.[13]

Within a month the State District Court of Appeals overruled Judge Murphy's order on bail, freeing Burns pending her appeal. The same month Defense Attorney McGovern filed the appeal based on double jeopardy, which they argued before the District Court of Appeals on November 8, 1947. The appellate court denied their motion; therefore McGovern requested a hearing before the Supreme Court of the State of California, which they denied on March 27, 1948. Three days later Burns, along with Mabel Spaulding, Musette Briggs, and Myrtle Ramsey, surrendered to the sheriff and was subsequently transported to Tehachapi State Prison for Women. Joseph "the Duster" Hoff went to San Quentin. On October 27, 1948, Burns lost her appeal to the U.S. Supreme Court. "They have come to the end of a long, gruesome, bloody, macabre road," Judge Murphy said.[14]

———

Following Inez Burns's conviction in September 1946, William A. Burkett, special agent for the investigative unit of the Internal Revenue at the San Francisco office, was assigned her tax case along with his superior, Donald Rogers. Six months later, Burkett wrote a letter to the district attorney's office requesting a statement from Tom Lynch detailing the circumstances surrounding the cash found in Burns's house on the day of the police raid. One year later, in October 1947, Burkett gave Rogers an update on the status of the case: "Full time work was given to an active investigation. Thirteen statements have been taken to date from witnesses. A personal diary and private ledgers of [the] taxpayer found and audited."[15]

Then months slipped by with no activity on the case. Burkett sent memos, made lists, and complained, but his superiors stalled. Ralph Reed, the bureau's intelligence chief for San Francisco, assured Burkett that as soon as they got the green light from the district attorney's office they would launch a full investigation.[16]

PART FIVE

Follow the Money

19 "Baghdad by the Bay"

San Francisco's . . . police force is graft-ridden and incompetent, and the municipal government is a dung heap of bungling phonies and clowning politicos.

—Reporter Robert Allen

In the first week of January 1946, Pat Brown announced the corruption case connected to Inez Burns's arrest would be the first order of business for the new grand jury and put one of his best men, Assistant District Attorney Norman Elkington, in charge. With supplementary funds promised by the state's attorney general, Brown pledged to investigate Burns's vice case with "all its ramifications."[1]

Brown believed, as Elkington did, that there were actually two tip-offs: the first, days before the raid, and the second, which sent Burns and her accomplices racing from the clinic five minutes before officers arrived. Witnesses testified that Burns and her employees did not carry enough with them to account for the large number of records missing when police gained access to the clinic. In addition, former employee turned state's witness Madeline Rand told the grand jury she remembered Burns received a "very important" phone call at least two days prior to the raid. The call excited her, Rand testified, and Burns immediately told everyone, "We have to get the hell out of here!" Speaking for the district attorney's office, Elkington insisted, "I'm sure the tip-off came from the police department," because, he continued, "I know it didn't come from our office."[2]

Elkington subpoenaed a total of twenty-six people before the grand jury, including those present at the planning meeting between Tom Lynch and Chief Dullea, which included Inspectors Frank Ahern and Alvin Corassa. Others called to testify had been privy to the raid only moments before it occurred. Newspaper accounts published Elkington's subpoena list, including a dozen names of other San Francisco policemen, before Superior Court judge Edward Murphy could get a gag order in place.[3]

By the third week of January, Brown launched a full scale vice investigation of the city's police and high-ranking public officials. He warned the probe would equal, and maybe even exceed, the scope of the 1935 Atherton investigation. On January 19, after weeks of media speculation and random insiders making various unsubstantiated claims, the district attorney's office issued a formal statement that they intended to "turn the spotlight off" on the Burns graft investigation. "We'll get nowhere fast if we announce our plans in advance," said Elkington.

Behind a veil of secrecy, the grand jury began hearing officer's testimonies: first Chief Dullea, then the captains, and then Inspectors Ahern and Corassa. They continued each day until all sixteen subpoenaed department members appeared.[4]

Over the next several days of testimony numerous other witnesses made their appearances before the grand jury, including two former Burns employees, three aides from the district attorney's office, and crooked bail bondsman Edward "Red" Maloney. Elkington also called the bartender known only as "Bruno," and Burns's accountant, state tax employee Tom Mitchell, whose name was not released to the press. The district attorney's office also questioned Dr. Joseph Visalli, the intern who treated Gerrylee Marsigli and consequently triggered the investigation into Burns's clinic. And finally, Burns herself was called. But Burns, escorted to the Hall of Justice by Homicide Inspector Corassa, refused to testify.[5]

By the end of February, the district attorney's office had turned its focus to Burns's abortion trial. Brown announced he would hold off until the trial ended before he would present further evidence of payoffs and protection money to the grand jury, thus tying both Burns cases together.[6]

When Inez Burns's third abortion trial ended with a conviction in September 1946, as promised, the grand jury resurrected the corruption case the following month. According to jury foreman Henry C. Maginn, they were most interested in examining the unexpected transfer of Inspector Al Corassa from the head of homicide to robbery detail to see if it connected in any way to Burns's case. When questioned, Corassa's superior, the captain of inspectors, denied any link, stating that Corassa asked for the transfer "when the grand jury began to investigate the Burns case." Despite rampant rumors that he might resign, Corassa went on the record stating, "I absolutely have no intention of quitting. No one has told me to quit, and I do not intend to."[7]

Then new evidence surfaced during the murder investigation of one of Burns's partners, Dr. Charles Caldwell, that shed light on the tip-off mystery in the Burns vice case. Dr. Caldwell, a part-time assistant to Burns who also performed abortions out of his Market Street office, was charged in the December 25, 1945, death of Signa Bredeson. According to his former receptionist, Edith Chappell, two days after Bredeson's death, while police conducted a "top secret" investigation of Caldwell, she received a call from the doctor telling her to stay away from her house between 8:00 and 8:30 p.m. that evening because the police planned to arrive at that time to question her. Chappell told the grand jury that Inspector Corassa, from the homicide division, and an assistant district attorney then showed up at her home at that specific time but she was gone. The receptionist also revealed that confidential information leaked to Dr. Caldwell from the coroner's office gave the doctor time to destroy key records prior to the police raid at his clinic.[8]

William Miller, a special agent for the telephone company, produced records to confirm Chappell's story that showed as many as ten calls from the home of Mrs. Hazel Grant, another employee of Dr. Caldwell, to the Hall of Justice and to homicide inspector Al Corassa's home. But Grant claimed she never made the calls and said neither she nor any member of her family knew Corassa. Finally, Corassa testified that he had no knowledge of a tip-off in either the Caldwell or the Burns case.[9]

The grand jury concluded they found no actual proof of who made the calls. However, Corassa, who headed up the homicide squad and was directly in charge of investigating abortion cases, left immediately following his testimony in February. According to his captain, the inspector went to a Northern California resort for vacation. Upon his return Corassa was quietly transferred to the robbery division.[10]

During the district attorney's investigation of the tip-offs and of Corassa specifically, an anonymous source within the police department leaked information to the *San Francisco Examiner* that implicated several other officers. According to the informant one officer obtained an even higher rank than Corassa after he engineered a "switch in the abortion payoffs" to eliminate a bail bondsman. Furthermore, once Burns's clinic came under investigation the situation became so "hot" it forced two other inspectors to resign.[11]

Meanwhile, the state insurance commissioner, Frank Fullenwider, began investigating bail bondsman Ed "Red" Maloney, who once lost his license after fronting for the city's "fountainhead of corruption," Pete McDonough, and who managed to post Burns's bail before her booking at the county jail. Fullenwider believed the timeline on Burns's bail application could aid in the grand jury investigation, but Maloney claimed it had mysteriously disappeared.

After weeks of diligent searching, Maloney recovered the missing documents and said his staff had misfiled them under "D" rather than "B" for Burns. But the application he produced failed to contain key information: the date and time of the application, information leading to the application, and the name of the person who arranged the bail. A Maloney employee testified at the hearing that his boss walked into the office on the day of Burns's arrest and announced, "Inez Burns just got arrested." Later that day, he said, Maloney got a security bond signed by Judge Leo Cunningham, who just happened to pass by Maloney's front door. Investigators for the grand jury felt sure that Burns's bail application, had it contained the necessary facts, would have aided in the tip-off investigation. Regrettably, it was a dead end.[12]

In October Brown announced the grand jury once again postponed its inquiry, this time until after the November 5 elections. With his own election on the horizon Brown began to back away from his earlier allegations of extensive citywide corruption. He pointed to reports of widespread graft and payoffs as political smear tactics against his election for state attorney general and emphasized they would only work to jeopardize policemen from winning pay raises. "Relatively few officers were involved in the tip-off," he declared, "and the inquiry will be confined to the illegal operations of this [abortion] case."[13]

"And I don't know of any police payoffs," he continued, "in these reports of alleged graft, and I cannot see any basis for action by the district attorney. These reports are about things one has heard about for years. . . . I can only act on evidence." Furthermore, he declared, "San Francisco is a white spot among cities. There may be isolated payoffs . . . but in general the San Francisco Police Department is a fine body of men." Finally, the three-member police commission went public and expressed its confidence in the integrity of inspector Al Corassa.[14]

Columnist Herb Caen, who coined the phrase "Baghdad by the Bay," summed it up the best: "The hollowest laugh of the season—the 'secrecy' surrounding the names of the police officers Inez Burns paid off during her reign as San Francisco's leading abortionist. The whole town has known—and shrugged—for years!"[15]

———

Pat Brown lost his initial bid for the attorney general's seat and continued as San Francisco's district attorney for one more term. Following the election he announced that, even though testimony clearly showed a tip-off in Burns's case, there was not enough evidence to bring an indictment. The only official record would be a brief mention in the grand jury's annual report.[16]

Unlike the district attorney's office and the grand jury, police reporter Charles Raudebaugh doggedly kept after corrupt city cops. Seven years after the grand jury closed its investigation, he wrote a twelve-article series for the *Chronicle* entitled "The Untold Story of S.F. Police Department." He began his précis by insisting, "There was a tip-off [in the Burns abortion raid], and it could have only come from the Hall of Justice."[17]

20 *Wise Guys*

In San Francisco . . . competition is not tolerated, either in business or the rackets.

—Police reporter Charles Raudebaugh

On the night of May 9, 1947, across town from Inez and Joseph Burns's home on Guerrero Street, police found a new black Chrysler Sports Coupe convertible abandoned on a dark side street. The keys were in the ignition, and the tail of a man's cashmere overcoat was hanging out of the trunk.[1]

The gray overcoat covered the body of Santa Rosa resident Vincent Rossi, who had been strangled and unceremoniously crammed into the trunk of his own car, a hair comb still clutched in his hand. Within hours detectives determined Rossi, who neighbors knew as a mild-mannered, retired furniture salesman, was in reality Nicholas DeJohn: Chicago thug, gambler, and former muscle for Al Capone.[2]

Further investigation revealed DeJohn was also related to Vincent "the Don" Benevento, a mafia figure known in Chicago as the "Cheese King," who only eight months before police found shot ten times while lying in bed next to his wife. Detectives believed Benevento's death, along with the subsequent mob clean up, prompted DeJohn to skip town with anywhere from $60,000 to $200,000 in dirty money.[3]

It soon became evident that Mrs. DeJohn either did not know her husband's whole story or refused to admit that she did. Regardless, she hired defense attorney Vincent Hallinan to represent her at the coroner's inquest. Following his advice, she testified that although married to DeJohn for twenty years, she knew nothing of her husband's occupation except "he worked days and retired because of stomach ulcers." Lena DeJohn insisted she never had occasion to inquire what her husband retired from—only that she supposed he had a business of his own, but he never told her, and she never asked. She did admit her husband recently invested $90,000 in "an Oceanside night spot." Other sources specified the nightclub was in North Beach (San Francisco's "Little Italy").

Captain of inspectors Barney McDonald put together a six-man task force headed up by the department's top detectives, homicide inspectors Frank Ahern and Thomas Cahill, to find the killers. With this power-packed team McDonald had every confidence they would solve the murder. The squad immediately went to work following up every lead and repercussions from the murder investigation quickly spread throughout the Bay Area underworld. Club operators found to have any gangland connections were placed under surveillance or closed down. State investigations into Northern California mafia activities were launched, and G-men suspecting narcotics trafficking moved in.[4]

In the first weeks of the investigation police found that at least eighteen former Chicago acquaintances visited DeJohn at his home in pictur-esque Santa Rosa. Apparent mobsters, these associates sported around in expensive cars, tipped lavishly, and insisted local launderers hand-clean their clothes.

Investigators believed these advance hoods snuck into the Bay Area as representatives of higher-ups, racketeers such as Benjamin "Bugsy" Siegel and Mickey Cohen, one-time Capone mobsters who were trying to take over racing, and Lucky Luciano, who dealt primarily in narcotics. They also believed that Waxey Gordon (Irving Wexler), who San Francisco police escorted to the city limits in 1941, came back, although investigators were unable to find him.[5]

On the night of his death DeJohn's wife was in Chicago visiting rela-tives. In a cryptic letter to her husband mailed two days before, Mrs. DeJohn wrote, "I hope I'm successful," which she finally admitted to police referred to her visit to a bank safe deposit box belonging to the couple. Investigators also discovered that Nick DeJohn wore a nine-carat diamond ring worth $25,000 and a gold watch, that he had cash in the "five figures," and carried a small personal notebook. None of these items were recovered at the scene. Ahern led the investigation and, unsatisfied with Lena DeJohn's explanation, believed she "was afraid to talk even if she did know anything."[6]

Police tracked the victim's movements on the night of May 7 and discovered the dead man ate his last meal at the Poodle Dog restaurant (owned by local mobster James Franzone) before heading to a North Beach tavern, LaRocca's Corner, on Columbus Avenue. Two hours later concerned neighbors remembered seeing DeJohn's convertible parked on Laguna Street.[7]

When the grand jury convened on May 28, small-time hood Leonard Calamia took the stand first. A native of Chicago's North Side, he reportedly was DeJohn's closest friend and the last person to see him alive, but Calamia refused to testify. Instead, the convicted dope peddler presented a 300-word, typewritten statement to the grand jury detailing the history of his arrest and asserting he became "confused and uncertain" in his statement because police interrupted his sleep throughout the questioning. His statement concluded with: "In view of my present condition . . . I exercise my constitutional right and refuse to testify."[8]

Officers went on the record that they questioned Calamia for more than eight hours but acquired nothing more from the ex-con than "See my lawyer." According to Calamia's lawyer, officers woke the suspect every fifteen to twenty minutes throughout the night to question him, and then grilled him continually throughout the day. "We'll talk to Calamia whenever we feel like it," Captain McDonald countered. "This is a murder case we're investigating here."[9]

But in fact, this was all a charade to protect Calamia from his mafia cohorts. The district attorney's office kept secret that after only two weeks in jail the desperate hoodlum squealed on his cronies and gave detectives detailed information naming the four individuals who plotted and carried out DeJohn's murder. Calamia made a full confession, even admitting his role as "the bait" to lure his unsuspecting friend into the trap. Finally, he described another witness—an unidentified woman who accidently overheard the plot to carry out the murder.[10]

In an effort to substantiate Calamia's statement and identify the woman, police questioned a number of the slain mobster's friends and associates, many for several hours. All proved hostile witnesses and professed to have no knowledge whatsoever of DeJohn's business activities, the source of his money, or his whereabouts on the night of his murder. Finally, Inspector Ahern admitted to the grand jury that the police had no eyewitness to the slaying.

For nineteen months investigators had no leads in Nick DeJohn's murder case. Then a year and a half later police raided a South Van Ness abortion clinic they had had under surveillance for several months and arrested a woman named Anita Rocchia de Venza, who provided authorities with enough information to dismantle the large Bay Area abortion ring she was connected to, including a clinic still operating under the direction of the incarcerated Inez Burns. More importantly, de Venza gave evidence that broke open the DeJohn murder case.

———

In November 1948 District Attorney Brown personally joined the abortion sweep that resulted in the arrests of five men and three women. Included in the roundup, the *Examiner* reported, was "ex-assemblyman Joseph F. Burns, notorious fixer, and husband of Inez Burns," who now operated a local nightclub. Police captain James English said his men also raided seven suspected establishments, including one in San Jose that authorities believed handled the overflow from the lucrative Bay Area clinics. The officers managed to catch one physician, Dr. Malcolm Hoffman, in the middle of an operation.[11]

Dr. Hoffman, a former army colonel and partner of Inez Burns, had worked at her Fillmore Street clinic prior to her arrest in September 1945. According to court records Dr. Hoffman also worked at Burns's Oakland clinic, where he was arrested in 1936, and sometimes used the Market Street office of Dr. Charles Caldwell (another associate of Burns), who was acquitted in the abortion death of Signa Bredeson in 1947. Following Burns's third trial and while she remained out on bail, police listed Dr. Hoffman in another complaint along with Burns's employee and codefendant Musette Briggs (also out on bail). It was clear from the evidence and the testimony of former employee Madeline Rand that Burns continued to manage her operation from her prison cell in Tehachapi, most likely through Dr. Hoffman.[12]

According to the district attorney's office, once they came down hard on the "Queen of Abortionists" Inez Burns, the newly developed abortion racket went to great lengths to stay hidden. "Women wanting abortions were picked up at their homes by taxi or private automobile," Ahern reported. "They were then blindfolded or forced to wear opaque glasses, and in some cases, even drugged to make them semiconscious," to keep them from later pinpointing the locations of the clinics.[13]

Following the raids Brown scheduled a press conference that included Police Captain English, Inspectors Ahern and Cahill, and Assistant District Attorney Tom Lynch where he confirmed the existence of a "protection mob" for the abortion providers and its connection to the dead Chicago gangster Nick DeJohn. The gangster was killed, he confirmed, because he became an obstacle to the international mafia already collecting payoffs from the city's abortionists.[14]

As it turned out, when police unraveled the abortion racket they swept into their net another ex-politician, millionaire Gus Oliva. The once-popular Oliva, a well-known former bootlegger who was given the keys to the city by Mayor James Rolph in 1928, was often referred to as the "boss of North Beach." Finally, police had both Oliva and irrefutable evidence that abortionists throughout the Bay Area had paid protection money to local mobsters.[15]

The key police informant, Anita de Venza, told police that Oliva demanded she pay $2500 monthly to keep her doors open. The thirty-three-year-old mother of three then told police an incredible story: She accidently overheard the murder plot of mobster Nick DeJohn. When Ahern took her statement he realized that after nineteen months of searching he had found the eavesdropping woman his secret informant had placed at the crime scene.[16]

With de Venza's statement it was only a matter of weeks before San Francisco police and the district attorney's office fit together the pieces that exposed the underworld conspiracy that had infiltrated the city, including gangsters from Chicago and Brooklyn who had moved in and taken control over several lucrative businesses in the Bay Area. This outfit—organized into the now defunct Sunland Olive Oil Company—investigators believed eliminated DeJohn as a threatening competitor. Police believed DeJohn had similar ambitions back in Chicago that caused him to be ousted by the remnants of Al Capone's gang.[17]

Captain English confirmed the racketeers currently received $2500 per month from local abortionists and planned to step up the sum to a weekly payoff of $2500. With Burns tucked away in a prison cell in Tehachapi, current Bay Area clinics did a business of approximately $60,000 per month—a significant sum, but far less than Burns's million-dollar annual take. Furthermore, local mobsters received an undisclosed sum from crab fishermen and were prepared to force payoffs from local gambling joints, nightclubs, bars, and restaurants.[18]

Taped phone conversations between de Venza and Oliva, evidence police collected over nineteen months, and de Venza's testimony were enough for the district attorney to bring charges of murder against six men. Originally named in the indictment were Sebastiano Nani, Michael Abati, Tony Lima, Frank Scappatura, Leonard Calamia, and Vincent Bruno. Nani and Abati had remained in jail since the investigation began. The victim's close friend Calamia, who police arrested and released, was picked up by FBI agents in New Mexico and held on $50,000 bail. Brown sent Ahern and Cahill to fetch Calamia, stating the case would be "very good" with him in San Francisco. Tony Lima, Frank Scappatura, and

Vincent Bruno remained fugitives. According to Inspector Ahern, who headed up the investigation, he had a complete case without all six, and "we only need one fifth of the evidence we have."[19]

The final indictment narrowed to five minus Vincent Bruno, the Stardust bartender who regularly referred clients to Burns and whose name showed up on the slip of paper Burns attempted to swallow during her arrest in September 1945. Key evidence, as it turned out, that someone tipped Burns off prior to the raid on her clinic.[20]

After a year and a half of coming up empty-handed, on November 30 police held three of the five in custody and put out an all-points bulletin for Lima and Scappatura. Following the arrests one prosecutor on the case began receiving threatening calls at his home. The caller identified himself only as "Johnnie" and promised the assistant district attorney he could expect "plenty of trouble" if he continued with the case. Also, in spite of police protection, de Venza began receiving threatening phone calls telling her to "break a leg or something."[21]

21 *Murder "Mis-Trial"*

I asked Brown the $64 question . . . and I got my answer.

—Inspector Frank Ahern

The Nick DeJohn murder trial began on the morning of January 28, 1949, with Assistant District Attorney Tom Lynch diligently guarding the identity of his key witness: Anita de Venza, whom he secreted into the Hall of Justice under heavy guard. With de Venza's testimony, along with that of twenty-four others (most unidentified for their own protection), he was confident he had "more than enough evidence" for a solid conviction. The notorious cast of characters that filed into the courtroom to face charges of murder and conspiracy included Sebastiano Nani, Michael Abati, and finger-man Leonard Calamia. The trio, decked out in pinstriped suits and flashy ties, were according to the *San Francisco Examiner* as "fancy a band of thugs and cutthroats" as were ever bred by the mafia. Prosecutor Lynch requested the death penalty, explaining to jury candidates that this was a gangland murder committed for greed and power, and not a crime of passion.[1]

When admitted abortionist Anita de Venza came to the stand, she testified of her longtime friendship with bar owner Vincenzo LaRocca, and stated she often frequented his establishment (LaRocca's Corner Bar), where the victim was last seen alive. De Venza then recounted for the jury how she came to be at the bar during the week of May 5, 1947, when she overheard the defendants plotting to "take out" DeJohn. De Venza said she visited LaRocca hoping to get a job to pay off a loan she owed him. But when she arrived that evening, he was unavailable and an elderly relative of his ushered her into the bedroom of a basement apartment nearby and told her to wait.

After sitting in the quiet bedroom for twenty to thirty minutes, de Venza testified that she heard several men enter the next room and sit down to play cards. Hidden behind the bedroom door, she overheard the men discuss their difficulties with newcomer Nick DeJohn and come to the conclusion that unless they "took care" of the pudgy Sicilian mobster, he would drive them out of business.

"They agreed they had to get rid of him," she told the jury.[2]

Still concealed in the next room, de Venza said she was startled when she heard the old man return to the apartment and asked the men, "Where's the lady?"[3]

"What lady!" one of the men demanded. With that, according to de Venza's account, all four men pushed into the adjoining room, saw her sitting on the bed, and angrily insisted she tell what she overheard. Afraid and crying, she admitted she heard their conversation but promised to say nothing. They told her things "were not going to go well" for her and demanded to know the whereabouts of her husband and children. Only moments later, de Venza explained, LaRocca arrived and convinced the men she was a trustworthy friend and he would make sure there would be no trouble. After several minutes of heated discussion they allowed her to leave.[4]

Two days later police arrested de Venza on a theft charge and sent her to the county jail. Released two weeks later, de Venza returned home to learn LaRocca's plotting friends had called her house. When she finally spoke to one he ordered her to come back to LaRocca's apartment, which she agreed to do on May 16.

On this visit she met Frank Scappatura, one of the four men she identified from the first meeting at the apartment. The other three were Sebastiano Nani, Michael Abati, and Tony Lima. Scappatura gave her $500 cash and told her to leave the state immediately and never come back. Taking no chances, de Venza testified that on May 23 she took her children and fled to Virginia City, Nevada, where she hid out at the Silver Dollar hotel.[5]

De Venza spent five days on the stand identifying each of the defendants. Nevertheless, the defense argued that Sicilian gangsters out of Chicago, not his clients, came to San Francisco and killed DeJohn for revenge. Defendant Nani, a bartender, took the stand to refute de Venza's testimony, telling the jury that he worked on the night of the murder and could not have been in LaRocca's apartment. But prosecutor Lynch produced Nani's grand jury statement that put him delivering dresses next door to LaRocca's bar on the night in question. Furthermore, evidence taken in a police raid of Nani's San Mateo home produced two pawn tickets officers traced back to a Brooklyn pawnshop. One was issued for a $50 loan on a gold wristwatch and the other for a loan of $825 on a diamond ring. Both items, the prosecution pointed out, were taken from the crime scene.[6]

Two weeks into the trial Lynch produced a surprise witness, Mrs. Eleanor Pierce, whose North Beach apartment sat directly above the one in which prosecutors believed the defendants killed DeJohn. Pierce immediately identified DeJohn's '47 Chrysler Coupe and testified she saw four men in and around his car, which was backed halfway into a garage below her window on the day of the murder. She also identified two of the four men from police photographs as Tony Lima and Frank Scappatura (both of whom were still fugitives). Pierce said that Lima and an unidentified man drove off in one direction in DeJohn's car while Scappatura and the fourth man sped away in the other direction.[7]

Following Mrs. Pierce, defense witness Frank Tornahene took the stand. Tornahene, a cab driver, contradicted Pierce's story and told the court that the victim left the North Beach bar alone on the night of May 7. Outraged, Lynch jumped to his feet.

"Isn't it true, you told the 1947 grand jury—" he stormed.[8]

But defense objections drowned out Lynch's attempt to interrupt Tornahene's testimony. A shouting match between the attorneys forced the judge to order the jury out and demand a reading of the grand jury transcript. The record confirmed Tornahene told the grand jury that DeJohn left the bar with "four or five" other men on the night of the murder.

Prosecutors knew Tornahene changed his story out of sheer panic. When the district attorney's office first located the cab driver as a possible witness he begged them not to identify him or force him to testify. Inspector Ahern remembered the young man even got down on his knees and said he would do anything but tell what he knew. "He said he knew he would be walking down the street someday and somebody would step out of a dark doorway and he'd get it," Ahern recalled.[9]

The young cabby was not the only witness to recant his testimony. The eyewitness who testified at the coroner's inquest that DeJohn's abandoned luxury automobile first caught his attention on the night of May 7 then swore at the trial that he actually first saw the car the night before. Frustrated, Brown threatened to prosecute the man for perjury but he could not shake his resolve.

To finally nail down the case the prosecution put Inspector Ahern on the stand as their final witness to go over all the evidence. When Ahern read from the statement given by Calamia two weeks after the slaying, the ex-con repeatedly interrupted him from the defense table.

"You're a liar," Calamia muttered. "You're a damn liar!"[10]

Ahern told the jury that Chicago mobster Leonard Calamia ratted out his companions in the plot and murder of his friend to save his own neck. Calamia told police he spent most of the "death day," May 7, with the deceased and led him under false pretenses to LaRocca's bar later that night. In his statement, Calamia named those at the bar and the four defendants who disappeared into the apartment a block away with the murder victim. According to Calamia, DeJohn went willingly with his killers to the basement apartment expecting to play a game of pinochle. Calamia not only pointed the finger at his buddies, he drew detectives a map detailing the location of LaRocca's bar and apartment and the seating arrangement of all involved. He then personally led police to the scene of the crime but denied ever going to the basement himself or being present during the slaying.

"I couldn't have done it myself," he repeatedly told police. "I needed help, I needed help!"[11]

The defense had no comment as the jury inspected Calamia's crudely drawn map; however, the stool pigeon shot nervous glances at his fellow defendants throughout Ahern's testimony and the jury inspection. The other two Sicilian mobsters stared coldly ahead. At the end of the day, when the bailiff returned the three to their cells, he put Calamia in a cell apart from the others for "precautionary" reasons.

Calamia's statement supported the testimony of de Venza that she overheard the murder plot. It also fit with the statement made by LaRocca's neighbor, Mrs. Pierce, who recalled seeing four men in and around DeJohn's car while it was parked at LaRocca's apartment.[12]

In the end, the prosecution presented twenty-four witnesses and introduced twenty-nine pieces of evidence. The judge gave the case over to the jury on the afternoon of March 7.

———

Two days later at 6:10 p.m. the jury of six men and six women, who had deliberated for thirty-one hours, twenty minutes, stood at 8–5 to convict. The jury requested a rereading of the transcript of Calamia's testimony and collectively agreed to continue their discussion. Then District Attorney Brown appeared and asked to meet with presiding judge Preston Devine in his chambers. To the astonishment of the jurors and police investigators, he requested the case be dismissed. Brown said he based his decision on "grave doubts" as to the veracity of Anita de Venza's testimony. When pressed, Brown only stated that he was "*not completely*" sure that de Venza was "telling the truth on all points."[13]

"Will you move to do it?" Judge Devine asked him.

"I will personally move to discharge the jury," Brown stated.[14]

Later that day in his official press conference Brown assured clamoring reporters that he did not consider the DeJohn case "washed up," but that the district attorney's office did not have enough evidence to bring a conviction at this time and they would continue to investigate.[15]

Brown's abrupt dismissal of the jury brought outrage from the San Francisco Police Department. One official who declined to use his name said, "Never in twenty years of experience have I seen a jury discharged while it was waiting for a transcript to be read—this case stinks from the district attorney's end." Furthermore, "It's customary to ask police to sit in on all cases of this kind when the judge is about to discharge a jury," the officer continued, "but, the police were not asked to sit in and the door was literally slammed" in Frank Ahern's face.[16]

Inspector Ahern was in fact infuriated at Brown's decision and angrily pushed through shouting reporters gathered on the steps of the Hall of Justice. "I'll have a statement for you later," he promised them. "One that will curl your hair!"

"I asked District Attorney Brown the $64 question," he added, "and I got my answer!"[17]

22   *The Corrupt and Contented IRS*

THE GUESSPEL THRUTH: Memo to anybody: Aren't the
local income tax probers interested in finding out how much
"protection" money Inez Burns paid to whom—and how
they managed to conceal it on their tax returns?

—Columnist Herb Caen

District Attorney Brown spent over two years and all the resources at
his disposal to take away Inez Burns's freedom, but try as he might he
could not get his hands on her money. Instead, it took the relentless moral
indignation of an unknown, lowly civil servant who resigned his position
in protest of the fraud and corruption he discovered in the San Francisco
IRS office. In the spring of 1951 former Internal Revenue investigator
William A. Burkett went to the press to expose corrupt agents and to
pressure officials into making examples of lawbreakers (Inez Burns being
at the top of his list). Eventually, Burkett, who Senator Estes Kefauver
credited in his book, *Crime in America*, with "originally breaking the
Internal Revenue scandal . . . for Northern California and Nevada," got
his public vindication. And his associate Edward S. Montgomery of the
San Francisco Examiner won a Pulitzer Prize.

Inez Burns lost everything.[1]

———

For years Inez Burns managed to dance around Uncle Sam. She was
first indicted in 1938 for her 1934 tax returns that stated her income was
$4,873—barely a tenth of the $45,113 that federal tax assessors believed
she took in. The following year she claimed only $3,621 in income and
paid $317 in taxes.[2]

After spending two years fighting federal indictments and at one point hiring a tax attorney to fly to Washington DC to meet with bureau chiefs, she pled guilty to defrauding the government and was given a paltry $10,000 fine. She paid the fine but coyly refused to tell Federal Judge Harold Louderback how she earned her money, prompting the judge to refer her to a probation officer—not for probation, he said, but to bring her record to light.[3]

In 1940 Tom Lynch, then working for the United States Attorney's office, prosecuted Burns for her 1935–36 tax returns, resulting in another $10,000 fine and a three-year suspended sentence. Court records show her 1936 assets—at least those they could find—at $202,956, or $3.5 million today. Almost immediately a collector for the Internal Revenue filed a lien for $64,800 for unpaid taxes on her income for the years 1928–35. Rather than test the patience of the court, Burns paid it with money she raised through a loan underwritten by bail bond king Pete McDonough.[4]

By December 1945 it appeared Burns had learned her lesson. A source (in a position to know, the *San Francisco Call* assured its readers) leaked details of Burns's tax records going back to 1942 to the editor, and according to the source she paid all her federal and state taxes for the years 1942, 1943, and 1944, which totaled $400,000, or more than $6.7 million in today's dollars.[5]

Burns's arrest in September 1945, along with the discovery of over $300,000 cash in her safe and another $700,000 unaccounted for, initiated another federal investigation. Her subsequent conviction on abortion charges and the discovery of $60,000 in water-soaked bills traced back to a local jeweler only added fuel to the fire. Then according to the report, while the district attorney's office built its abortion case against her, Brown followed up by turning over seized records that showed Burns earned a minimum of $50,000 per month from approximately 500 abortions in her Fillmore Street clinic alone. The following year a spokesman for the special intelligence unit of the IRS confirmed Burns was again under investigation.[6]

In August 1948 two agents (Burns later identified one as William Burkett) from the IRS drove out to Tehachapi prison to quiz Burns on her bank records and other pertinent documents. After several days of questioning that the agents described as "an uphill battle," Burns finally conceded—on some points. However, one agent who asked not to be identified made it clear that the questioning did not go into the so-called police payoffs.[7]

"We're not interested in 'payoffs' because they are not tax deductible," he stated.

He also indicated that they intended to present the collected evidence to the federal grand jury immediately, and if it returned an indictment Burns would stand trial for tax evasion.[8]

No grand jury was convened to examine the case. In fact, nothing happened.

———

For the next two years Inez Burns's tax case remained on an in-house U.S. Treasury Department list as still pending. In February 1950 William Burkett listed it along with the case files of other "racketeers," now five years old, on a handwritten memo addressed to his superior with the notation: First Order of Business.[9]

Finally, getting nowhere and fed up with stall tactics from his superiors, Burkett wrote a report detailing corruption and bribery in the San Francisco Internal Revenue office. His report claimed his unit chief cautioned him "not to air our dirty Internal Revenue linen before the justice department in Washington." One month later, Burkett left his position with the agency and offered to turn over his information to the Estes Kefauver Senate Committee, which investigated crime in interstate commerce. In his report the thirty-seven-year-old war veteran and father of two said he resigned in protest over official cover-ups of his investigations, which he alleged included tax fraud and extortion rackets throughout the state of California and nationwide.[10]

After his resignation Burkett joined forces with investigative reporter Edward Montgomery of the *San Francisco Examiner*. The two went public, insisting there was a general tolerance toward big-shot crooks that cried out for action. They accused IRS officials of an estimated $20 billion a year take and of concealing the names of "high lords of interlocking racketeer syndicates" who lived lavish lifestyles, lolled around in expensive hotels, and made handsome gifts to politicians and law enforcement friends—even sometimes giving them a percentage of their profits. These common criminals and the IRS agents who covered for them, Burkett asserted, owned luxuries few others could afford and wintered in Miami and Palm Springs. Furthermore, many of them purchased legitimate businesses with their ill-gotten gains—fashionable restaurants, hotels, cigar stores, and liquor distributorships.[11]

Federal and state tax investigators held the resources, Burkett said, to "smash" California's and the nation's leading racketeers overnight. But this almost never happened. In fact, at the time of his resignation Burkett's caseload included Burns, two treasury agents, and nine others—all well hidden beneath layers of favors, bribes, and payoffs. While exposing the bureau in San Francisco he singled out Burns, who among his cases owed by far the most in back taxes, fines, and penalties.[12]

Exactly one week after Burns walked out of Tehachapi State Prison on November 9, 1950, the California Commission on Organized Crime, headed by Admiral William H. Standley, spotlighted her stagnated tax case in its final report and pointed an accusing finger at the Treasury Department for its negligence in not prosecuting her.[13]

The following February, only five months after Burkett dropped his bombshell and under pressure from the California Commission on Crime report, the Bureau of Internal Revenue went after Burns and revealed her undeclared income for 1944 to be $243,500 and not the $31,100 she claimed. Furthermore, the assistant U.S. attorney stated Burns's federal income tax liability for the period 1934–45 totaled $936,700.[14]

Burkett's perseverance paid off and Burns was indicted for tax evasion in February 1951. Three months later she stood in federal court with her veiled head bowed, quietly dressed in a matronly black dress. Speaking in a low voice she told the judge she had nothing to say in her own defense, only that she pleaded guilty. Internal Revenue agents estimated her business grossed at least $500,000 in 1944 alone, and they estimated her total tax debt over a ten-year period at over $1 million with penalties and interest, or $13.6 million in today's dollars.[15]

Rising in her defense, attorney Frank J. Ford pleaded with the judge. "Next Sunday is Mother's Day," he said. "I would hate to see her separated from her family."

Ford described his black-draped client as a good, kind, and generous mother, devoted to her large family. He reminded the court that Burns spent a total of two years and seven months in Tehachapi prison and since her release suffered from numerous ailments, including sclerosis, arthritis, and dizzy spells, and lived a life filled with depression and pain. With considerable emotion, Ford painted Burns's life as one with "two strikes against her" since early childhood.

"Such a life sears the soul of some people," Ford told the court.

Unmoved by the condition of Burns's soul, presiding judge George Bernard Harris had a few choice words of his own. "This case transcends ordinary sentimentality," he snapped.[16]

Nor was the judge taken in by Burns's flair for theatrics. He fined her the maximum of $10,000 and sentenced her to a year and a day in federal prison after rejecting fervent pleas from her attorney to allow the "elderly grandmother" time with her four children and ten grandchildren. Furthermore, as a federal physician had examined Burns and found her to be physically fit, Judge Harris determined that she be transported immediately to the federal women's prison at Alderson, West Virginia.[17]

23   The Kefauver Committee

ITEMS OVERLOOKED BY SENATOR KEFAUVER? The details behind "The Big Fix" that permitted Inez Burns, the abortion queen, and a few other gilt-edge characters to run unmolested for long and lucrative years.

—Columnist Herb Caen

In March 1951 the United States Special Senate Committee to Investigate Crime in Interstate Commerce descended on the city of San Francisco to conduct hearings into the state's organized crime. The committee, granted broad powers by President Harry Truman, was headed up by Senator Estes Kefauver and focused on certain local underworld figures including betting commissioner Tom Kyne, San Francisco gambling kingpin Elmer "Bones" Remmer, Emilio "Gombo" Georgetti, Mickey Cohen, and Inez Burns, to name a few. Its hearings were held in cities throughout the nation and broadcast daily on live television with committee members grilling lawmen, mobsters, and con men, captivating millions of Americans. In the end the Kefauver Committee, as it came to be known, produced an 11,000-page report on organized crime in America.[1]

In examining Burns's case the senators first questioned newly elected state attorney general, Pat Brown, and San Francisco's newly appointed district attorney, Tom Lynch, while seeking to substantiate ex-Internal Revenue agent William Burkett's claim of a tax fraud conspiracy. At the committee's request Lynch detailed the 1945 raid on Burns's clinic and home including the confiscation of cash from her safe, her "little black books," and her medical records, all of which the San Francisco district attorney's office used to build the criminal case against her:

"Was she entitled to keep that money?" Senator Charles W. Tobey asked.

"Yes," Lynch said. "Under the law she could keep it."

"Was it in a safety deposit box?" asked committee chief counsel Rudolph Halley.

"No, in a safe in her home closet," Lynch told the members.

"What I want to know," Senator Tobey interrupted, "Was she hard to look at?"

"Hard as nails," Lynch smiled, "and in addition to the $300,000 there was evidence of at least $700,000 more."

"Did you report that several hundred thousand dollars to the Bureau of Internal Revenue?" Halley asked.

"Yes," Brown assured them, "and we turned over all the notebooks as well."

"Was she prosecuted?"

"Not to my knowledge," Lynch said.[2]

"I will tell you what happened," Brown jumped in. "I was interviewed on several occasions by a number of members of the Internal Revenue staff, and by one gentleman in particular, for whom I have very high regard, and I believe the gentleman will appear here, Mr. Burkett. It is my opinion," Brown continued, "Mr. Burkett worked very hard and conscientiously with the information I furnished to him, of course at his request, but also in my opinion, there was substantial evidence of a large income-tax violation by Mrs. Burns."

"What did they do about it?" Tobey asked.

"Senator," Brown said, "you are going to have to ask Burkett about that."[3]

When called before the committee, Burkett described how his immediate supervisor, Donald Rogers, first assigned him Burns's tax case. According to Burkett, Rogers informed him through a letter that he was assigned to a joint investigation in the case, and that the file was to remain in Rogers's office. Also, he needed to make case progress reports at the end of each month only to Rogers. Finally, Rogers sent him to speak with District Attorney Brown, Tom Lynch, and the San Francisco police inspectors Frank Ahern and Tom Cahill concerning their investigation.

"What happened to her case?" Senator Kefauver asked Burkett.

"It's over in the Intelligence Unit, United States Treasury, in San Francisco; I left there on March 15," Burkett explained.[4]

The committee then questioned Michael Schino, chief field director in the Northern District collections office for the Internal Revenue Service located in San Francisco:

"Well, I can tell you—what was her name—this Brown woman, we picked her up for a lot of taxes—Brown," Schino said, nodding assuredly to the committee.

"Inez Burns?" Halley asked.

"Burns . . . ha, yes," Schino recalled. "Pardon me, oh my gosh."

"Did she go to jail for income tax evasion?"

"That I don't know. . . . No, I think she paid her taxes. She went to jail the last time, I understand," Schino stammered. "I have to look at my records."

"You can't offhand think of anyone who did go to jail?"

"Well yes, there were several of them who went to jail, but I just can't think of their names," Schino replied.

"Are you a married man?" Chairman Kefauver asked.

"No, sir; I'm a single man."

"There have been a lot of complaints about the company you keep."

"That is what I hear," Schino nodded again.

"Did you ever have anything to do with Inez Burns?"

"No!" The field director countered adamantly, "and I didn't have her case, the men in the investigation office had it."[5]

Michael Schino was in fact named in the complaint submitted by Burkett that he later believed to be covered up. Also, Burkett testified, he attempted to subpoena books and records to complete his cases but his superior prevented him from obtaining the evidence, claiming "legal issues."[6]

Burkett's revelations eventually led to the convictions of six individuals connected to fraud, bribery, prostitution, and various other crimes. This included chief field deputy E. Mike Schino and, of course, "abortion queen" Inez Burns.[7]

Burkett's work so impressed Senators Estes Kefauver and John L. Williams that in March 1953 they sponsored a senatorial bill designed to restore him to his former position with the Internal Revenue Service.[8]

———

While the Kefauver committee weeded through the state's organized crime and internal whitewashing, *San Francisco Examiner* columnist Herb Caen, with his usual "acid penchant for the distaff twist," as attorney Melvin Belli liked to point out, stepped up and asked the question that was on everyone's mind: Where are the "details behind 'the Big Fix?'"[9]

24 *"Hello Again"*

WASHING THE LINEN: A lot of San Franciscans, prominent and otherwise, may now relax. There is no "little black book" in the Inez Burns abortion case THIS time.

—Columnist Herb Caen

In March of 1952 Inez Burns, now sixty-six years old, was released from Alderson federal prison. Her husband, Joe, traveled to Virginia to meet her and together they boarded the train for San Francisco. Soon whispers began circulating around town that she was back in business, and newly elected district attorney Tom Lynch wasted no time putting together a task force to drag her back to jail. After weeks of patient observation, Lynch brought in Adrienne Scheuplein, a young woman working as an investigator for the district attorney's office, to set up the sting.[1]

On October 21 the "pregnant" Miss Scheuplein went to the Hyde Street office of Burns's old partner Dr. Adolphus A. Berger, who also happened to be a district federal jail physician and former autopsy surgeon. Scheuplein introduced herself as Kathryn Phillips and told Berger that when she became pregnant a friend referred her to him. Berger, thinking that he had established her pregnancy through laboratory results, scheduled another office appointment where she met Burns. (Investigators later boasted they used some "very sophisticated scientific tricks" to dupe Berger.) At the consultation, Burns told Scheuplein the procedure could not be done at Berger's office and asked to do it at her home. Scheuplein agreed and that night Carl Warfield, a relative of Burns, came to the investigator's house, gave her instructions to prepare her for surgery, and delivered a suitcase.

Early the next morning Burns arrived alone and went into the kitchen, where she took her surgical instruments from the suitcase and placed them in pots of water to boil. She then hung a sheet over the front window before arranging pillows on the table and setting out containers of Pitocin, Ergotrate, metsol, and ammonia, along with cotton and a large roll of gauze. According to Scheuplein's report, the setup and preparation took approximately forty-five minutes, during which time Burns talked about her past operations and reassured Scheuplein that she had nothing to worry about as she had years of experience. Scheuplein paid Burns $525— the price went up $25 at this point—in marked bills, and as the water began to boil, went upstairs to change.

The trap was set. Burns, caught off guard, was standing over the stove in "Kathryn Phillips's" Richmond district home removing her sterilized instruments when her old adversary Tom Lynch, together with Homicide Inspector Frank Ahern, walked in and surprised her.

"Hello again," Lynch smiled.[2]

Overwhelmed, Burns collapsed and immediately admitted her guilt as officers carried her out. Locked up in the city jail, Burns refused to get out of bed, claiming illness and demanding to see a doctor. When the prison physician thoroughly examined her he determined she had some arthritis but was otherwise fine and did not need hospitalization.[3]

Newspaper headlines announced that "Queen Incz Burns" was back in her old rut. But the once flamboyant Queen Bee of the abortion racket had no desire to fight her fate. "I've lived too long anyway; I want to go back to jail and get it over with," Burns declared, in her ever-dramatic fashion. This time she served concurrent sentences of two to five years on each of four counts of abortion, attempted abortion, and conspiracy.[4]

PART SIX

The Bone Rattler

25 *Official Closets*

No man is just a little bit crooked.

—William A. Burkett

In 1954 Inez Burns was serving her time at the California Institution for Women in Corona, and the corruption investigation surrounding her seemed all but forgotten. The only one who had not let it go, as it turned out, was William Burkett, the state's self-appointed moral compass and newly appointed state director of employment. On the evening of August 11 Burkett stood before the members of the Commonwealth Club of San Francisco and resurrected the crusade he began as an Internal Revenue investigator four years before. In his speech entitled "How Much Morality Can There Be in Government?" he called for a moral rearmament to fight tax fraud and corruption in local government. While working in San Francisco, he told his audience, he had the unpleasant experience of watching dishonesty and corruption at work within its powerful governmental bureaucracy. So powerful, he asserted, that when he initiated a probe into tax investigations, his reports were not only ignored, but they also provoked anonymous threats to him and his family. Nevertheless, following the lead of another Internal Revenue agent, John V. Lewis, whose 1935 speech to the San Rafael Rotary Club triggered the famous Atherton graft investigation, Burkett also determined to expose the commonly accepted corruption that "greased the wheels" of city government.[1]

The *San Francisco Chronicle* labeled Burkett "the bone-rattler," accusing him of making "skeleton-rattling" in official closets his hobby.

After quitting his job with the Bureau of Internal Revenue for the San Francisco office and testifying before the Kefauver Senate Committee in 1951, Burkett went after the State Department of Employment. In 1953 Burkett accused jobless workers of bilking the State of California out of at least $20 million in unemployment insurance funds. When the State Director of Employment lost his job in the ensuing cleanup Burkett, appointed to the position, blew the lid off the mess he inherited in that department.[2]

In his Commonwealth speech Burkett attributed much of the fraud and corruption to a weakening of the moral fiber of America—a continuation of the New Deal philosophy, as he saw it, that a man should grab all he can for himself. "No man is just a little bit crooked," Burkett insisted, "and bribers should be punished as well as the persons accepting the bribe."[3]

Burkett told his audience that in the course of his former assignment he had access to details of city corruption involving organized crime, bookies, prostitution, and abortion—specifically payoffs made by Inez Burns. Burkett's attack on city officials and the San Francisco Police Department resurrected the conveniently buried protection scandal surrounding Burns, who had been quietly hustled off to jail while her official cohorts got off scot-free.

"While I was investigating Inez Burns for tax evasion," Burkett told the members, "I drove out to Tehachapi prison and talked with her; at that time she gave me the name of the person to whom she had been making police payoffs in the amount of $125 per day while operating her million-dollar abortion business. I reported it, but nothing happened."[4]

In fact, Burkett had included this information in his statement before the Kefauver Senate Committee in 1951. In the course of his testimony, Burkett told the committee that several months after he completed Burns's tax case his supervisor, Donald Rogers, sent him back to Tehachapi to interrogate Burns, but gave him specific instruction not to attempt to get any information regarding payoffs. When the committee called Rogers to testify, he stated that he instructed Burkett to take with him the "little notebooks," seized during the 1945 raid on Burns's home and upon which Burns's taxes had been set at over $1.3 million with penalties—but, only for her to identify and initial.[5]

Addressing Rogers, Senator Kefauver demanded, "Did you tell him not to get information about payoffs to policemen?"

"Well," Rogers attempted to explain, "I didn't want him running afield, trying to start up another series of cases. . . . We had considerable trouble [with him] in that respect."[6]

Burkett told the committee that as a safeguard, Rogers sent another agent, Guy Marshall, along to report back on the interview with Burns. En route to the prison, Marshall let it slip to Burkett that Rogers instructed him to watch Burkett and make sure he only questioned Burns with regard to her income tax. "I warned Marshall," Burkett said, "I'm going to go into the protection money that was paid by Inez Burns, and you can just tell Mr. Rogers that I did." Following Burkett's testimony the Kefauver Committee did not revisit this issue, and neither did anyone in the Internal Revenue Regional office in San Francisco.[7]

Within a week of his speech to the Commonwealth Club the clatter of Burkett's latest "skeleton" reached the grand jury and launched another full-scale investigation into charges of police corruption connected to Burns's abortion clinic. When acting police chief George Healy heard the allegations he responded that he was not aware of any such report and he passed it off to homicide inspector Frank Ahern, who had handled the Burns investigation in 1945–46.[8]

Ahern also refused to take responsibility and stated, "To my knowledge no report of this nature was ever forwarded to the San Francisco Police Department." Ahern recalled that he spoke with Burkett on several occasions, but said the tax investigator never mentioned the charges to him. Nevertheless, according to Burkett the asserted payoffs occurred back in the days of Mayors Rossi and Lapham, when Ahern worked in homicide, and at least one of the principal payees Burns named during his interview still held a high position in public office.

Hoping to put the Burns case behind him, District Attorney Tom Lynch also tried to ignore Burkett's latest airing of the city's dirty laundry, but he too was unsuccessful. After weeks of media speculation he committed to try to fit in an appointment with Burkett, even though "it all happened seven or eight years ago."[9]

Weeks later Burkett noted that he had yet to be contacted by the district attorney's office, but he assured reporters he had the evidence and was willing to turn it over to the proper authorities. Burkett also made it clear he would not discuss the matter with the district attorney before appearing before the grand jury. Furthermore, he would not "force it on San Francisco authorities." When pressed, Lynch responded, "The statute of limitations has run out on any Burns allegations."[10]

But Norman Elkington, who led the "tip-off" investigation, felt more optimistic and stated that Burns's testimony might implicate bribes that still continued. He pointed out there was no statute of limitations on civil code provisions for the removal of corrupt officials by the grand jury; furthermore, he considered the issue of the statute of limitations to be just a "shield for bribe takers." The grand jury "might well be considering the possible removal of a public official, or officials, for an offense that may relate beyond the statute of limitations," Elkington argued.[11]

Finally, at 9:10 p.m. on August 30, Burkett, accompanied by Lynch and Elkington, marched into the grand jury chamber and revealed the true identity of the police officer Burns described to Burkett as "Mr. Hill, the insurance agent." According to Burkett, Burns revealed that "Mr. Hill" did the collecting for the rest of the police in the department on her payroll and called her at stated intervals to give her a heads-up when she had a "premium" due, usually around $12,000 a month. At the time of the interview Burns had hesitated to reveal the true name of Mr. Hill, so Burkett testified that he spelled out the names of several officers phonetically on cards and showed them to her. Burns warily picked the card with the name of the officer who handled the bulk of the payoffs.

She nodded her head, affirming that was the correct one. "But you don't know how to spell it," she added.[12]

After the grand jury hearing, neither Burkett nor jury foreman Dr. Charles Ertola would reveal the name of the police official Burns disclosed, stating only that while the man no longer worked in the police department, he had seemed a man of excellent reputation.

In fact, Burkett told the grand jury that while reviewing his notes before his testimony he discovered more damning information on at least ten more individuals, including another former member of the police department and three men who still worked in the department. Others he named as important witnesses were key figures in the state income tax department, and two former associates—a man and a woman—of Inez and Joseph Burns. Burkett insisted that some on the list remained in important public positions, and he demanded that these revelations, which the jury heard off the record, be placed into the official record. This, in effect, challenged jury members to take action on the charges.[13]

During his testimony, Burkett revealed that Burns also disclosed the name of Navy physician Dr. Larry Everson, who had lived in Oakland while serving on Treasure Island and who worked as her partner. According to Burns, when the former lieutenant completed his daily tasks at the naval infirmary he traveled by cab to her clinic on Fillmore Street. There he performed abortions five afternoons a week and frequently on Saturday mornings. She also confirmed that unbeknownst to her Everson kept a journal (the orange diary placed in evidence at her trial) of the amount of business coming in and sums paid out for protection money, salaries, and other general business.[14]

Lynch, finally, if only reluctantly, on board with Burkett's crusade, agreed to make the records from Burns's Fillmore Street clinic, including a slip of paper listing $125 a day for payoffs, available to the grand jury. He also took Everson's journal into the grand jury chambers. The notebook, according to Lynch, contained entries of protection money, the number of patients operated on each day, and payroll expenses. Lynch turned the entire notebook containing the collaborating evidence over to the grand jury.

As a final point, William Burkett faced the grand jury and reminded them of their most important function in the community: to maintain morality and good government. They could investigate the information he supplied to them, Burkett said, but if they chose not to, he would see to it that a future grand jury did.[15]

26 *"That Big Wind"*

These rumors are a ghost that has been haunting this department for nearly a decade. . . . It's time the ghost is laid to rest.

—Chief of Police Michael Gaffey

District Attorney Lynch reluctantly reopened the Burns graft investigation. He told the grand jury he agreed with William Burkett, but it was important to remember that even if the investigation proved police payoffs or other derogatory conduct, criminal offenses were governed by the statute of limitations. Nevertheless, after the grand jury heard Burkett's testimony, they insisted Lynch obtain a court order to bring Burns from the women's state prison at Corona to testify.

The grand jury held no legal authority to subpoena a prisoner to testify, so the jurors made an exceptional effort to induce Burns to come of her own volition. They not only promised to devote the entire evening to her testimony, but also Lynch agreed to personally appear at the session. Although not entirely unprecedented, it was highly unusual for the district attorney to appear instead of one of his assistants. When the grand jury's enticements failed, Superior Court judge Milton D. Sapiro ordered Burns brought from her Corona jail cell to San Francisco's Hall of Justice.[1]

In the weeks leading up to her testimony, every newspaper in the city pursued Burns for her sensational story. She was initially undecided, but after years of living in a cramped cell and donning prison grays she longed for the touch of fine silk, diamonds, and the flash of the photographer's bulb. More than anything she missed the excitement afforded her by sensational stories of insider deals and backroom corruption. Of the reporters clamoring to write her final exposé, only one qualified as far as she was concerned. Fraud, graft, and vice were the bread and butter of popular *San Francisco Examiner* reporter Edward S. Montgomery, whose stories of Internal Revenue corruption, together with the testimony of William Burkett, resulted in high profile criminal investigations and convictions in 1951. The tax scandal exposés garnered Montgomery a Pulitzer Prize—and Burns a six-by-eight-foot jail cell in Alderson. Nevertheless, when the award-winning journalist courted her—no, begged her—to "let her hair down" one last time, Inez obliged and gave Montgomery her inside story for the *Examiner*.[2]

The newspaper headlined her story: "Inez Burns Tells Full Story of Huge Payoffs to Police." Montgomery's interview with Burns spread out over several days and detailed her audacious life, immune from police harassment for twenty-five plus years while operating openly in the heart of San Francisco. In fact, she confided, it was because individuals highly placed in police circles shared in protection payoffs totaling hundreds of thousands of dollars. Burns estimated it cost her $125 per day in protection payoffs "just to keep the doors open" and another $5000 a week to the "brass downtown." She also paid a representative of a state agency regularly and made numerous campaign contributions and other required "gifts." In all, according to Burns, police protection cost "nearly one half the take" of her $1 million-a-year abortion business.[3]

Burns gave Montgomery the names of a number of police officials, past and present, and politicians to whom she paid large sums of protection money. Only three individuals handled the payoffs, she said—sometimes with her present, and always in cash. She confided that a former trusted employee, a bookkeeper, could corroborate her allegations but she refused to involve him.

Burns admitted that she had, in fact, revealed the name of a highly placed official on her payroll to William Burkett during his jailhouse visit in 1950. Burns recalled Burkett as a perfect gentleman "just doing his job," and for the record, she told the reporter, she held no animosity for the former investigator. However, Burns hesitated to confirm the identity of that official to Montgomery, stating she still saw herself as vulnerable, in jail, and hoping for a chance at parole.[4]

Burns finally confided the facts behind the now famous tip-off that facilitated her last minute getaway before the special police unit and district attorney detail raided her Fillmore Street clinic in September 1945. The tip, she revealed with a smile, came from someone in the homicide division who quietly called someone at the front desk of the police department. That individual then contacted a third party outside the department. The third person in the relay then called Burns's clinic to give the signal. Burns gave up the name of the other two individuals involved to Montgomery. "As it turned out," she added, "we had less than fifteen minutes to get away."[5]

With a sly gleam in her eye, Burns described the mysterious "B. Hill," a name that continued to crop up in the allegations of police corruption. There was never any B. Hill, she said, waving her hand contemptuously. It was "Captain Hill." Actually, Burns revealed, no Captain Hill existed at that time; it was just a code name for whoever happened to be the headman at the moment. "Whoever we called on for favors," she said. "It could be someone in the front office or collecting the money." For example, she continued, "If a beat cop was spending too much time on the corner and it was worrying some of the patients, I'd simply tell someone to call 'Captain Hill' and have him get that cop out of here."[6]

So why, at the eleventh hour, did Burns grant an interview with such a high-profile journalist and agree to blow the whistle on a host of individuals who she claimed reaped a financial harvest for years at her expense? The answer was simple, she said: With the heat on, everyone disappeared, leaving her holding the bag. Jailed and virtually penniless, Burns told Montgomery she felt terribly alone and bitter with the knowledge that those she supported became leeches that bled her dry. Through others she liquidated thousands of dollars in stock in PG&E, AT&T, the Regal Amber Brewery, and other companies, all to pay off her tax liabilities. But to her shock and dismay she learned that not one penny of the money went to the IRS. Gone too, she lamented, were the proceeds from her daughter's annuity, which she now needed as a last resort. Property she purchased and thought she owned or at least had an interest in she now learned no longer belonged to her, but was in others' names. Friends she supported for years and those who came to her in times of need had forgotten her. "I owe them nothing," she cried. "I'm not obligated to anyone!" Burns concluded the interview by telling Montgomery that she only wished to go home, straighten out her affairs, and see her grandchildren.[7]

In the days following the headlining publication of Montgomery's story, Burns went into virtual seclusion and refused to see anyone. Alarmed, her husband, Joe Burns, traveled to Corona and spent three days attempting to see her. When he arrived on Friday she refused to see him, and on Saturday and Sunday he sent notes that she ignored. Then mysteriously, on the day before her scheduled flight to San Francisco to testify before the grand jury, an unidentified woman arrived at the prison and conferred privately with Burns in her jail cell. No records exist to indicate the identity of the woman or the nature of her visit, but what is clear is that Burns clammed up and refused to answer any further questions except to say that San Francisco attorney Molly Minudri would now represent her.

Initially, Burns had told Montgomery she would not refute Burkett's testimony. Now making a sudden about-face, Burns, dressed in her prison garb, met with reporters in the small waiting area outside the warden's office. "I believe nothing would result from my testimony," she told them. "A lawyer has been retained for me, and I am convinced that I should follow her advice." Standing at her side Molly Minudri (Lady Gadfly, as Tom Lynch liked to call her) confirmed, "I have advised her not to talk," and she added, "Inez Burns is old, ill, feeble, and her memory is impaired. Furthermore, she is a prisoner, and so many factors are involved—her right to parole and a tax case that is still pending." In spite of Minudri's arguments, Judge Sapiro ordered the sixty-eight-year-old Burns to appear before the grand jury on September 14, 1954.[8]

Flown from Los Angeles International Airport, Burns, escorted by detectives, arrived at the San Francisco County jail to wait her turn before the grand jury. Back in the limelight, she forgot her earlier moments of doubt and made her grand entrance in a tasteful (albeit a bit overdone) black satin dress and a three-quarter-length fur coat topped off with a matching brown hat decorated with two large pom-poms. Smiling coyly and making elaborate gestures for the jurors, Burns was questioned for ninety minutes by District Attorney Lynch.

At one point during Lynch's lengthy questioning, Burns turned to the district attorney and snapped, "Why, Mr. Lynch, you know I'm supposed to have paid you, too!"

"You tell that story to the grand jury right now!" Lynch demanded.

"Oh," Inez smiled and shrugged, "I can't remember all of it now."[9]

For the dozens of reporters awaiting her long-heralded appearance, her testimony ended in disappointment. Burns spent over an hour before the grand jury but it added up to complete denial on her part, and at times roars of laughter throughout the chamber. In the end, Burns insisted she "didn't pay a penny of protection money to anyone." Lynch, who conducted the questioning, asked her specifically about several present and former police officers. His list included former chief of police Charles Dullea; John Engler, a supervising police captain; the present chief, Michael Gaffey; and Al Corassa, now a police inspector in burglary.[10]

Burns emphatically told the grand jury that she personally knew several prominent San Francisco officials and policemen, but she had never given money to anyone at any time. When she emerged from the jury room she smiled and joked with reporters.

"What lovely people," she said of the jurors. "They're all Santa Clauses!" she laughed.

When asked about former chief of police Charles Dullea, now a member of the State Adult Authority, Burns replied, "Sure, I've known Charlie for many, many years—why, we even went to school together."

"They asked me if I ever gave him any money," she told reporters, her eyes wide with shock. "I said I did not!"

Ever enjoying the attention of the press, Burns held court in the marble breezeway of the Hall of Justice. Captivating her subjects by divulging tidbits of her confidential testimony, she continued,

"I was asked about a lot of men," she told them. "I couldn't even remember them all—Like John Engler, they asked me about him and I told them I never even met Johnny," Burns smiled.

One reporter shouted from the back, asking if she took the Fifth Amendment.

"Did I take a constitutional?" She laughed. "Why, I don't know, I took something! I answered some of their questions, but I didn't say anything incriminating, if that's what you want to know."

Others wanted her to elaborate on her long-term relationship with the late bail bondsman Pete McDonough, a question she chose to ignore. Then they wanted to know her connection with former homicide inspector Al Corassa, now assigned to burglary. "Yes, they asked about him," she said. "I told them, 'Oh yes, now that is a good man.'"

"But then they asked me if I ever gave him any money, can you imagine that?" Burns smirked, "I told them, of course not."

The jury even wanted to know the present whereabouts of her husband, Joe Burns, to which she retorted, "How should I know where he is?"

"Look," she told reporters, "I never had any protection," and laughed.[11]

Hustling Burns back to reality, the bailiff took her by the arm and escorted her to the holding cell to await transfer back to Corona. Burns left the courthouse, head held high and hips swaying. "My, I've had a wonderful time!" she smiled and waved one last time to friendly shouts, flashing blue-white bulbs, and handsome, fedoraed men.[12]

When told of Burns's testimony, Burkett declared, "I have no comment to make at this time other than to say there was a second treasury agent present the day I obtained the information from Mrs. Burns. Two of us heard what she had to say."[13]

The next day grand jury foreman Dr. Charles Ertola admitted they had no place to go with the matter now that Burns officially denied any payoffs. Former police chief Charles Dullea weighed in on Burns's grand jury appearance stating, "At least she told the truth."[14]

"Inez talked a lot but said nothing," Lynch declared. "On questions of any consequence she stood on her constitutional rights and declined to answer." Lynch went on to describe the rest of Burns's testimony as "very evasive" and stated that his office planned no further jury sessions on the subject. "As far as I am concerned the Burns phase of any inquiry is a dead duck." And San Francisco, the "perfectly imperfect city," returned to business as usual.[15]

With his usual satirical flair, Herb Caen pointed out, "That big wind Monday night—didn't you feel it? Was caused by the sighs of relief coming from the Halls of Justice, when Inez Burns said nothing (while talking a lot!) before the grand jury."[16]

Epilogue   Death and Taxes

It will be years before physicians will be
properly trained . . . to do it well and safe.

—Inez Brown Burns

In the end, Pat Brown's celebrated conviction of Inez Burns did little to
curb the deep-rooted corruption in San Francisco's police department.
Regardless, homicide inspector Frank Ahern proudly wore the nickname
"honest Frank" even though he was passed over for promotion many times
when he refused to go along with the department's "program" of palm
greasing and payoffs. Then in 1951 when the Kefauver Senate Committee
came to town, Ahern's testimony of mob activity on the West Coast so
impressed the members that the committee borrowed him to aid in their
nationwide investigation.[1]

In his biography *Christopher of San Francisco* author George Dorsey
said that ten years after Burns went to jail, newly elected Mayor George
Christopher was so impressed by the way Ahern took on "Inez Burns,
operator of the biggest abortion mill in the West" that he passed over
many others with seniority and appointed Ahern chief of police. "I
want an honest cop," Christopher declared, to come in and "straighten
out the department." Within the first eight months the mass cleanup
Ahern initiated, which included transferring every district captain and
demoting his former supervisor, Chief of Inspectors James English,
became legendary.[2]

Two years later, Ahern took a rare afternoon off and drove with his
wife Gertrude to watch the San Francisco Giants battle it out with the

Los Angeles Dodgers at Seals Stadium. At the top of the sixteenth inning, as Ahern jumped to his feet to cheer Giants' slugger Willie Kirkland on to home plate, he was overcome with chest pain and slumped to the ground. Gertrude cradled her husband's head in her lap as he died of a heart attack. He was fifty-eight years old.[3]

In remembering his friend, Thomas Cahill (Ahern's successor as police chief) recounted the story of Burns's arrest as told to him by Ahern—a slightly different account from the court records:

> Frank said when he got there [Burns's Guerrero Street home], her attorney, she already had him at the house. . . . Walter McGovern— went over the back fence with $50,000 in cash to bail her out. Then when they searched the piano, in the strings they found $350,000 in cash. And Frank said, "Come over here, Iney and sit down and watch me count this money." But she [Burns] said, "Don't be a fool Frank, take it and get out of here." But he told her, "You got the wrong man, Iney." And he made her sit there as he counted it out in front of her.[4]

Frank Ahern's obituary also retold the famous attempted bribery episode that all of San Francisco knew so well but always loved to hear again. In this particular version the incorruptible cop was quietly led by the city's notorious "abortion queen" into the back of her bedroom closet, where she unlocked a large safe.

"Help yourself," she said, pointing to the $300,000 in cash.

"Come on, Inez," smiled Ahern, shaking his head as he led her out the door to a waiting patrol car.[5]

———

Throughout Inez Burns's three trials, Pat Brown's office managed to keep her onetime partner, Loraine Everson, the handsome Navy doctor who kept the incriminating orange diary, out of the newspapers. But prosecutor Tom Lynch kept his promise to the editor of the *Wisconsin State Journal* and tipped him off when the doctor's illegal association with Burns came into evidence in the spring of 1946. It is unclear how much influence Lynch's information had on federal authorities, but it appears the long arm of the San Francisco district attorney's office reached halfway across the country to Madison, Wisconsin, for within eighteen months federal agents arrested Dr. Everson.

According to the charges Everson had prescribed large amounts of Dilaudid, a strong narcotic, to a local woman without filing the proper reports. The woman testified that Everson gave her the medication to relieve migraines and intentionally got her addicted to the drug. He then charged her $85 for a tube of tablets, or $2000 ($24,000 in today's dollars) for a bottle of 500. The woman admitted to federal agents that when her money ran out, she began forging prescriptions in Everson's name in desperation. However, the evidence showed that Everson wrote most of the prescriptions and cashed thousands of dollars in checks from the woman. On April 20, 1948, while Inez Burns was locked away in Tehachapi prison, Everson was making a deal with prosecutors to plead guilty to three counts of narcotics violations.

At Everson's sentencing on May 10 the judge declared, "It is possible in good faith [for a physician] to be fooled by an addict . . . but, the government does not feel this was a possibility in this case." He went on to condemn Everson, who he pointed out was clearly only interested in making money and "did not care how he did it." The judge sentenced the doctor to the maximum—six months in the federal penitentiary at Sandstone, Missouri. Ten days later the Wisconsin Medical Board revoked his license to practice medicine.

Two months into his six-month sentence, the thirty-three-year-old doctor strapped his trouser belt around his throat, tied the other end to a bedpost, and hanged himself.[60]

—

Following the advice of her attorney, six months after her September 1945 arrest Inez Burns sold her abortion headquarters at 325–27 Fillmore Street. The new owner turned it into a convalescent home for the aged.[7]

———

Gloria Shannon's scandalous tell-all manuscript, *My Memoirs in the Midstream of Life after an Intimate View of San Francisco's Slaughter-House for Babies*, from which District Attorney Brown gleaned key evidence against Inez Burns, was sold to William Randolph Hearst in January 1946. Hearst subsequently printed the first two chapters in the *Examiner* just weeks before Burns's first trial began in February 1946. Although future chapters were promised, suddenly and without explanation they stopped. According to archival records chapters three through seven of the manuscript were received, cataloged, and photographed in March 1946, then stored with the *Examiner*'s photograph collection. This is the final record of Shannon's scathing account, as it is missing from the collection.

———

Always reaching for the next rung on the political ladder, Pat Brown campaigned for the state attorney general's seat throughout the spring and into the fall of 1946. Convinced the high profile conviction of San Francisco's abortion queen would be the catalyst to propel him to the state capital, Brown promised voters he intended to devote the remainder of his term to bringing law and order to the city and to "discovering how Inez Burns was allowed to operate for twenty years without interference."[8]

In May, with the primary election only one month away, Brown went so far as to return his salary back to the city coffers because, he told reporters, "I'm not spending my entire time in my office and it's only right that I should return my salary." The September 1946 guilty verdict handed down in Burns's case proved Brown's relentless pursuit of justice had paid off and he was capable of cleaning up graft in San Francisco—no small feat. Even though Brown lost his first statewide election, he made an impressive showing and returned to win four years later.[9]

Pat Brown became state attorney general in 1950. At the age of forty-five, he was the only Democrat elected to hold a statewide office, and subsequently became the leader of California's Democratic Party. Brown's reputation spread and before long he enjoyed the same popularity throughout California that he had in San Francisco. After two terms as attorney general he tossed his hat in the ring for the governorship, running against Republican William Knowland in 1958. On Election Day, he and wife Bernice teed off their traditional Election Day round of golf at the Olympic Club, and Brown beat Knowland by more than one million votes.

Pat Brown, the son of a bookie, made it to Sacramento.

———

The San Francisco district attorney's office never re-opened the investigation into the death of Chicago mobster Nick DeJohn. Police detectives shouted their outrage—but let it go. Lead investigator in the case Frank Ahern never revealed the answer Pat Brown gave to his "$64 question," and Nick DeJohn's murder remains unsolved.[10]

In February 1950, six months after the judge declared a mistrial in the case, Anita de Venza, the key witness, was convicted on abortion charges and sentenced to serve two to five years at Tehachapi State Prison. She was never charged with perjury.[11]

———

Continuing financial difficulties clouded Inez Burns's final years. She was a sixty nine year-old grandmother when she was released from Corona Prison for Women in the spring of 1955. Within a month she lost her sister Nellie, the dressmaker, who had quietly stayed by her side from the beginning, often living with her or in the flat below her Fillmore Street clinic.

The following year the IRS came down on Burns full force. The government wanted its money from the estimated $1.3 million (or $15 million in today's dollars) she made in the final three years of her operation. Burns attempted to hold off the taxman by claiming that a large sum of money had been eaten by termites and that she inflated the value of her business in her "little black books" to discourage interested buyers. Furthermore, she pointed out, the government made no allowance for the money she paid out to middlemen, physicians, and hospitals (not to mention protection payoffs) for "services rendered." In the end, she agreed to a settlement of $745,325, and she was allowed to live in her Guerrero Street home (which Herb Caen sarcastically pointed out was "inappropriately" decorated out front with the statue of a little boy), until her death.[12]

"All I've got is my life," she told reporters. "They can have that if they want it—I don't think it's worth $800,000."[13]

Before the year was out she lost her son William. Always a bit of a disappointment, he never had the drive of his older brother Robert and mostly worked cleaning carpets at the Palace Hotel, an irony not lost on Burns. Still, throughout her three trials it was Willie who held her arm as she walked through the Hall of Justice. It pained her when tax agents seized her property in the upscale neighborhood of Atherton, forcing William to move his family to a small bungalow in San Carlo where he lived until his death.

In May 1971 the *San Francisco Examiner* sent a reporter to interview Burns on the new abortion case *Roe v. Wade* pending before the U.S. Supreme Court. "It will be many years before physicians will be trained properly for this type of surgery," she said, "in order to do it well and safe." When questioned about her payoffs to city cops, she still refused to give specifics, but insisted that her fondest memories were connected to the policemen she had known over the years.

"Ah, the sweet old days," she sighed, "you can't hardly find sensible men like that anymore."[14]

In the summer of that year she lost her son Robert—always Bobby to her. He had been her pride and joy, the child she thought most like herself. After years of struggle Robert succumbed to the bottle he battled most of his adult life.

"How could life be so cruel?" She asked Joe. He had no answer.

It was no secret that Burns always favored Robert. She wanted a better life for him, paying his way through medical school at Cornell University and even accepting his decision to open a "legitimate practice" unsoiled by her less-than-respectable work. In fact, after establishing himself at a local hospital Robert further removed himself from his mother's operation and refused to be added to her long list of local physician fixers. During her three trials, Tom Lynch included him on the prosecution's witness list but never called him to the stand. The child she groomed to take her place shamefacedly watched from the shadows.[15]

———

In July 1975 Joseph "the Fixer" Burns died, leaving Inez to rattle around alone in her five-bedroom mansion. She spent her mornings staring out into the foggy street watching neighborhood children as they passed below her window on their way to school. She rarely dressed beyond her pink silk robe, now faded and frayed at the sleeves.

One month after she buried Joe, Inez, then eighty-seven years old, moved to the Moss Beach Hospital and Rehabilitation Center nursing home where she spent her final six months. The floors, once white tile now yellow with age, met at the corners with institution-green walls. It reminded her of Tehachapi, she said.

She had one visitor in those final months: her sweet Caroline made the drive every Sunday afternoon. The two women, grandmother and granddaughter, best friends and co-conspirators, continued a tradition they started many years ago when Caroline was just a girl.

Caroline, the smuggler and designated lookout, stood at the open door to Inez's room watching for the ever-spying orderlies to leave the floor, giving Inez time to pour two steaming cups of black coffee and top each off with a healthy splash of Jim Beam.

"To all the men," Caroline giggled.

"To Buster Brown!" Inez raised her cup.

"Yes! To those sons-of-bitches!" they both laughed. The two women settled back in gray Naugahyde chairs, drank strong black coffee and reminisced.[16]

———

On January 25, 1976, Inez Burns died. The *San Francisco Chronicle* memorialized her as the "Queen of San Francisco Abortionists." She was laid to rest with a simple prayer and only a handful of mourners there to remember her. As the silent graveside attendees huddled beneath dripping umbrellas, a middle-aged woman joined them, face and eyes concealed behind large dark glasses. It was Alice, so long gone from her mother. She had missed the short service, but pressed close to quietly watch the modest casket lowered into the ground before she quickly walked away, speaking to no one.

Only Caroline noticed the long black town car that paused for a moment before winding its way along the gravel path and pulling to a stop at the edge of the wet grass. A darkened rear window rolled partway down to reveal the round, weathered face of a stately, old gentleman staring out behind wire-rimmed glasses. Caroline started toward the unexpected visitor, but the window closed and the car pulled away. She could only assume it was one of her grandmother's many admirers.[17]

———

Three months after Burns's death, U.S. marshals put her custom-built Guerrero Street home on the auction block. The house, once a show-place, had been stripped bare by vandals; chandeliers, carpets, marble fireplaces—all gone. The winning bid of a mere $80,150 came from a less-than-reputable local lawyer.[18]

———

According to witnesses and court documents, Inez Burns kept meticu-lous, day-by-day records of absolutely everything and everyone. So what happened to those "little black books," the voluminous, detailed and dark secrets she hid away under lock and key? How many city officials, cops, judges, and politicians were on her list? Did she really write down every bribe and to whom? And was it true that she recorded every single client—from local women who paid as little as $50, to Hollywood stars who paid as much as $2000? What about the lawyers, physicians, priests, and businessmen who recommended her?

After District Attorney Pat Brown led the September 1945 raid on Burns's clinic he called a press conference and announced that he was in possession of the little black notebooks. But as the investigation heated up and drew more and more public attention Brown hedged on questions about the notebooks and refused to name names of persons in public life with whom Burns associated. Finally he disclosed that "various prominent persons" had pressured him to back off the Burns investigation. Others, he said, repeatedly threatened that it would be political suicide to prosecute her. Nevertheless, Brown pressed on and Burns was finally convicted after two hung juries.[19]

Six years later the five-member Kefauver committee came to town and Burns's secret ledgers were brought in as evidence at the senate hearings. However, any information cited from the books was kept explicitly off the record. When the hearings ended, no one seemed to know what became of them.

The Special Committee to Investigate Crime in Interstate Commerce disbanded after its extensive fourteen-city national tour. Then almost thirty years later, in 1980, the Bancroft Library at the University of California at Berkeley received thirty large cardboard boxes of evidence. The truckload of boxes marked as evidence for organized crime in the State of California were unceremoniously dropped off and are now housed offsite at the University's Richmond Field Station, where they have gathered dust for more than three decades.

The boxes contain a binding restriction: they cannot be opened until the year 2028.[20]

Notes

Note: CPI: Consumer Price Index; EGB: Edmund G. (Pat) Brown; JCAH: Joint Commission on Accreditation of Hospitals.

PREFACE

1. Miller, *The Worst of Times*, 314–15.
2. Reagan, *When Abortion was a Crime*, 45.
3. Reagan, *When Abortion was a Crime*, 190–91; for further study on the history of abortion see Linda Gordon's *The Moral Property of Women: A History of Birth Control Politics in America* (Chicago: University of Illinois Press, 2002).

PROLOGUE

1. See testimony of Madeline Rand, The People v. Inez Burns et al. District Court of Appeals of the State of California, First Appellate District, Brief for Respondent (1948); descriptions of clothing, seating, and posture in the courtroom taken from court photographs and newspaper accounts.
2. "New Turn in Burns' Case," *San Francisco Chronicle*, February 28, 1946.
3. "Mrs. Burns Returns; Trial Slated Today," *San Francisco Chronicle*, February 17, 1946.
4. Raudebaugh, "San Francisco," 352; EGB oral history, 122.

1 ON TRIAL

Epigraph: "Mrs. Burns Returns; Trial Slated Today."
1. "Delay Barred in Burns' Case," *San Francisco Examiner*, February 17, 1946; "Burns' Trial Opens Today," *San Francisco Examiner*, February 18, 1946; "Mrs. Burns Returns; Trial Slated Today."
2. Lynch oral history, 57–89; Flamm, *Hometown*, 151; "Burns Defense Hits 'Politics' in Picking Jury," *San Francisco Examiner*, February 20, 1946.
3. "Burns Defense Hits 'Politics' in Picking Jury."

4. Lynch oral history, 57–89; "Burns Defense Hits 'Politics' in Picking Jury."

5. Lynch oral history, 57–89.

6. "Burns Defense Hits 'Politics' in Picking Jury"; "Burns Trial Opens Today," *San Francisco Examiner*, February 18, 1946; Lynch oral history, 57–89.

7. Lynch oral history, 57–89.

8. "Burns Abortion Trial," *San Francisco Examiner*, February 13, 1946.

9. "Abortion Case," *San Francisco Chronicle*, January 15, 1946.

10. "Jury Selected in Burns' Trial: 5 are Women," *San Francisco Examiner*, February 21, 1946; "Inez Burns' Abortion Trial: Shannon Relative Found on Jury," *San Francisco Chronicle*, February 20, 1946.

11. "Trial Begins for Inez Burns, Four Others," *San Francisco Examiner*, February 19, 1946.

12. "Trial Begins for Inez Burns, Four Others."

13. "Trial Begins for Inez Burns, Four Others"; "Abortion Case," *San Francisco Chronicle*, March 5, 1946; "Mrs. Burns Sobs at Trial in S.F.," *Oakland Tribune*, March 4, 1946.

14. Descriptions of Burns's clinic can be found in The People v. Inez Burns et al. District Court of Appeals of the State of California, First Appellate District, Reporter's Transcript, F 2452 (1948).

15. *People v. Inez Burns* et al., F 2452.

16. *People v. Inez Burns* et al., 74–77.

17. Flamm, *Hometown*, 151; *People v. Inez Burns* et al., F 2452.

18. *People v. Inez Burns* et al., 2–8.

2. FROM THE PALACE TO A TENT

Epigraph: Nolan, *Hammett: A Life at the Edge*, 38–39.

1. Caroline Carlisle (Burns's granddaughter), interviews with author, 2009–11; "The Inez Burns Story, parts 1–10," by June Morrall on Half Moon Bay Memories & El Granada Observer, accessed January 2010. http://halfmoonbaymemories.wordpress.com/category/caroline-carlisle/.

2. Carlisle interview; "The Inez Burns Story."

3. Advertisement, *San Francisco Examiner*, October 12, 1904; for further examples see *San Francisco Examiner* and *San Francisco Chronicle* advertisements 1885–1910; Reagan, *When Abortion was a Crime*, 89.

4. See various articles *San Francisco Call*, October–December 1895; Duke, *Celebrated Criminal Cases of America*, 92–95.

5. Burns's association with Dr. West, Carlisle interview; "The Inez Burns Story"; for references on Dr. Eugene West see various Bay Area newspapers beginning 1885–1910.

6. Inez had multiple abortions, the first by Dr. West. Carlisle interview; "The Inez Burns Story."

7. *Crocker Langley City Directory*, 1899; Carlisle interview; "The Inez Burns Story."

8. Carlisle interview; "The Inez Burns Story."

9. Carlisle interview; "The Inez Burns Story"; for extensive photographs, first-hand accounts, and newspaper articles on life in the camp at Golden Gate Park see the Special Collection at the University of California, Berkeley Bancroft Library, http://www.lib.berkeley.edu/libraries/bancroft-library/pictorial-collection. Also see Dan Kurzman, *Disaster: The Great Earthquake and Fire of 1906* (New York: W. Morrow, 2001); Richard and Gladys Hansen, *1906 San Francisco Earthquake* (Charleston: Arcadia Publishing, 2013); Gary Kamiya, *Cool Gray City of Love*, 239–57; Dennis Smith, *San Francisco is Burning*, 107, 155–57; James Russel Wilson, *San Francisco's Horror*, 208–10.

10. *Crocker Langley City Directory*, 1919.

11. See *"The Garment Worker" Official Journal of the United Garment Workers of America*, 1912–20; "Labor News," *San Francisco Chronicle*, various dates 1914–19; also see Pastorello, *A Power Among Them*.

12. "Police Probe Death of Girl," *San Francisco Examiner*, May 23, 1920.

13. "Police Probe Death of Girl."

14. "Police Probe Death of Girl."

15. "Mystery Veils Death of Union Labor Woman," *San Francisco Chronicle*, May 25, 1920.

16. "Edith Suter's Death Laid to Malpractice," *San Francisco Chronicle*, May 26, 1920.

17. "Edith Suter's Death Laid to Malpractice."

18. "Professional Notes," *Pacific Coast Journal of Homoeopathy*, 314; "Edith Suter's Death Laid to Malpractice"; "Experts Will Pass on Physician's Diagnosis," *San Francisco Chronicle*, May 27, 1920; "Illegal Operation," *San Francisco Chronicle*, June 3, 1920.

19. "Woman Arrested Malpractice Charge," *San Francisco Chronicle*, April 2, 1921.

20. Description of Burns's clinic and home, Carlisle interview; "The Inez Burns Story"; and *People v. Inez Burns*, F 2452.

21. Carlisle interview; "The Inez Burns Story"; *People v. Inez Burns*, F 2452.

22. A list of Burns's associates can be found in *People v. Inez Burns*, F 2452.

23. Carlisle interview; "The Inez Burns Story."

24. Carlisle interview; "The Inez Burns Story."

25. Carlisle interview; The Inez Burns Story"; Flamm, *Hometown*, 5; for a comprehensive study on the history of plastic surgery see Elizabeth Haiken's *Venus Envy: A History of Cosmetic Surgery* (Baltimore: Johns Hopkins University Press, 1999).

26. Gentry, *Madams of San Francisco*, 268.

27. Flamm, *Hometown*, 51; Herb Caen was the longtime San Francisco journalist whose contribution as the voice and conscience of the city won him a Pulitzer Prize in 1996; Belli, *My Life on Trial*, 138.

28. Kamiya, *Cool Gray City of Love*, 16–17; Flamm, *Hometown*, 51; Worthen, *Governor James Rolph and the Great Depression in California*, 75.

29. For example, see "Death Tales Told in Court," *Oakland Tribune*, August 5, 1937.

3. LOVE PIRATE

Epigraph: "So Says S.F. Woman in Divorce Suit Revealing New and Novel Matrimonial Pact," *San Francisco Examiner*, December 10, 1927.

1. Examples of these articles can be found in *San Antonio Light*, *Ogden Standard*, and *Havre Daily News* as well as newspapers throughout the state of California.

2. *Crocker Langley City Directory*, 1925; Burns made every effort to shield her daughter from her abortion business by sending her away to an East Coast boarding school.

3. Carlisle interview; "The Inez Burns Story."

4. "Jacob Gets 6 Speeders," *Woodland Daily Democrat*, October 19, 1925.

5. "Burns Sued for $150,000 by Granelli, Rich S.F. Man," *San Francisco Chronicle*, November 4, 1927.

6. "Burns Sued for $150,000 by Granelli, Rich S.F. Man."

7. "Connivance Laid By Wife To Granelli," *San Francisco Chronicle*, December 10, 1927; "Rich S.F. Man in New Divorce Suit," *San Francisco Examiner*, May 9, 1928.

8. "Hubby Gets Cash to Let Wife Flirt," *San Francisco Examiner*, December 10, 1927. Examples of these articles can be found in *San Antonio Light*, *Ogden Standard*, and *Havre Daily News* as well as newspapers throughout the state of California.

9. "Connivance Laid By Wife To Granelli"; "So Says S.F. Woman in Divorce Suit Revealing New and Novel Matrimonial Pact."

10. "Rich S.F. Man to Proceed With Battle to Obtain Divorce Decree," *San Francisco Chronicle*, May 11, 1928; "So Says S.F. Woman in Divorce Suit Revealing New and Novel Matrimonial Pact"; "Rich S.F. Man in New Divorce Suit."

11. "Rich S.F. Man in New Divorce Suit"; "S.F Suit Dismissed," *Berkeley Daily Gazette*, May 11, 1928; "End of Love Row," *Woodland Daily Democrat*, May 12, 1928; "Granelli Love Suit Against Burns Dropped," *San Francisco Examiner*, May 11, 1928; "Politics Charged by Assemblyman in Suit," *San Francisco Chronicle*, November 5, 1927.

12. F. Adler v. Granelli, District Court of Appeals of the State of California, First Appellate District, Division Two, 297, 592 (1931).

13. "Burns in Love Suit Charges Politics," *Oakland Tribune*, November 5, 1927; "Politics Charged by Assemblyman in Suit."

14. "United States Senator Hiram Johnson Prepares to Defend Title Against All Comers," *Oxnard Daily Courier*, November 1, 1927.

15. "Voting Returns," *Oakland Tribune*, August 29, 1928.

4. OFF THE HOOK

Epigraph: In 1935 the city of San Francisco, clouded by tales of police officers and public officials involved in corruption and graft, forced District Attorney Matthew Brady and Mayor Angelo Rossi to act and hire private investigator and former FBI agent Edwin N. Atherton. The results of this investigation, the so-called *Atherton Report*, prompted the firing of dozens of policemen and the resignation of the entire police commission over reports of police payoffs. Bail bond skimming, unpaid loans to public officials, and loan sharking were laid at the door of Peter McDonough, described in the report as "the fountainhead of corruption." For a full text of the report see: "The Atherton Graft Report," *San Francisco Chronicle*, March 17, 1937.

1. *Western Journal of Medicine*, 112; also see *San Francisco Examiner*, June 7 and June 19, 1936; *San Francisco Call-Bulletin*, June 18, 1936; U.S. Department of Labor Bureau of Labor Statistics, CPI inflation calculator: http://data.bls.gov/cgi-bin/cpicalc.pl.

2. "Inez Brown's Place Raided Again," *San Francisco News*, May 4, 1938.

3. "Inez Brown's Place Raided Again."

4. Ehrlich, *A Life in My Hands*, 97; Gentry, *The Madams of San Francisco*, 100–101; also see *Los Angeles Evening News*, June 6, 1936; *San Francisco Examiner*, June 7, 1936; *San Francisco Call-Bulletin*, June 18, 1936; *San Francisco Examiner*, June 19, 1936; *Los Angeles Times*, October 8, 1936. For a full text of the *Atherton Report* see: "The Atherton Graft Report."

5. Stanford, *The Lady of the House*, 66–68.

6. Caen, *Don't Call it Frisco*, 147; Shaw, *The Tenderloin*, 49–53; Flamm, *Hometown*, 50–53; also see Stanford, *Madam of the House*.

7. Flamm, *Hometown*, 33.

8. "Shannon Would be Lieutenant-Governor," *Oakland Tribune*, June 18, 1919; "SF Shannon Face Grilling," *Oakland Tribune*, January 28, 1929; "Huge Throng to Witness Golden Gate Bridge Fete," *Oakland Tribune*, February 25, 1933; *San Francisco Municipal Record*, vol. 2 (1936–37), San Francisco: Ca. SF Municipal Pub Co., 1937.

9. Dyble, *Paying the Toll*, 31, 51; Langmead, *Icons of American Architecture*, 122.

10. "Fete to Mark Opening of Gate Bridge Work," *Oakland Tribune*, February 19, 1933; "Bay Cities Join S.F. in Bridge Fete," *San Francisco Chronicle*, May 28, 1937; "Shannon Divorce," *San Francisco Chronicle*, September 2, 1941; "Shannon to Wed G. Davenport," *San Francisco Chronicle*, August 12, 1942; "Rites to be Held in New York for Warren Shannon," *Oakland Tribune*, March, 27, 1948.

5. "MISS X"

Epigraph: "S.F. Abortion Mill Operates Openly: Proprietor Boasts, 'We've Thousands of Clients,'" *San Francisco News-Call Bulletin*, May 4, 1938.

1. Arthur Sherry later became chief assistant attorney general under Governor Edmund "Pat" Brown.
2. "S.F. Abortion Mill Operates Openly."
3. "S.F. Abortion Mill Operates Openly."
4. "S.F. Abortion Mill Operates Openly."
5. "S.F. Abortion Mill Operates Openly."
6. "S.F. Abortion Mill Operates Openly."
7. "S.F. Abortion Mill Operates Openly."
8. "S.F. Abortion Mill Operates Openly."
9. Mary Ellen Leary, oral history, 20–21.
10. "Inez Brown's Place Raided Again," *San Francisco News-Call Bulletin*, May 5, 1938.
11. "Inez Brown's Place Raided Again."
12. "Inez Brown's Place Raided Again."
13. "Inez Brown's Place Raided Again"; "Abortions admitted by Patients," *San Francisco Examiner*, May 5, 1938; "Police Raid Flat As Abortion Hospital," *San Francisco News-Call Bulletin*, May 5, 1938.
14. "Inez Brown Wins Freedom," *San Francisco Examiner*, June 1, 1938.
15. "Abortion Case Figure Indicted on Tax Charges," *San Francisco Examiner*, October 12, 1939; U.S. Treasury Department: Bureau of Internal Revenue, Statistics of Income for 1936; CPI inflation calculator: http://data.bls.gov/cgi-bin/cpicalc.pl.

6. THE FIXER

Epigraph: "Burns's Raid," *San Francisco News*, May 6, 1938

1. "Inez Brown's Husband: J. F. Burns Married to Suspect," *San Francisco Examiner*, May 8, 1938.
2. "Burns's Raid"; "Inez Brown's Husband: J. F. Burns Married to Suspect."
3. *South of Market Journal*, vol. 11–16, 1936–41; Flamm, *Hometown*, 49–50; "Sporting Green," *San Francisco Chronicle*, September 11, 1938; Lotchin, "John Francis Neylan," 86–105.

4. See *San Francisco Examiner*, September 1937 through January 1938.

5. "Inez Brown's Husband: J. F. Burns Married to Suspect."

7. "FIVE-TO-ONE" ODDS

Epigraph: As quoted in Carey McWilliams's *California: The Great Exception*, 172.

1. Rapoport, *California Dreaming*, 22–23; EGB oral history, 1–29, 74–75, 108; Harold Brown, EGB oral history, 13; for a more complete list of Brown's civic activities refer to EGB Papers, carton 149, folder 56, also carton 183, folder 2. For the most comprehensive look at Edmund G. Brown's life see Ethan Rarick's *The Life and Times of Pat Brown: California Rising*.

2. In 1928, Brown ran for the legislature as a Republican when the party outnumbered Democrats two to one. By the 1936 election when Brown voted Democrat, the ratio was almost reversed; Starr, *Golden Dreams*, 119; also see Carney, *The Rise of the Democratic Clubs in California*.

3. Letter from EGB to Mr. and Mrs. Norval Fast, July 6, 1939, EGB Papers, carton 183, folder I, "Brown, personal"; Letter from EGB to Howard Ellis, February 13, 1940, EGB Papers, carton 154, folder 19, "Brown, Edmund G."

4. See *San Francisco Chronicle*, February 20, 1923, August 10, 1927 and September 6, 1939; Starr, *The Dream Endures*, 141; For full text, see: "The Atherton Graft Report."

5. EGB oral history, 122; Flamm, *Hometown*, 33, 134.

6. EGB oral history, 122; Harris oral history, 82, 94–95; Matthew Brady went on to serve as a justice in the municipal court. In his autobiography, *My Life on Trial*, attorney Melvin Belli gives an account of a drunk Brady handing down a sentence from the bench, an action that caused the bar association to bring him up on charges.

7. Rapoport, *California Dreaming*, 28–33; White, *Earl Warren: A Public Life*; Letter from EGB to Mr. and Mrs. Norval Fast, July 6, 1939, EGB Papers, carton 183, folder 1, Brown, personal; Lynch oral history, 115.

8. Rapoport, *California Dreaming*, 32.

9. EGB oral history, 124; Allen, *Our Fair City*, 4; Flamm, *Hometown*, 47.

10. "Brady Blasts Opponent's Record," *San Francisco Examiner*, October 29, 1943; "Brown Revealed as Counsel for 2 S.F. Gambling Clubs," *San Francisco Examiner*, October 31, 1943; for reference on the power of the press see Wirt, *The Power of the City*, 168.

11. "Brown Replies to 'Unfair Attack,'" *San Francisco Examiner*, November 2, 1943.

12. EGB oral history, 124; Rarick, *The Life and Times of Pat Brown*, 38.

13. "Brown's Speech: 'I will Act on Behalf of All—Not a Few,'" *San Francisco Chronicle*, January 9, 1944; See photos in the *San Francisco Chronicle* and the *San Francisco Examiner*, January 9, 1944; EGB oral history, 127.

14. Rarick, *California Rising*, 87; Lynch oral history, 97, 123; also see various quotes in EGB oral history.

15. "Shannon Divorce"; "Shannon to Wed G. Davenport"; "Rites to be Held in New York for Warren Shannon"; "Fete to mark Opening of Gate Bridge Work"; "Bay Cities Join S.F. in Bridge Fete"; "The City's Abortion Case," *San Francisco Chronicle*, January 21, 1946.

8. A "NEW BROOM"

Epigraph: Raudebaugh, "San Francisco," 364.

1. Boyd, *Wide Open Town*, 40–42.

2. EGB oral history, 101; *San Francisco Examiner*, January 9, 1944.

3. EGB oral history, EW, 22–23; Raudebaugh, "San Francisco," 364–65; Stephen Bloom, "San Francisco's Worst-Kept Secret," 40–48.

4. "Slaughter Charged to Abortion Mills," *San Francisco Examiner*, January 16, 1946; Lynch oral history, 71–85.

5. Elkington oral history, EGB, 17–22.

6. EGB oral history, 102.

7. Elkington oral history, EGB, 17–22; Lynch oral history, 79–85; "Second Arrest in Suspected Abortion Mill," *San Francisco Chronicle*, September 28, 1946.

8. *Hearings*, 419–629; CPI inflation calculator: http://data.bls.gov/cgi-bin /cpicalc.pl.

9. "What Started the Abortion Inquiry?" *San Francisco News*, January 25, 1946; also see *Ex parte Burns et al. on habeas corpus*. District Court of

Appeals of the State of California, First Appellate District, F2440, 2452 (1948), 445–96; Lynch oral history, 58; Elkington oral history, EGB, 17–22; "Second Arrest in Suspected Abortion Mill."

10. "Burns Abortion Case—Brown to Call Clients," *San Francisco Chronicle*, January 1, 1946; Carlisle interview; "The Inez Burns Story"; CPI inflation calculator: http://data.bls.gov/cgi-bin/cpicalc.pl.

11. Lynch oral history, 57–89; "Burns Abortion Case—Brown to Call Clients"; also see *Hearings*, 419–629.

12. Lynch oral history, 57–89; "Burns Abortion Case—Brown to Call Clients"; Raudebaugh, "San Francisco," 364; "The Abortion Case," *San Francisco Examiner*, December 18, 1945.

13. "Probe of Alleged 'Abortion Mill' to Continue, Says D.A.," *Oakland Tribune*, November 8, 1945.

14. "California: The Mill," *Time*, October 8, 1945.

15. "Mrs. Burns Booked on Abortion Conspiracy Charge," *San Francisco Chronicle*, September 29, 1945; Also see District Court of Appeals of the State of California, F 2452, for the testimony of Madeline Rand and Levina Queen.

16. For descriptions of Burns's clinic see *People v. Inez Burns*, F 2452; Carlisle interview; "The Inez Burns Story."

17. "New Inquiry Called in S.F. Vice Charges," *San Francisco Examiner*, January 19, 1946; "More About the Inez Burns Abortion Case Situation," *San Francisco Chronicle*, January 20, 1946; Elkington oral history, EGB, 17–22; Raudebaugh, "San Francisco," 364; "Abortion Tipoff Investigation," *San Francisco Chronicle*, January 20, 1946.

9. COPS AND ROBBERS

Epigraph: "What Started the Abortion Inquiry? 'An Honest Cop!'" *San Francisco News*, January 25, 1946.

1. *People v. Inez Burns et al.*, Brief for Respondent, 495; Al Corassa's name was sometimes spelled Corrasa in newspaper reports and trial coverage. However, I use the spelling Corassa as it was the most common use in official documents.

2. "More About Two Tipoffs in Burns Abortion Case," *San Francisco Examiner*, January 25, 1946.

3. "Abortion Hearing," *San Francisco Examiner*, January 31, 1946.

4. "Abortion Hearing"; "Cops Testify in Burns Tipoff," *San Francisco Examiner*, February 6, 1946; "The Abortion Mill Case," *San Francisco Chronicle*, January 31, 1946. In April 1948 another bartender, Angelo Antonini, was arrested for taking $550 to set up an abortion with Burns that he could not deliver, as she was already in Tehachapi State prison.

5. Lynch oral history, 57–89.

6. "Shannons Linked to U.S. Tax Case Against Mrs. Burns," *Oakland Tribune*, December 9, 1945.

7. "Burns Couple Won't Testify," *San Francisco Examiner*, January 28, 1946; "Bribe Offer Also Told," *San Francisco Examiner*, January 22, 1946.

8. "Full Jury Quiz in Burns Tipoff Report Slated," *San Francisco Examiner*, January 25, 1946.

9. "3 Held in S.F. Dope Ring," *San Francisco Examiner*, March 19, 1946.

10. "Full Jury Quiz in Burns Tipoff Report Slated"; "Abortion Hearing."

11. "Abortion Case," *San Francisco Chronicle*, January 15, 1946.

12. "Cop Neighbor of Inez Talks," *San Francisco Examiner*, December 22, 1945.

13. "Abortion Case."

14. "Shannons Hint at Big Abortion Mill Payoff," *San Francisco Examiner*, December 21, 1945.

15. Elkington oral history, EGB, 17–22.

16. "The S.F. Abortion Payoff Investigation," *San Francisco Examiner*, January 19, 1946; "Dullea Order Housecleaning," *San Francisco Chronicle*, January 19, 1946.

17. "Sensational Shannon Volume Aids Widening Vice Inquiry," *San Francisco Examiner*, January 20, 1946; Lynch oral history, 58; Sides, *Erotic City*, 36.

18. Lynch oral history, 57.

19. Raudebaugh, "San Francisco," 354.

20. "General Vice Inquiry By Grand Jury Proposed," *San Francisco Examiner*, January 18, 1946; "Abortionists Paid Off, Says Brown," *San Francisco Chronicle*, January 18, 1946; Raudebaugh, "San Francisco," 355.

21. "Abortionists Paid Off, Says Brown"; "14 to Testify in Burns Tipoff," *San Francisco Examiner*, January 29, 1946; "Abortion Tip-Off," *San Francisco Chronicle*, January 25, 1946.

22. "10 More Police Tip Witnesses," *San Francisco Examiner*, February 7, 1946.

23. "Letter Urges Vice Inquiry," *San Francisco Examiner*, January 19, 1946.

24. "General Vice Inquiry by Grand Jury," *San Francisco Examiner*, January 18, 1946; Brown also criticized the three-member police commission. For reference to the structure and power of this commission see Wirt, *Power in the City*, 115–17.

25. "Jury to Hear 14 in Tipoff," *San Francisco Examiner*, January 29, 1946; "Abortion Blackout," *San Francisco Chronicle*, January 29, 1946.

26. "Deductive Case," *San Francisco Chronicle*, January 7, 1946.

10. DISAPPEARED

Epigraph: "Questions to Answer," *San Francisco Call*, December 6, 1945.

1. "Probe of Alleged 'Abortion Mill' to Continue, Says D.A.," *San Mateo Times*, December 22, 1945.

2. "Surgery Mill Case Goes On Minus Indictment," *San Francisco Examiner*, October 4, 1945.

3. Elkington oral history, EGB, 18; also see Lynch oral history, 57–62; Raudebaugh, "San Francisco," 364; "Surgery Mill Case Goes On Minus Indictment," *San Francisco Examiner*, October 4, 1945; "The Abortion Cases in San Francisco," *San Francisco Chronicle*, January 9, 1946.

4. "Wife Describes Surgery Mill at Burns Trial," *San Francisco Examiner*, November 26, 1945.

5. "Wife Describes Surgery Mill at Burns Trial."

6. James Brennan was replaced as Burns's attorney following the preliminary hearing.

7. "Wife Describes Surgery Mill at Burns Trial."

8. "Wife Describes Surgery Mill at Burns Trial."

9. "'Surgery Mill' Witness Gets Police Protection," *San Francisco Examiner*, November 28, 1945.

10. "Wife Describes Surgery Mill at Burns Trial."

11. "Another Woman Tells of 'Mill' Operation," *San Francisco Examiner*, November 29, 1945; "More About the Burns Trial," *San Francisco Chronicle*, November 30, 1945.

12. "The Burns Abortion Case and the New Grand Jury," *San Francisco Chronicle*, January 3, 1946.

13. "More About the Abortion Cases in S.F.," *San Francisco Chronicle*, January 10, 1946; "Full Jury Quiz in Burns Tipoff Report Slated"; "Abortion Hearing."

11. HOUSEGUESTS

Epigraph: "Shannon Tells of Horror House Visit," *San Francisco Examiner*, January 20, 1946.

1. "Shannon Called Author of Surgery Mill Book," *San Francisco Examiner*, December 10, 1945.

2. *People v. Inez Burns et al.*, Brief for Respondent, 291; Lynch oral history, 60; "Abortion Mill Lawyer Hits at Shannon," *San Francisco Chronicle*, November 29, 1945.

3. "Shannon Quits Bakersfield for 'Operation Mill' Quiz," *Oakland Tribune*, December 2, 1945; "Shannon Pair Vanish Again," *The Bakersfield Californian*, December 3, 1945.

4. "More on the Abortion Case," *San Francisco Chronicle*, December 4, 1945; "Grand Jury to Study Shannon 'Mill' Case Angles," *Oakland Tribune*, December 11, 1945; *People v. Inez Burns et al.*, Brief for Respondent, 474–487; "Probe of Alleged 'Abortion Mill' to Continue, Says D.A.," *Oakland Tribune*, November 8, 1945; *Hearings*, 431.

5. "Questions to Answer," *San Francisco Call*, December 6, 1945.

12. ON THE LAM

Epigraph: "Couple Sought in Abortion Inquiry Stops in El Paso," *El Paso Herald-Post*, December 18, 1945.

1. "The Shannon Search," *San Francisco Chronicle*, December 15, 1945; "Former S.F. Supervisor is Hunted," *Oakland Tribune*, November 30, 1945.

2. "Statewide Hunt on for Shannon," *San Francisco Examiner*, December 1, 1945; "Shannon Pair Vanish Again," *The Bakersfield Californian*, December 3, 1945; "Shannon Says She is Star Witness," *San Francisco Examiner*, December 18, 1945.

3. "Shannon Quits Bakersfield for 'Operation Mill' Quiz"; "Shannon Pair Vanish Again"; "Shannons—A Call from El Paso," *San Francisco Chronicle*, December 15, 1945.

4. "Shannon Says She is Star Witness."

5. "Shannons' Threat Exposed," *San Francisco Examiner*, December 15, 1945.

6. "Statewide Hunt on for Shannon"; "Shannons Phone They'll Be Back," *Oakland Tribune*, December 18, 1945.

7. See Elkington, EGB oral history; "Shannons on Way Back to S.F.," *Oakland Tribune*, December 21, 1945.

8. "Coast Abortion Mill Witness 'Talk' Here," *Arizona Republic*, December 20, 1945; "Shannon Says She is Star Witness."

9. "Couple Sought in Abortion Inquiry Stops in El Paso"; "Shannons Reported on Way Back to Bay City," *The Bakersfield Californian*, December 18, 1945.

10. "Shannons on Way Back to S.F."; "D.A. Questions Shannons on Abortion Mill," *San Francisco Examiner*, December 21, 1945; "Shannon Called Author of Surgery Mill Book," *San Francisco Examiner*, December 10, 1945.

11. "Shannon Says She is Star Witness"; "Shannons' Threat Exposed."

12. "Shocking and Disgusting," *San Francisco Examiner*, February 19, 1946.

13. "Shannon Says She is Star Witness"; "Brown Will See Shannon," *Oakland Tribune*, December 19, 1945; "Coast Abortion Mill Witness 'Talk' Here"; "Abortion Case," *San Francisco Chronicle*, January 15, 1946.

14. "Shannons Due in S.F. Friday; They'll Tell All," *Oakland Tribune*, December 26, 1945.

15. "Letter From Shannon Denies Charge," *San Francisco Chronicle*, December 28, 1945.

16. "The City's Abortion Case," *San Francisco Chronicle*, January 21, 1946.

17. "The City's Abortion Case"; "Mrs. Burns Blasts Abortion Mill Tale by Shannons," *Nevada State Journal*, January 22, 1946.

18. "The Shannon Search"; "The City's Abortion Case."

13. "THE PROPHET"

Epigraph: Photograph collection, BANC PIC 2006.029: 127616-A.04-NEG Box 922, Bancroft Library, Berkeley, California.

1. "Police Knew of Alleged Mill Charges Shannon," *Oakland Tribune*, December 30, 1945; "Missing Burns Figure Identified," *Oakland Tribune*, December 31, 1945.
2. "Mill Case No. 1 For New Jury," *Oakland Tribune*, January 3, 1946.
3. "Pair Deny Threatening The Shannons," *San Francisco Examiner*, January 13, 1946.
4. Photograph collection, BANC PIC 2006.029: 127616-A.04-NEG Box 922, Bancroft Library, Berkeley, California.
5. Photograph collection, BANC PIC 2006.029: 127616-A.04-NEG Box 922, Bancroft Library, Berkeley, California; "Bribe Offer Also Told."
6. "The Abortion Investigation," *San Francisco Chronicle*, January 12, 1946.
7. Ehrlich, *Life in My Hands*, 85–86.
8. Raudebaugh, "San Francisco," 352; Boyd, *Wide Open Town*, 50–51; Nolan, *Hammett*, 57–77.
9. Raudebaugh, "San Francisco," 352; Boyd, *Wide Open Town*, 50–51; Nolan, *Hammett*, 57–77; "Abortion Tip-Off"; "Shannon tells of Transaction," *San Francisco Examiner*, January 1, 1946; "Burns Abortion Case—Brown to Call Clients," *San Francisco Chronicle*, January 1, 1946; "Missing Burns Figure Identified"; "'Mill' Case No. 1 for New Jury," *Oakland Tribune*, January 3, 1946; Flamm, *Hometown*, 43.
10. "Threat on Testimony Charged by Shannons," *San Francisco Examiner*, January 12, 1946; "S.F. Defender, Sleuth Deny Shannon Story," *San Francisco Examiner*, January 13, 1946.
11. Belli, *My Life on Trial*, 83.
12. "Threat on Testimony Charged by Shannons"; "Pair Deny Threatening The Shannons."
13. "Threat on Testimony Charged by Shannons"; "Pair Deny Threatening The Shannons."
14. "Slaughter Charged To Abortion Mills," *San Francisco Examiner*, January 16, 1946.

15. "Shannons Ask Church Aid in Fight on Abortion Mills," *San Francisco Examiner*, January 12, 1946.

16. "The Abortion Investigation"; "Shannons Ask Church Aid in Fight on Abortion Mills."

14. DEATH HOUSE

Epigraph: "Inez Burns' House of Horrors," *San Francisco Examiner*, January 20, 1946.

1. "Inez Burns' House of Horrors."

2. "Inez Burns' House of Horrors."

3. "Inez Burns' House of Horrors."

4. "Inez Burns' House of Horrors."

5. "Inez Burns' House of Horrors."

6. "Inez Burns' House of Horrors."

7. "Inez Burns' House of Horrors."

8. "Inez Burns' House of Horrors."

9. "Inez Burns' House of Horrors."

10. "Inez Burns' House of Horrors."

11. "Inez Burns' House of Horrors."

12. "Shannon Tells of Horror House Visit," *San Francisco Examiner*, January 21, 1946.

13. "Shannon Tells of Horror House Visit."

14. "Shannon Tells of Horror House Visit."

15. "Shannon Tells of Horror House Visit."

16. "Shannon Tells of Horror House Visit."

17. "Shannon Tells of Horror House Visit."

18. "Shannon Tells of Horror House Visit."

19. In the spring of 1945, as the war was coming to an end, representatives from fifty nations came together in San Francisco to map out a plan for a new international body aimed at ensuring world peace and stability. By late June, these delegates hammered out a charter that would form the United Nations; see Phillip, R., ed., "The Trial of Josef Kramer and Forty-Four Others: The Belsen Trials," 1949.

20. "Inez Burns' House of Horrors."

21. "Calling of Inez Burns by Grand Jury," *San Francisco Examiner*, January 22, 1946.

22. "S.F. Jury May Call Shannons," *Oakland Tribune*, January 22, 1946; "Operation Case Inquiry Tuesday," *Oakland Tribune*, January 23, 1946; "Sensational Shannon Volume Aids Widening Vice Inquiry," *San Francisco Examiner*, January 29, 1946.

23. "New Plea to Shannons," *San Francisco Examiner*, February 14, 1946; "Burns Abortion Trial," *San Francisco Chronicle*, February 13, 1946; "Shannons Sued by Attorney," *San Mateo Times*, March 14, 1946.

15. THE LONE HOLDOUT

Epigraph: "Burns Jury," *San Francisco Examiner*, April 11, 1946.

1. Flamm, *Hometown*, 148.

2. Flamm, *Hometown*, 148; *People v. Inez Burns et al.*, F 2452, 320–26.

3. "Burns Trial—Girl Says 'Mabel' Paid Hospital Bill, *San Francisco Chronicle*, March 6, 1946; "Oakland Branch of 'Mill' Hinted," *Oakland Tribune*, February 28, 1946; also see *People v. Inez Burns et al.*, F 2452, 285–97.

4. "Address Here Linked to Burns," *Oakland Tribune*, March 5, 1946.

5. *People v. Inez Burns et al.*, F 2452, 313–19.

6. "Burns Abortion Trial," *San Francisco Chronicle*, March 1, 1946; "Burns Trial—Girl Says 'Mabel' Paid Hospital Bill," *San Francisco Chronicle*, March 6, 1946; also see *People v. Inez Burns et al.*, F 2452, 313–19.

7. "Illegal Mill Doctor Traced, Official Says," *San Francisco Examiner*, January 28, 1946.

8. Lynch oral history, 57–89.

9. Lynch oral history, 57–89.

10. "New Turn in Burns Case," *San Francisco Chronicle*, February 28, 1946.

11. *People v. Inez Burns et al.*, F 2452, 154–247.

12. *People v. Inez Burns et al.*, F 2452, 154–247.

13. "New Turn in Burns Case"; also see Rand's testimony in *People v. Inez Burns et al.*, F 2452.

14. "Two Surprise Witnesses at Mrs. Burns' Trial," *San Francisco Examiner*, February 27, 1946; *People v. Inez Burns et al.*, F 2452, 154–247.

15. "Burns Trial—Girl Says 'Mabel' Paid Hospital Bill," *San Francisco Chronicle*, March 6, 1946; *People v. Inez Burns et al.*, F 2452, 409–37.

16. "Abortion Case," *San Francisco Chronicle*, March 5, 1946; "Gap in Testimony at Burns Trial," *San Francisco Examiner,* March 5, 1946; District Court of Appeals, Reporter's Transcript, 402.

17. *People v. Inez Burns et al.*, 15; "Records Show Mill Prospered," *Oakland Tribune*, March 1, 1946.

18. "More on Burns's Defense Plea to Jury, 'Don't be Pawns,'" *San Francisco Chronicle*, March 7, 1946.

19. "Burns Jury Deadlocked, Told to 'Keep Trying,'" *San Francisco Examiner*, March 9, 1946.

20. "Burns Jury Deadlocked, Told to 'Keep Trying.'"

21. "Burns Jury Deadlocked, Told to 'Keep Trying.'"

22. "More on the Burns Trial," *San Francisco Chronicle*, March 10, 1946.

23. "Burns Friend Explains Aid to Holdout Juror," *San Francisco Examiner*, March 14, 1946.

24. "Burns Jury," *San Francisco Examiner*, April 11, 1946.

25. "Burns Jury."

26. "Burns Jury is Discharged," *Oakland Tribune*, March 10, 1946.

27. "Burns Jury Hung: Hopeless Deadlock," *San Francisco Chronicle*, March 10, 1946; "Local News Front," *Oakland Tribune*, May 31, 1946.

28. "Lawyers in Clash," *San Francisco Examiner*, February 28, 1946; "Local News Front."

29. "Girl Witness in Burns Case Tries Suicide," *San Francisco Examiner*, March 17, 1946; "Girl in Burns Case Improves," *San Francisco Examiner*, March 18, 1946.

16. "ACCOMPLICES AND CO-CONSPIRATORS"

Epigraph: "Burns Abortion Case," *San Francisco Examiner*, May 15, 1946.

1. "Burns Abortion Case."

2. "Mother of Four Testifies at Burns Operation Trial," *Oakland Tribune*, May 23, 1946; "Defense Wins Skirmish," *Oakland Tribune*, May, 13, 1946.

3. "Burns Abortion Case."

4. "Defense May Hold Back in Burns Case," *San Francisco Examiner*, May 20, 1946.

5. "Burns' Jury Locked Up," *San Francisco Examiner*, May 27, 1946; "Defense May Hold Back in Burns' Case."

6. "Burns' Jury Locked Up"; "Burns' Jury Locked Up: 2nd Deadlock Hinted," *San Francisco Examiner*, May 28, 1946.

7. "Burns' Jury Questioned," *San Francisco Examiner*, May 30, 1946.

8. "Inez Burns, Four Co-Defendants Face 3rd Trial," *Oakland Tribune*, May 29, 1946; "Burns Will Be Tried a Third Time," *San Francisco Examiner*, May 29, 1946; "Burns' Jury Questioned," *San Francisco Examiner*, May 30, 1946.

9. "Inez Burns' Home Robbed," *Oakland Tribune*, June 4, 1946.

10. DeJohn's undercover life is detailed in various newspapers following his murder, also in *Hearings*, 497–503.

17. A GRAND FIGHT

Epigraph: Flamm, *Hometown*, 149.

1. "Judge Quits Burns' Trial," *San Francisco Examiner*, September 11, 1946; "Judge Murphy Opens Burns Trial Today," *San Francisco Examiner*, September 17, 1946; "Third Burns Trial Begins," *San Francisco Chronicle*, September 18, 1946; "Brown Tells Situation in Burns Case," *San Francisco Chronicle*, September 19, 1946.

2. "Judge Quits Burns' Trial"; "Judge Murphy Opens Burns Trial Today."

3. "Third Burns Trial Begins," *San Francisco Chronicle*, September 18, 1946; Lynch oral history, 54; Flamm, *Hometown*, 149–151.

4. *People v. Inez Burns et al.*, Reporter's Transcript, c-1.

5. "Third Burns Trial Begins," *San Francisco Chronicle*, September 18, 1946; also see *People v. Inez Burns et al.*, Reporter's Transcript, c-1.

6. *People v. Inez Burns et al.*, Reporter's Transcript, B; "Burns Jury Locked Up," *San Francisco Chronicle*, September 19, 1946; "Court Orders Jury Isolated," *Oakland Tribune*, September 20, 1946; "Burns Jury Sees a Movie—Under Guard," *San Francisco Chronicle*, September 21, 1946. The last time a San Francisco jury was sequestered was the Mooney "Preparedness Day Parade" trial in 1917: Starr, *Inventing the Dream*, 275; Ralston, *Fremont*, 195.

7. *People v. Inez Burns et al.*, 2–6.

8. "More Surprises in the Burns Trial," *San Francisco Chronicle*, September 20, 1946; "Burns Trial," *San Francisco Chronicle*, September 25, 1946.

9. *People v. Inez Burns et al.*, Reporter's Transcript, 497–551.

10. *People v. Inez Burns et al.*, Reporter's Transcript, 497–551.

11. *People v. Inez Burns et al.*, Reporter's Transcript, 497–551.

12. Photograph collection, BANC PIC 1959.010: 140948.8:6-NEG Box 180, Part 2, Bancroft Library, Berkeley, California.

13. *People v. Inez Burns et al.*, Reporter's Transcript, 497–551.

14. *People v. Inez Burns et al.*, Reporter's Transcript, 19–35.

15. *People v. Inez Burns et al.*, Reporter's Transcript, 19–35.

16. *People v. Inez Burns et al.*, Reporter's Transcript, 19–35.

17. *People v. Inez Burns et al.*, Reporter's Transcript, 111–42.

18. *People v. Inez Burns et al.*, Reporter's Transcript, 339–73.

19. *People v. Inez Burns et al.*, Reporter's Transcript, 339–73.

20. *People v. Inez Burns et al.*, Reporter's Transcript, 335, 388–97; Lynch oral history, 57–89.

21. *People v. Inez Burns et al.*, Reporter's Transcript, 335, 388–97.

22. *People v. Inez Burns et al.*, Reporter's Transcript, 36–73.

23. Raudebaugh, "San Francisco," 364.

24. *People v. Inez Burns et al.*, Reporter's Transcript, 480–96.

25. For Ahern's testimony see *People v. Inez Burns et al.*, Reporter's Transcript, 480–96; for reference to earlier Burns trials see "More on Abortion Case," *San Francisco Chronicle,* January 20, 1946; "Mrs. Burns Sobs at Trial in S.F.," *Oakland Tribune,* March 4, 1946; "Burns Trial," *San Francisco Chronicle*, March 7, 1946.

26. *People v. Inez Burns et al.*, Reporter's Transcript, 445–96.

27. *People v. Inez Burns et al.*, Reporter's Transcript, 445–96; for reference to earlier Burns trials see "Burns Trial," *San Francisco Chronicle*, March 5, 1946; "'Little Brown Books' Spark Burns Trial," *Oakland Tribune*, March 5, 1946; "Ahern Quizzed on Mystery Letter in Burns Trial," *Oakland Tribune*, March 6, 1945; Flamm, *Hometown*, 151.

18. THE END OF THE ROAD

Epigraph: "Inez Burns and 3 Lose Fight," *Oakland Tribune*, March 30, 1948.

1. "The Burns Case," *San Francisco Chronicle*, September 25, 1946.

2. For coverage of San Francisco during WWII see Starr, *Embattled Dreams*, 85–89; "The Burns Case"; for reference to earlier Burns trials see "More on

Burns' Defense Plea to Jury, 'Don't be Pawns,'" *San Francisco Chronicle*, March 7, 1946; "Defense Charges Politics in Raid on Burns 'Mill'" *Oakland Tribune*, March 7, 1946.

3. "The Burns Case," *San Francisco Chronicle*, September 25, 1946; for reference to earlier Burns trials see "More on Burns' Defense Plea to Jury, 'Don't be Pawns'"; "Defense Charges Politics in Raid on Burns 'Mill.'"

4. "The Burns Case"; for reference to earlier Burns trials see "More on Burns' Defense Plea to Jury, 'Don't be Pawns'"; "Defense Charges Politics in Raid on Burns 'Mill.'"

5. "The Burns Case"; for reference to earlier Burns trials see "More on Burns' Defense Plea to Jury, 'Don't be Pawns'"; "Defense Charges Politics in Raid on Burns 'Mill.'"

6. "Police Worries Over Burns Case Inquiry," *San Francisco Chronicle*, September 25, 1946; *People v. Inez Burns et al.*, Reporter's Transcript, 579–606; for reference to earlier Burns' trials see "More on the Burns Trial."

7. "Police Worries Over Burns Case Inquiry"; *People v. Inez Burns et al.*, Reporter's Transcript, 579–606.

8. "Police Worries Over Burns Case Inquiry"; *People v. Inez Burns et al.*, Reporter's Transcript, 579–606.

9. "Inez Burns Convicted," *San Francisco Chronicle*, September 26, 1946.

10. Ex parte Burns et al. on habeas corpus. District Court of Appeals of the State of California, First Appellate District, F. 2440, 574–612; "Inez Burns Convicted," *San Francisco Examiner*, September 26, 1946.

11. *Ex parte Burns et al.*, F. 2440, 574–612; "Inez Burns Convicted," *San Francisco Examiner*.

12. *Ex parte Burns et al.*, F. 2440, 574–612; "Inez Burns Convicted," *San Francisco Examiner*.

13. "Brown Plans Wider Inquiry on Abortions," *San Francisco Chronicle*, September 27, 1946; "Burns Case Sentence," *San Francisco Chronicle*, September 27, 1946.

14. "Mrs. Burns Wins Petition for Release on Bail," *San Francisco Examiner*, October 4, 1946; *Ex parte Burns et al.*, F. 2440, 1–6; *Inez Burns, Mabel Spaulding, Myrtle Ramsey, Joseph Hoff and Musette Briggs v. the People of the State of California*, Supreme Court of the United States, no. 219

(1948); "Inez Burns and 3 Lose Fight," *Oakland Tribune*, March 30, 1948; "U.S. Supreme Court Denies Inez Burns' Plea for Review," *San Francisco Examiner*, October 27, 1948.

15. "Mrs. Burns' Income Investigated Again," *San Francisco Examiner*, January 4, 1946; Letter to Edmund G. Brown, April 4, 1947, William A. Burkett Papers, carton 9, folder 17; U.S. Treasury Memo to Special Agent in Charge from Burkett, October 24, 1947, William Burkett Papers, carton 9, folder 17.

16. U.S. Treasury Memo to Special Agent in Charge from Burkett, October 24, 1947, William Burkett Papers, carton 9, folder 17.

19. "BAGHDAD BY THE BAY"

Epigraph: Allen, "Still, 'Corrupt and Content,'" 5.

1. "Offer State Funds in Inez 'Tipoff' Quiz," *San Francisco Examiner*, January 2, 1946.

2. "Abortion Tipoffs," *San Francisco Examiner*, January 25, 1946.

3. "Abortion Tipoffs"; Elkington oral history, EGB, 13–18.

4. "Case Against Inez Burns is Sharpened," *San Francisco Chronicle*, February 4, 1946.

5. "Calling of Inez Burns By Grand Jury Delayed," *San Francisco Examiner*, January 21, 1946; "Full Jury Quiz in Burns Tipoff Report Slated," *San Francisco Examiner*, January 25, 1946; also see photograph collection, BANC PIC 2006.029: 127616.04.06-NEG Box 922, Bancroft Library, Berkeley, California.

6. "10 More Police Tip Witnesses," *San Francisco Examiner*, February 7, 1946; "Burns Tipoff Quiz Ends," *San Francisco Examiner*, February 12, 1946.

7. "Grand Jury Maps Action," *San Francisco Examiner*, October 15, 1946; "Grand Jury to Consider Abortion Tipoffs," *San Francisco Examiner*, October 16, 1946; "New Evidence Tonight in Surgery Tipoff Case," *San Francisco Examiner*, November 18, 1946.

8. "Police Tipoff Probe Told of Mystery Calls," *San Francisco Examiner*, November 20, 1946.

9. "Police Tipoff Probe Told of Mystery Calls."

10. "Sullivan Pledges 2d Probe; Corassa Testifies," *San Francisco Examiner*, November 19, 1946; "Police Tipoff Probe Told of Mystery Calls," *San Francisco Examiner*, November 20, 1946.

11. "More on Police Worries Over Burns Case Inquiry," *San Francisco Examiner*, November 20, 1946.

12. "Burns' Bail Application 'Found' in Broker Quiz," *San Francisco Examiner*, September 13, 1946.

13. "District Attorney Claims Evidence on Two Police," *San Francisco Examiner*, October 22, 1946.

14. "District Attorney Claims Evidence on Two Police"; "Lack of Evidence Halts Police Quiz on Tipoffs," *San Francisco Examiner*, November 27, 1946.

15. "Herb Caen: Baghdad by the Bay," *San Francisco Examiner*, September 15, 1954.

16. "Surgery Mill Inquiry Ends," *Oakland Tribune*, November 26, 1946.

17. "The Untold Story of S.F. Police Department," *San Francisco Chronicle*, February 1, 1955.

20. WISE GUYS

Epigraph: Raudebaugh, "San Francisco," 350.

1. It was later learned the killers intended to take the body over the bridge but were stopped and warned by a motorcycle policeman for speeding. Afraid to go further, they left DeJohn's car containing his corpse on a side street.

2. *Hearings*, 497–503.

3. "'Cheese King' Murdered After a Year of Hiding," *Statesville Record*, September 23, 1946.

4. "Gangster's Death Probe Clues Go into Secret File," *San Francisco Examiner*, May 18, 1947.

5. Noble and Averbuch, *Never Plead Guilty*, 134; "Gang War Opens in San Francisco with Mobster's Murder," *San Francisco Examiner*, May 10, 1947.

6. *Hearings*, 495–503.

7. *Hearings*, 495–503; "Slaying Time Bared at DeJohn Inquest," *San Francisco Examiner*, June 4, 1947; "Gangster's Death Probe Clues Go into Secret File"; Kefauver, *Crime in America*, 30.

8. Reid, *The Grim Reapers*, 283; "2 Mafia Suspects Held by Police in DeJohn Mystery," *San Francisco Examiner*, May 23, 1947.

9. "2 Mafia Suspects Held by Police in DeJohn Mystery"; "Calamia Claims 'Night Snack' as Alibi," *San Francisco Examiner*, May 26, 1947.

10. *Hearings*, 496–503; "DeJohn Witness Threatened Police out to Smash Mafia," *Oakland Tribune*, December 1, 1948.
11. "Six Sought in DeJohn Case," *San Francisco Examiner*, November 26, 1948.
12. "McDonough Withdraws Plea," *Oakland Tribune*, November 1, 1946; "DeJohn Probe Takes New Turn," *San Francisco Examiner*, November 23, 1948; "Six Sought in DeJohn Case."
13. "Gus Oliva, Joe Burns, Six Others in Gangland Net," *San Mateo Times*, November 24, 1948.
14. "Nick DeJohn Death Linked to Vice Ring," *Oakland Tribune*, November 24, 1948.
15. Flamm, *Hometown*, 146; "Police Hide Woman in S.F. Racket Cleanup," *San Francisco Examiner*, November 24, 1948; Reid, *The Grim Reapers*, 198.
16. "DeJohn Case Indictments," *San Francisco Examiner*, November 28, 1948.
17. "DeJohn Case Web Tightens," *Oakland Tribune*, November 26, 1948.
18. Five Indicted in DeJohn Killing," *Oakland Tribune*, November 30, 1948; "8 Arrested in Gangland Net," *San Francisco Examiner*, November 24, 1948.
19. "DeJohn Case Web Tightens"; "Two Detectives Go for Calamia," *San Francisco Chronicle*, December 24, 1948.
20. "DeJohn Case Web Tightens"; "Two Detectives Go for Calamia"; "Three Face Trial Today in Slaying of DeJohn," *San Francisco Examiner*, January 28, 1949. See Chapter 9 for details of the tip-off in Burns's case.
21. "Five Indicted in DeJohn Killing"; "DeJohn Witness Threatened Police Out to Smash Mafia," *San Francisco Examiner*, November 30, 1948; also see Frank Ahern's testimony in *Hearings*, 493–501.

21. MURDER "MIS-TRIAL"

Epigraph: "DeJohn Jury Dismissed; D.A. to Drop Indictments," *Oakland Tribune*, March 9, 1949.
1. "Three Face Trial Today in Slaying of DeJohn," *San Francisco Examiner*, January 28, 1949.
2. "Alibi Hit at DeJohn Trial," *San Francisco Examiner*, February 8, 1949.
3. "Alibi Hit at DeJohn Trial."

4. "Alibi Hit at DeJohn Trial."

5. Reid, *The Grim Reapers*, 198; "Alibi Hit at DeJohn Trial."

6. "3 On Trial in DeJohn Murder Case," *San Francisco Examiner*, January 27, 1949; "Defense Starts Wednesday in DeJohn Trial," *San Mateo Times*, February 19, 1949; "Nani Denies Part in Plot Against DeJohn," *San Francisco Examiner*, February 28, 1949.

7. "State Witness Tells of Seeing DeJohn's Car," *San Francisco Examiner*, February 11, 1949.

8. "DeJohn Trial Witness Faces Perjury Rap," *San Francisco Examiner*, February 1, 1949.

9. *Hearings*, 599; "DeJohn Trial Witness Faces Perjury Rap."

10. "DeJohn Suspect Squealed on Pals, SF Murder Jury Told," *Oakland Tribune*, February 18, 1949.

11. "DeJohn Suspect Squealed on Pals, SF Murder Jury Told."

12. "DeJohn Trial Witness Faces Perjury Rap"; "DeJohn Suspect Squealed on Pals, SF Murder Jury Told"; "DeJohn Murder Trial Nears Close," *San Francisco Examiner*, March 5, 1949; *Hearings*, 495–505.

13. Emphasis added; EGB oral history, 131–32;

14. EGB oral history, 131–32; Brown, as governor, appointed Judge Divine first to the appellate court, then made him presiding judge of the district court of appeals; "DeJohn Jury Dismissed," *San Francisco Chronicle*, March 9, 1949.

15. "DeJohn Jury Dismissed."

16. "Police Irate at Dismissal of DeJohn Jury," *San Francisco Examiner*, March 9, 1949.

17. "Police Irate at Dismissal of DeJohn Jury"; "DeJohn Jury Dismissed"; "D.A. to Drop Indictments," *Oakland Tribune*, March 9, 1949.

22. THE CORRUPT AND CONTENTED IRS

Epigraph: Herb Caen: "Baghdad by the Bay," *San Francisco Examiner*, June 13, 1951.

1. Kefauver, *Crime in America*, 243; "The IRS, Corrupt and Contented," as quoted in William Burkett's speech to the Lion's Club of San Mateo, January 24, 1951, William Burkett Papers, carton 9, folder 24.

2. "Abortion Case Figure Indicted on Tax Charges," *San Francisco Examiner*, October 12, 1939.

3. See *San Francisco Examiner*, July 1938; December 1939; and February–March 1940.

4. "Woman Facing New Tax Debt," *San Francisco Examiner*, February 29, 1940; "Taxes Owed by Inez Burns," *San Francisco Examiner*, March 17, 1940; "Inez Burns," *The Call Bulletin*, March 16, 1940; "Burns Owes Tax," *San Francisco Examiner*, February 14, 1951; also see City and County of San Francisco Office of the Assessor-Recorder, federal tax lien 87732, June 30, 1955; CPI inflation calculator: http://data.bls.gov/cgi-bin/cpicalc.pl.

5. "Inez Pays $400,000 in Taxes," *San Francisco Call*, December 27, 1945; CPI inflation calculator: http://data.bls.gov/cgi-bin/cpicalc.pl.

6. "Calling of Inez Burns by Grand Jury Delayed," *San Francisco Examiner*, January 21, 1946.

7. "Profits from Abortion Mill," *San Francisco Examiner*, August 24, 1948.

8. "Profits from Abortion Mill."

9. U.S. Treasury Memo to Read from Burkett, November 23, 1949, William Burkett Papers; Handwritten "Note to Read," February 29, 1950, William Burkett Papers.

10. "Extortion Charge," *San Francisco Chronicle*, September 2, 1950; "Burkett Raps Att'y General," *San Francisco Chronicle*, December 5, 1950.

11. Tax Fraud Report, William Burkett Papers.

12. Tax Fraud Report, William Burkett Papers.

13. Special Crime Study Commission, *Final Report*, 50.

14. "Inez Burns is Indicted on 1944 Income Tax Charge," *San Francisco Chronicle*, February 15, 1951.

15. CPI inflation calculator: http://data.bls.gov/cgi-bin/cpicalc.pl; see City and County of San Francisco Office of the Assessor-Recorder, federal tax liens 61399, 87732, April 21, 1952, and June 30, 1955.

16. "Year Sentence for Inez Burns," *San Francisco Chronicle*, May 19, 1951.

17. "Inez Burns Fined, Sent to Prison in Tax Case," *San Francisco Examiner*, May 19, 1951; "Year Sentence for Inez Burns," *San Francisco Chronicle*, May 19, 1951.

23. THE KEFAUVER COMMITTEE

Epigraph: "Monday Medley: Herb Caen," *San Francisco Examiner*, March 26, 1951.

1. See City and County of San Francisco Office of the Assessor-Recorder, federal tax lien 61399 (Inez Burns), April 21, 1952; Raudebaugh, "San Francisco," 365.
2. *Hearings*, 419–629.
3. *Hearings*, 419–629.
4. *Hearings*, 419–629.
5. *Hearings*, 419–629.
6. *Hearings*, 419–629.
7. Kefauver, *Crime in America*, 248; "Report Borne Out," *The Washington Post*, September 2, 1951.
8. "Treasury Agent Burkett," *Science Monitor*, March 18, 1953.
9. "Monday Medley: Herb Caen," *San Francisco Examiner*, March 26, 1951; Belli, *My Life on Trial*, 84.

24. "HELLO AGAIN"

Epigraph: Herb Caen: "Baghdad by the Bay," *San Francisco Examiner*, October 22, 1952. Herb Caen wrote different and regular columns, one entitled "Baghdad by the Bay," and I used portions of his columns from various dates throughout the manuscript.

1. "Prefers Tehachapi to W. Va. Prison," *San Francisco Examiner*, March 2, 1952.
2. "Baghdad by the Bay: Herb Caen," *San Francisco Examiner*, October 24, 1954.
3. The People, Respondent, v. Adolphus A. Berger, et al., District Court of Appeals of the State of California, Transcript. Crim. No. 3028 (February 28, 1955).
4. "Queen, Inez Burns Back in Old Rut," *San Francisco Examiner*, October 23, 1952; "Inez Burns, Federal Doctor Arrested on Illegal Surgery Plot," *Oakland Tribune*, October 23, 1952; "Inez Burns Under Doctor's Care," *Oakland Tribune*, October 25, 1952; "Inez Burns Will Not Fight Prison," *Oakland Tribune*, October 24, 1952.

25. OFFICIAL CLOSETS

Epigraph: "Speech to Commonwealth Club of San Francisco," August 11, 1954, William Burkett Papers.

1. "Speech to Commonwealth Club of San Francisco"; Raudebaugh, "San Francisco," 352.
2. "San Francisco: The Bone Rattler," *San Francisco Chronicle*, September 13, 1954.
3. "Speech to Commonwealth Club of San Francisco."
4. "Speech to Commonwealth Club of San Francisco."
5. *Hearings*, 419–629.
6. *Hearings*, 419–629.
7. *Hearings*, 419–629.
8. "S.F. Grand Jury to Quiz Burkett," *Oakland Tribune*, August 25, 1954.
9. "Lynch to Act on Charges of Pay-Offs," *San Francisco Chronicle*, August 22, 1954.
10. "Inez Burns to Tell S.F. Grand Jury of Payoffs," *Oakland Tribune*, August 31, 1954.
11. "Inez Burns Ordered to Face Jury Payoff Quiz," *San Francisco Chronicle*, September 5, 1954; "Burkett Won't be Ignored," *San Francisco Chronicle*, August 22, 1954; "S.F. Grand Jury to Quiz Burkett."
12. "Jury will Probe S.F. Cop Graft," *The Call Bulletin*, August 24, 1954.
13. "Full Scale Police Probe Forecast in Charges of Payoff," *San Francisco Call Bulletin*, August 25, 1954; "Hint Quiz of Cops on Inez 'Payoff,'" *San Francisco Chronicle*, August 30, 1954.
14. It was erroneously believed that Everson was serving time in a Midwest prison on an abortion conviction in September 1954, when in fact he died in prison in 1948.
15. "Hint Quiz of Cops on Inez 'Payoff.'"

26. "THAT BIG WIND"

Epigraph: "Top Police Welcome 'Payoff' Probe," *San Francisco Chronicle*, September 1, 1954.

1. "The Jury to Seek 'Payoff' Story by Inez Burns," *The Call Bulletin*, August 30, 1954.

2. "Examiner Reporter Wins Pulitzer Prize," *San Francisco Examiner*, May 8, 1951.

3. Ed Montgomery, "Surgery Mill Protection Names Given," *San Francisco Examiner*, August 28, 1954.

4. Montgomery, "Surgery Mill Protection Names Given."

5. "Surgery Mill Protection Names Given."

6. "Surgery Mill Protection Names Given."

7. Ed Montgomery, "Inez Burns Tells Full Story of Huge Payoffs of Police," *San Francisco Examiner*, August 29, 1954.

8. "The Jury to Seek 'Payoff' Story by Inez Burns"; "Inez Burns to be Silent at Jury Quiz," *San Francisco Examiner*, September 2, 1954; "Inez Burns Must Face the Grand Jury," *San Francisco Chronicle*, September 13, 1954.

9. "My, I've Had a Wonderful Time," *San Francisco Call*, September 14, 1954.

10. "Inez Burns Denies Bribes," *San Francisco Examiner*, September 14, 1954.

11. "Down Memory Lane," *San Francisco Chronicle*, September 19, 1954; "Inez Burns Denies Bribes," *San Francisco Examiner*, September 14, 1954; "Inez Quiz 'Flops,'" *San Francisco Call*, September 14, 1954.

12. "Inez Burns Leaving the Grand Jury Room," *San Francisco Call-Bulletin*, September 14, 1954; "I didn't Pay Anyone, Says Inez Burns," *Oakland Tribune*, September 14, 1954; "Inez Quiz 'Flops.'"

13. "Inez Burns Denies Bribes," *San Francisco Examiner*, September 14, 1954.

14. "Inez' Denial Put an End to Jury Probe," *San Francisco Chronicle*, September 15, 1954.

15. "Inez' Denial Put an End to Jury Probe"; "Prosecutor Will Drop Inez Burns Payoff Quiz," *San Francisco Examiner*, September 15, 1954; Caen, *One Man's San Francisco*, 232.

16. "Pocketful of Notes: Caenfetti," *San Francisco Examiner*, September 15, 1954.

EPILOGUE

Epigraph: "Inez Burns Raps Abortion Law," *San Francisco Examiner*, May 25, 1971.

1. Kefauver, *Crime in America*, 28–29.

2. Dorsey, *Christopher*, 114; "Chief Ahern," *San Francisco Examiner*, September 2, 1958; Starr, *Golden Dreams*, 120.

3. Dorsey, *Christopher*, 119.

4. As quoted in Flamm, *Hometown*, 149.

5. See various articles following Ahern's death September 2, 1958 in *San Francisco Examiner, San Francisco News Call-Bulletin*, and *San Francisco Chronicle*; "Honesty v. Graft: A News CB Survey of Police Dept.," *San Francisco News-Call Bulletin*, October 12, 1959; "Ahern Bull-Dozed S.F. Police into Top Force," *San Francisco News-Call Bulletin*, October 19, 1959; Garvey, *San Francisco Police Department*, 71.

6. Lynch oral history, 57–89; *La Crosse Central High School Yearbook*, 1932, La Crosse, Wisconsin; United States Military Register 1942–43, Medical Corp, 1944, 267, U.S. National Archives; *The Wisconsin State Journal*, various dates between January 1945 and July 1948; Missouri Division of Health: Standard Certificate of Death, File No. 22898, July 24, 1948; "Special Burns Fund Approved," *San Francisco Examiner*, March 19, 1946.

7. "Inez Burns' Headquarters," *San Francisco Chronicle*, March 13, 1946.

8. "New S.F. Grand Jury Selected, Will Conduct Abortion Mill Investigation," *San Francisco Examiner*, January 10, 1946.

9. "New S.F. Grand Jury Selected, Will Conduct Abortion Mill Investigation."

10. In 1953, California's Commission on Organized Crime summarized the Nick DeJohn case this way:

The murder of Nick DeJohn underlines the necessity for constant vigilance to ward off the infiltration of hoodlum gangs and continued alertness to the activities of the members of L'Unione Siciliano [Black Hand]. DeJohn was a rich and powerful figure in the Chicago underworld syndicates, including the infamous Capone gang. With his background, DeJohn's appearance in San Francisco a few months before his assassination was discovered by the police, was regarded with some fear by the city's Sicilian underworld. Frank Scappatura, a part owner of the Sunland Sales Company, Leonard Calamia, its sales manager, Tony Lima, an olive oil and cheese salesman, Mike Abati, and Sebastiano Nani, a hoodlum from Brooklyn, were indicted for DeJohn's murder. The prosecution, hampered by typical reticence on the part of gang members and victims alike, and crippled by perjury, came to naught. It became plain, however, that those implicated in the DeJohn killing had associated in a criminal organization extending all over the world. (Special Crime Study Commission, Final Report, 64).

11. "Prison Term for Mrs. Venza," *San Mateo Times*, February 7, 1950.

12. "Inez Burns Denies Tax Settlement," *San Francisco News Bulletin*, March 17, 1956; Herb Caen Column, *San Francisco Examiner*, May 10, 1951.

13. "Inez Burns Denies Tax Settlement."

14. "Inez Burns Raps Abortion Law," *San Francisco Examiner*, May 25, 1971.

15. "Inez Burns' Kin Dies in Redwood," *San Francisco Examiner*, April 29, 1955; Obituary, *San Mateo Times*, September 20, 1956; "Peninsula Deaths," *San Mateo Times*, June 25, 1971.

16. Carlisle interview; "The Inez Burns Story."

17. Details of Inez's funeral, Carlisle interview; "The Inez Burns Story"; "Famed Abortionist Dies," *San Francisco Chronicle*, January 29, 1976.

18. "Abortion Queen's House Vandal-Stricken, for Sale," *San Francisco Examiner*, April 13, 1976; "Inez Burns' House Sold for $80,150," *Oakland Tribune*, April 29, 1976; "Notice of United States Marshal's Sale of Real Property," *San Francisco Examiner*, April 8, 1976.

19. "Burns Abortion Case—Brown to Call Clients," *San Francisco Chronicle*, January 1, 1946.

20. Lynch oral history, 57–89; "Burns Abortion Case—Brown to Call Clients"; also see *Hearings*, 419–629.

Bibliography

Allen, Robert S. "Still, 'Corrupt and Content.'" In *Our Fair City*, edited by Robert S. Allen, 1–10. New York: Vanguard Press, 1947.

Belli, Melvin. *My Life on Trial: An Autobiography*. New York: William Morrow, 1976.

Bloom, Stephen. "San Francisco's Worst-Kept Secret." *The Californians* 13, no. 2 (1996): 40–48.

Boyd, Nan Alamilla. *Wide Open Town: A History of Queer San Francisco to 1965*. Berkeley: University of California Press, 2003.

Brown, Edmund G., Sr., interview by Amelia Fry, "The Governor's Lawyer," in *Earl Warren: Fellow Constitutional Officers*. Earl Warren Oral History Project. University of California, Berkeley Bancroft Library, 1969. Cited in notes as EGB oral history EW.

———, interviews by Malca Chall, Amelia Fry, Gabriella Morris, and James Rowland, *Years of Growth, 1939–1966: Law Enforcement, Politics, and the Governor's Office*. Regional Oral History Office, University of California, Berkeley Bancroft Library, 1977–81. Cited as EGB oral history.

———. Papers, 1907–96. University of California, Berkeley Bancroft Library.

Brown, Harold C., interview by Amelia Fry; Julie Gordon Shearer, "A Lifelong Republican for Edmund G. Brown," in *Brown Family Portraits*. Goodwin Knight and Edmund G. Brown Gubernatorial Eras in California, 1953–66 Project. Regional Oral History Office, University of California, Berkeley Bancroft Library, 1978–81.

Burkett, William A. Papers, circa 1916–2000. University of California, Berkeley Bancroft Library.

Caen, Herb. *One Man's San Francisco*. New York: Doubleday, 1976.

———. *Don't Call It Frisco*. New York: Doubleday, 1953.

Carney, Francis. *The Rise of the Democratic Clubs in California*. New York: Henry Holt, 1958.

Crocker Langley City Directory, 1899, 1910, 1919, 1925. San Francisco Public Library.

Dolan, Edward R., Jr. *Disaster 1906: The San Francisco Earthquake and Fire*. New York: Julian Messner, 1967.

Dorsey, George. *Christopher of San Francisco*. New York: MacMillan, 1962.

Duke, Thomas S. *Celebrated Criminal Cases of America*. San Francisco: James H. Barry, 1910.

Dyble, Louise Nelson. *Paying the Toll: Local Power, Regional Politics, and the Golden Gate Bridge*. Philadelphia: University of Pennsylvania Press, 2009.

Ehrlich, J. W. *A Life in My Hands*. New York: G. P. Putnam's Sons, 1965.

Elkington, Norman. Interview by Amelia Fry, Eleanor Glaser, and Julie Shearer. "From Adversary to Appointee: Fifty Years of Friendship with Pat Brown," in *Pat Brown: Friends and Campaigners*. Goodwin Knight and Edmund G. Brown Gubernatorial Eras in California, 1953–66 Project. Regional Oral History Office, University of California, Berkeley Bancroft Library, 1978–79. Cited as Elkington oral history, EGB.

Flamm, Jerry. *Hometown San Francisco: Sunny Jim, Phat Willie, & Dave*. San Francisco: Scottwall Associates, 1994.

Garvey, John. *San Francisco Police Department*. San Francisco: Arcadia Publishers, 2004.

Gentry, Curt. *San Francisco: An Irreverent History of the City by the Golden Gate*. New York: Doubleday, 1964.

Harris, George B. Interview with Morris, Gabrielle. "Memories of San Francisco Legal Practice and State and Federal Courts, 1920s–1960s." Regional Oral History Office, University of California, Berkeley Bancroft Library, 1981. Cited as Harris oral history.

Hearings Before a Special Committee To Investigate Organized Crime in Interstate Commerce, United States Senate, Eighty-First Congress, Second Session, Pursuant to S. Res. 202, pt. 10. Washington DC: Government Printing Office, 1950.

Kamiya, Gary. *Cool Gray City of Love: 49 Views of San Francisco*. New York: Bloomsbury, 2013.

Kefauver, Estes. *Crime in America*. New York: Doubleday, 1951.

Langmead, Donald. *Icons of American Architecture: From the Alamo to the World Trade Center*. Westport CT: Greenwood Press, 2009.

Leary, Mary Ellen. Interview by Shirley Biagi, for the Washington Press Club Foundation as part of its *Women in Journalism* project, 1990. http://beta.wpcf.org/oralhistory/lear.html.

Lotchin, Roger W. "John Francis Neylan: The San Francisco Irish Progressive." In *The San Francisco Irish: 1850–1976*, edited by James P. Walsh, 86–105. San Francisco: The Executive Council of the Irish Literary and Historical Society, 1978.

Lynch, Thomas C. Interview by Amelia Fry. "A Career in Politics and the Attorney General's Office." Goodwin Knight and Edmund G. Brown Gubernatorial Eras in California, 1953–66 Project. Regional Oral History Office, University of California, Berkeley Bancroft Library, 1978. Cited as Lynch oral history.

McWilliams, Carey. *California: The Great Exception*. New York: Current Books, 1949.

Miller, Patricia G. *The Worst of Times*. New York: HarperCollins, 1993.

Noble, John Wesley, and Bernard Averbuch. *Never Plead Guilty: The Story of Jack Ehrlich the Brilliant Criminal Lawyer*. New York: Farrar, Straus and Cudahy, 1955.

Nolan, William. *Hammett: A Life at the Edge*. New York: Congdon & Weed, 1983.

Pastorello, Karen. *A Power Among Them: Bessie Abramowitz Hillman and the Making of the Amalgamated Clothing Workers of America*. Chicago: University of Illinois Press, 2008.

Phillip, Raymond, ed., "The Trial of Josef Kramer and Forty-Four Others," in *The Belsen Trials*. Vol. 2 of *War Crimes Trials*. London: William Hodge, 1949.

"Professional Notes," *Pacific Coast Journal of Homoeopathy* 31, no. 8 (August 1920).

San Francisco Municipal Record, vol. 2 (1936–1937), San Francisco: Municipal Pub. Co., 1937.

Ralston, John C. *Fremont Older and the 1916 San Francisco Bombing: A Tireless Crusade for Justice*. Charleston SC: History Press, 2013.

Rapoport, Roger. *California Dreaming: The Political Odyssey of Pat & Jerry Brown*. Berkeley: Nolo Press, 1982.

Rarick, Ethan. *California Rising: The Life and Times of Pat Brown*. Berkeley: University of California Press, 2005.

Raudebaugh, Charles. "San Francisco: The Beldam Dozes." In *Our Fair City*, edited by Robert S. Allen, 347–69. New York: Vanguard Press, 1947.

Reagan, Leslie J. *When Abortion Was a Crime: Women, Medicine, and Law in the United States, 1867–1973*. Berkeley: University of California Press, 1997.

Reid, Ed. *The Grim Reapers: The Anatomy of Organized Crime in America*. Chicago: Henry Regnery, 1969.

Shaw, Randy. *The Tenderloin: Sex, Crime, and Resistance in the Heart of San Francisco*. San Francisco: Urban Reality Press, 2016.

Sides, Josh. *Erotic City: Sexual Revolutions and the Making of Modern San Francisco*. New York: Oxford University Press, 2008.

Smith, Dennis. *San Francisco Is Burning*. New York: Penguin Group, 2005.

South of Market Journal, vol. 11–16, 1936–1941.

Special Crime Study Commission on Organized Crime, State of California. *Final Report of the Special Crime Study Commission on Organized Crime*. Sacramento, California, 1950, 1953.

Stanford, Sally. *The Lady of the House*, New York: G. P. Putnam's Sons, 1966.

Starr, Kevin. *Embattled Dreams: California in War and Peace 1940–1950*. New York: Oxford University Press, 2002.

——. *Golden Dreams: California in an Age of Abundance 1950–1963*. New York: Oxford University Press, 2009.

——. *Inventing the Dream: California Through the Progressive Era*. New York: Oxford University Press, 1985.

——. *The Dream Endures: California Enters the 1940s*. New York: Oxford University Press, 1997.

U.S. Treasury Department: Bureau of Internal Revenue, Statistics of Income for 1936. Washington DC: Government Printing Office, 1938.

U.S. Treasury Department: Bureau of Internal Revenue, Statistics of Income for 1936: *United States San Francisco Municipal Record*. vol. 2 (1936–1937), San Francisco: Municipal Pub. Co., 1937.

Western Journal of Medicine 45, no. 1 (July, 1936).

White, G. Edward. *Earl Warren: A Public Life*. New York: Oxford University Press, 1987.

Wilson, James Russel. *San Francisco's Horror of Earthquake and Fire: Terrible Devastation and Heart Rending Scenes*. Issued by Memorial Publishing Co., San Francisco, 1906.

Wirt, Fredrick M. *Power in the City: Decision Making in San Francisco*. Berkeley: University of California Press, 1974.

Worthen, James. *Governor James Rolph and the Great Depression in California*. Jefferson NC: McFarland and Company, 2006.

Index

Burkett, William A., 136–37, 160–68, 173–79, 182, 184

Burnell's Smokery, 28

Burns, Inez: aliases of, 55, 100, 101, 124; appeal of verdict, 117; arrests of, xviii, 31, 39, 49, 54, 55, 92, 144–45, 153, 188; confrontations with police, 19, 20, 38, 52, 127; convictions of, 134–36, 168, 170, 190; death of, 194; defense team of, xviii–xix; early life of, 13, 14, 16; employees of, xvii–xviii, 7–9, 23, 49, 52, 54, 65, 67, 71, 77, 78, 91–95, 99–105, 111, 119, 120–21, 126, 129–30, 132, 142, 150–51, 177–78; escape from raid, 57, 58; extortion of, 5–7, 71–73, 80, 81, 87, 104–5; illness of, 164, 170; letter to *San Francisco Chronicle*, 80–81; marriages of, 17, 25–28; physical appearance of, xvii, 21–22, 90, 133, 183–84; private life of, xiv, 23, 25, 31, 32, 164, 181–82, 192–94; refusals to testify, 59, 182; releases from prisons, 163, 169–70; reputation of, 31–32, 37, 51, 54, 99–100, 124, 179–80; sale of properties, 64–65, 71, 190; on tip-off source, 58, 59, 176–77, 181; training of, 14–15; trials of, xvii–xix, 3, 8–9, 67, 99, 105, 109–11, 114, 116–17, 131, 136, 142–43, 164, 188, 192; wealth of, 25–28, 31, 32, 39–40, 90, 91, 107, 160–64, 181–82, 191–92

Burns, Joseph F.: affair with Inez Granelli, 26–28; death of, 193; friends of, 32, 51, 59–60, 177; Gloria Shannon's description of, 92; ownership of clinics, 100; political career of, 28, 41–42; questioning by investigator, 41–42; and raids of clinics, 57, 150; in Virginia, 169; visit to prison, 182; during wife's grand jury appearance, 184

Caen, Herb, 23, 31, 145, 168, 185, 192, 223nEpigraph

Cahill, Thomas, 148, 151, 167, 188

Calamia, Leonard, 149–52, 154, 157–58, 226n10

Caldwell, Charles B., 5, 143–44, 151

California: abortion laws in, xiv; employment department in, 173, 174; IRS in, 160; Pat Brown in, 191; Progressive Era politics in, 50; vice in, 162–63, 168, 195

California Assembly, 28

California Board of Medical Examiners, 39, 41–42

California Commission on Organized Crime, 163, 226n10

California Constitution, 135

California Department of Employment, 173, 174

California District Court of Appeals, 136

California Institution for Women (Corona), 173, 179, 184, 191

Ehrlich, Jack "the Master," 84

Elkington, Norman: on abortion, 51; on Charles Dullea, 60–61; and corruption cases, 141–42, 176; and leaks about investigation, 63; and raid of clinic, 52, 57–59, 127; threat to, 66–67

El Paso TX, 77

"Emilys" ("Emmas"), 120

Engler, George, 39

Engler, John, 58, 183, 184

Englis, John, 101

English, James, 150–52

Ertola, Charles, 177, 185

Everson, Larry (Loraine): at abortion clinic, 120–21, 124; arrest of, 189; death of, 189, 224n14; diary of, 92, 101–2, 121, 127, 129, 130, 177–78; payment of, 91–92; as witness, 5, 101, 188–89

Excelsior Avenue, 17, 25, 26

Exposition, Affairs, and Industrial Development Committee, 33

Eyman, Andrew J., xviii, 102, 122, 127, 128

Fairbanks, Charles Warren, 80

Fairmont Hospital, 19

Fairmont Hotel, 90

Federal Bureau of Investigation, 152. *See also* U.S. government

Fillmore Street clinic: clients at, 3, 8, 53–58, 65–66, 93–95, 126, 129–30, 177–78; deliveries to, 100, 126–27; description of, 7, 55, 92–95, 102–3, 128; earnings at, 161; evidence from, 58, 95, 101–2, 114, 127–29, 134, 165–66, 177–78, 194–95; journalists at, 33–37; knowledge about, 23; Levina Queen's residence at, 120; Nellie Ingenthron at, 191; physicians employed at, 120–21, 177; public curiosity about, 114; raid of, 29–30, 49, 51–52, 55–58, 65, 71, 77, 110, 126–27, 181; sale of, 190; Shannons' photographs of, 71, 72, 100. *See also* abortion clinics

Finn, Thomas ("Boss Finn"), 33, 42

Flahaven, Stephen, 60

Flamm, Jerry, 32, 46, 116

Florida, 119

Ford, Frank J., 164

Franzone, James, 149

Frazee, Winnie Bell, 126

Frenchy, 83

Fritz, Alfred J., 117

Fullenwider, Frank, 144

Furner, Thomas J., 117, 135

Gaffey, Michael, 183

gambling: establishments for, 28, 46–48; at Inez Burns's house, 21, 51, 59, 60, 92, 95; and organized crime, 148, 165; Pat Brown's tolerance of, 50; in San Francisco, 174

Gentry, Curt, 23

Georgetti, Emilio "Gombo," 165

Gilmour, Addie, 13–14
glantham, 91–92, 95–96. *See also* money
Golden, John R., xix
Golden Gate Bridge, 33
Golden Gate Park, 15–16
Gordon, Waxey. *See* Wexler, Irving
grand jury: on corruption, 58–59, 62, 67–68, 127, 141–46, 175–85; on DeJohn murder, 149, 156–57; on extortion, 73; failure to indict Inez Burns, 64, 73–74, 108; Inez Burns's appearance before, 179, 182–85; Shannons to appear before, 79, 80, 82–83, 86–87, 95; on tax evasion, 162. *See also* juries
Granelli, Alice Lorine, 25, 27, 114, 194
Granelli, Charles A., 25–28
Grant, Hazel, 143–44
Grant Drug Store, 72, 100
Great Depression, 32, 45
Grese, Irma, 94
Guerrero Street home: auction of, 194; break-ins at, 114; description of, 20–21; evidence from, 56–57, 121, 174–75; Inez Burns's final days at, 192, 193; ownership of, 27; police at, 52, 56–57, 59–60, 127, 188; Shannons at, 91; surveillance of, 41

Hagen, Sarah, 18
Half Moon Bay, 32
Halley, Rudolph, 166

Hallinan, Vincent, 147
Hamilton, Leah, 6
Harris, Judge, 164
Hayworth, Rita, 53
Healy, George, 175
Hearst, William Randolph, 89, 190
Henie, Sonja, 53
Hill, B., 176–77, 181
Hilton, Norma, 120
Hoff, Joseph "the Duster," xviii, 9–10, 55, 57, 100, 101, 124, 127, 133–36
Hoffman, Malcolm, 150–51
Hollywood CA, 29, 53
Hotel Lankershim, 18
Hubbard, H. R., 83
Hufft, Virginia, 123–24
Hughes, Glen, 60
Hunter, Thomas, 41–42

Icons of American Architecture (Langmead), 33
Ingenthron, Alice Bell Cross, 13, 15–16
Ingenthron, Frederick, 13
Ingenthron, Harry, 12, 13
Ingenthron, Inez Lillian. *See* Burns, Inez
Ingenthron, Nellie, 12–16, 191
Ingenthron, Walter, 12, 13
IRS. *See* Bureau of Internal Revenue
Italy, 26, 27

Johnson, Hiram Warren, 50

Sausalito CA, 14

Scappatura, Frank, 152–56, 226n10

Scheuplein, Adrienne, 169–70

Schino, E. Michael, 167, 168

Scott, Edmund A., 72, 100, 101

Seattle WA, 29

Shannon, Elise Bennet, 33

Shannon, Gloria Davenport: at abortion clinic, 7, 49, 72, 87, 100, 101, 128; book by, 71, 72, 77–80, 89–95, 99, 190; extortion accusations against, 5–7, 71–73, 81, 87; as "law and order," 78, 92; on Mabel Spaulding, 121; return to San Francisco, 82–88, 89; search for, 71, 75–77; and trial of Inez Burns, 5–7, 78–79, 95–96

Shannon, Warren A.: at abortion clinic, 7, 49, 72, 87, 100, 101, 128; acquaintance with Inez Burns, 90; career of, 32–33; extortion accusations against, 5–7, 71–73, 80, 81, 87; at poker games, 60; return to San Francisco, 82–89; search for, 71, 75–77; and trial of Inez Burns, 5–7, 78–80, 95–96

Shannon, William, 32

Sheridan, Joe, 33–37, 39

Sherry, Arthur, 33, 202nEpigraph

Siegel, Benjamin "Bugsy," 148

Sig (screenwriter), 77

Silver, Margie, 39

Southern Pacific Railroad, 12

South of Market Street Boys, 42

South Van Ness Avenue, 150

Spaulding, Mabel: in court, xvii, 55, 134–36; on day of raid, 65; duties of, 9, 91–94, 105, 107, 121, 124, 133

Special Committee to Investigate Crime in Interstate Commerce. See Kefauver Committee

St. Agnes Church, 42

Standley, William H., 163

Stanford, Sally, 23, 31

Stardust Bar, 58, 59, 153

Starr, Kevin, 45, 46

St. Claire, William, 107

Stern, Samuel, 120

St. Francis (social hot spot), 31

St. Francis Hospital, 23, 105, 124–26

St. Francis Wood neighborhood, 32

St. Mary's Hospital, 126

Strauss, Joseph, 33

Stuart Oxygen Company, 100–101

Stuck, Lewis A., 5

Sullivan, Jerd, 61–63

Sunland Olive Oil Company (aka Sunland Sales Company), 152, 226n10

Suter, Edith, 17–19, 31

taxes. See Bureau of Internal Revenue

Taylor, Dorothy, 124–26

Tehachapi State Prison for Women, 136, 151, 162–64, 174–75, 191, 193, 206n4

television, 165. See also newspapers